access to history

The American Civil War: Causes, Course and Consequences 1803–77

FOURTH EDITION

Alan Farmer

HODDER
EDUCATION
PART OF HACHETTE LIVRE UK

Study guides revised and updated, 2008, by Angela Leonard (Edexcel) and
Geoff Woodward (OCR)

The publishers would like to thank the following individuals, institutions and
companies for permission to reproduce copyright illustrations in this book:
© Bettmann/CORBIS, pages 16, 17, 47, 52, 65, 68, 75, 78, 104, 131, 160, 163, 166,
180, 204; © CORBIS, pages 44, 66, 105, 130, 137, 159 (top & bottom), 178, 197,
212, 221, 237; Getty Images, page 225; Mary Evans Picture Library, page 67;
© Medford Historical Society Collection/CORBIS, page 118; Private Collection/
Bridgeman Art Library, page 181; © Stapleton Collection/CORBIS, page 43.
**The publishers would also like to thank the following for permission to
reproduce material in this book:** Edexcel Limited for extracts used on
pages 194, 240.
The publishers would like to acknowledge use of the following extracts:
Addison Wesley Publishing Company for an extract from *The Origins of the Civil War*
by B.H. Reid, 1996; W.W. Norton for extracts from *The Political Crisis of the 1850s* by
M.F. Holt, 1979; Penguin for an extract from *The Growth of the U.S.A.* by R.B. Nye
and J.E. Morpurgo, 1965.

Every effort has been made to trace all copyright holders, but if any have been
inadvertently overlooked the publishers will be pleased to make the necessary
arrangements at the first opportunity.

Although every effort has been made to ensure that website addresses are correct
at time of going to press, Hodder Murray cannot be held responsible for the
content of any website mentioned in this book. It is sometimes possible to find a
relocated web page by typing in the address of the home page for a website in
the URL window of your browser.

Orders: please contact Bookpoint Ltd, 130 Milton Park, Abingdon, Oxon OX14 4SB.
Telephone: (44) 01235 827720. Fax: (44) 01235 400454. Lines are open 9.00–5.00,
Monday to Saturday, with a 24-hour message answering service.
Visit our website at www.hoddereducation.co.uk

© Alan Farmer 2006
Third edition published in 2006 by
Hodder Education,
Part of the Hachette Livre UK
338 Euston Road
London NW1 3BH

This fourth edition published in 2008.

Impression number   5 4 3 2 1
Year   2012 2011 2010 2009 2008

Cover photo shows *Emancipation Proclamation* by A.A. Lamb,
© Francis G. Mayer/Corbis.
Typeset in Baskerville 10/12pt and produced by Gray Publishing, Tunbridge Wells
Printed in Malta

A catalogue record for this title is available from the British Library

ISBN: 978 0340 965870

Contents

Dedication

Keith Randell (1943–2002)

The *Access to History* series was conceived and developed by Keith, who created a series to 'cater for students as they are, not as we might wish them to be'. He leaves a living legacy of a series that for over 20 years has provided a trusted, stimulating and well-loved accompaniment to post-16 study. Our aim with these new editions is to continue to offer students the best possible support for their studies.

Introduction

Confederate
Supporter of the Southern states that seceded from the Union in 1861.

Republican
A form of government without a monarch (or someone who supports such a government).

Federal
A government in which several states, while largely independent in home affairs, combine for national purposes.

Democratic
A form of government in which ultimate power is vested in the people and their elected representatives.

In April 1861 **Confederate** guns opened fire on Fort Sumter, situated on an island in Charleston harbour. These were the first shots of the American Civil War. Americans have tended to regard the Civil War as *the* great topic in American history – an event that helped to define modern America. Writer Shelby Foote saw the war as a watershed: before the war, he thought the collection of 'United' States were an 'are'; after the war the USA became an 'is'. (Foote might have added that had the Confederates won, the USA would have become a 'was'.) No other topic in American history has had so much written about it.

The Success of the 'Great Experiment'

Before 1861 the history of the United States had been in many ways a remarkable success story. The small, predominantly English settlements of the early seventeenth century had expanded rapidly, so much so that by the end of the eighteenth century they had been able to win independence from Britain. The United States, which in 1776 had controlled only a narrow strip of land along the Atlantic seaboard, expanded westwards. In 1802–3 the United States doubled in size when it purchased the Louisiana territory from France (see Figure 1.2, page 10). By 1860 the original 13 states had increased to 33 and the nation extended from the Atlantic to the Pacific.

By 1860 white Americans enjoyed a better standard of living than any other people on earth. Prosperity and the rapidly expanding economy attracted large-scale immigration. In 1860 the USA had a population of 31 million people (slightly more than Britain): four million were foreign-born.

The USA's political system – **republican, federal** and **democratic** – was the pride of most Americans and the envy of most British and European radicals. By the mid-nineteenth century, many Americans considered themselves to be the world's most civilised and fortunate people.

American Failure

Not everyone benefited from the '**great experiment**'.

- During the 250 years that had elapsed since the coming of the first English settlers, **Native Americans** had lost a huge amount of land.
- The other major ethnic group that might have questioned the notion of a 'great experiment' were African Americans, whose ancestors had been transported to America as slaves. The fact that slavery continued in the American South was a great anomaly in a country based on the **Declaration of Independence's** assertion 'that all men are created equal'.

In the opinion of many Northerners, the fact that slavery still existed was the major failing of the 'great experiment'.

If slavery was the USA's main failing pre-1861, the Civil War (1861–5) remains the greatest failure in US history. Some 620,000 Americans were to die in the conflict, as many as in almost all America's subsequent wars put together.

Should the War be Called a 'Civil War'?

Since 1861 scholars have argued over a name for the conflict. Most called it a civil war at the time. And it was a civil war in states like Missouri and Kentucky where brother sometimes did fight brother. However, this was not the norm. In general, the war was waged by two separate regions: most Northerners were on the Union (or Federal) side and most Southerners on the Confederate (or rebel) side. Moreover, the term civil war implies that two different groups were fighting for control of a single government. In reality the Confederacy was seeking to exist independently.

After 1865 Southerners frequently called the conflict 'The War Between the States'. This title was not quite correct: the contest was waged not by states but by two organised governments: the Union and the Confederacy.

Northerners sometimes referred to the conflict as 'The War of the Rebellion'. However, the struggle, fought by two governments respecting the rules of war, was more than a rebellion.

Other names occasionally used to describe the conflict include 'The War for Southern Independence', 'The Confederate War' and 'The War for Secession'.

It should be said that virtually everyone now calls the conflict the Civil War. This book will be no exception.

North Versus South

By withdrawing from the Union in 1860–1, the Southern states were embarking on a course of nation-making. Southerners came to believe that the South possessed a character quite distinct from that of the North, distinct enough to qualify their region (or section) for separate nationhood. However, it may be that the

Key terms

Great experiment
Americans saw themselves as doing things differently to, and more successfully than, the rest of the world. The USA was thus an example for other countries to follow.

Native Americans
American Indians; the people who first inhabited North America.

Declaration of Independence
Thirteen American colonies declared independence from Britain on 4 July 1776.

Civil War had more to do with developing Southern nationalism than Southern nationalism had to do with bringing about the Civil War. Arguably there was more uniting than dividing North and South in 1861. White Northerners and Southerners spoke the same language, had the same religion and shared the same legal system, political culture and pride in their common heritage. Most also held similar, racist, views, accepting without question that blacks were inferior to whites. Common economic interest seemed to bind the two together. 'In brief and in short', said Senator Thomas Hart Benson of Missouri, 'the two halves of the Union were made for each other, as much as Adam and Eve'.

In the mid-twentieth century some historians were convinced that, given these similarities, civil war was far from 'irrepressible' or inevitable. Historians, like James Randall and Avery Craven, blamed a small minority of extremists – Northern **abolitionists** and Southern '**fire-eaters**' – for raising tensions in the years before 1861, and blamed blundering politicians for failing to find a solution to the 'impending crisis'.

Most historians today tend to absolve the politicians. They stress that Northerners and Southerners were deeply divided. In particular, they held irreconcilable views about slavery – especially the desirability of its expansion. Thus, the Civil War was – to a large extent – 'irrepressible'.

Southern Guilt?

With hindsight, it was Southern, rather than Northern, politicians who blundered into war in 1861. After Lincoln's election success in 1860 many Southerners determined to **secede** from the Union, embarking on a course of action that was always likely to lead to war – and a war that they were always likely to lose. This was apparent to some Southerners and most Northerners in 1861. It is thus fair to point the finger of blame at Southern leaders and the Southern electorate.

There are many similarities between Southern actions in 1861 and Japanese actions in 1941. Both Southerners and Japanese felt that they had been pushed into a corner from which there was no honourable escape. Ignoring the likely outcome of their actions, both fired the first shots: Southerners at Fort Sumter in 1861, the Japanese at Pearl Harbor in 1941. By so doing they succeeded in provoking conflict and uniting against them the whole of the United States in 1941 and what remained of the United States in 1861.

Winston Churchill commented that the Japanese, by attacking Britain and the USA, had embarked on 'a very considerable undertaking'. The same could be said of the South's decision to risk war in 1861. As a result, one in four white male Southerners of military age died, and slavery – the institution that Southerners had gone to war to defend – ended.

Why the South acted as impulsively as it did is a central issue of this book. Why it was defeated is another. And how the Union was reconstructed is a third.

Key terms

Abolitionist
Someone who wanted to end slavery in the USA.

Fire-eaters
Southerners who wanted to leave the Union.

Secede
To leave or quit.

The USA in the Mid-nineteenth Century

1 | The US Political System

The Constitution

The 1787 Constitution, drawn up by the **Founding Fathers**, had created a system whereby power would be divided between the **federal government** in Washington and the individual states. The Founding Fathers, accepting that **sovereignty** should be founded on the people, set out to create a system of checks and balances that would prevent any branch of government being in a position to tyrannise the people or any group of people being able to ride roughshod over the rights of others. The federal government had well-defined executive, legislative and judicial branches, each of

Key question
How did the US system of government operate?

Key date
Founding Fathers drew up the US Constitution: 1787

Founding Fathers
The men who drew up the American Constitution.

Federal government
The national government.

Sovereignty
Supreme power.

which was able to check the actions of the others (see Figure 1.1). And the people, in theory, were able to check the actions of each branch.

State governments tended to replicate the federal government: each state had its governor, its own legislative body and its own Supreme Court. In the late eighteenth century the USA had devised a system for admitting new states. New areas first assumed territorial status, electing a territorial government. Once the population of a territory had reached 60,000 it could submit its proposed constitution (invariably cribbed from other states) to Congress and apply to become a state. By 1850 the USA comprised 30 states.

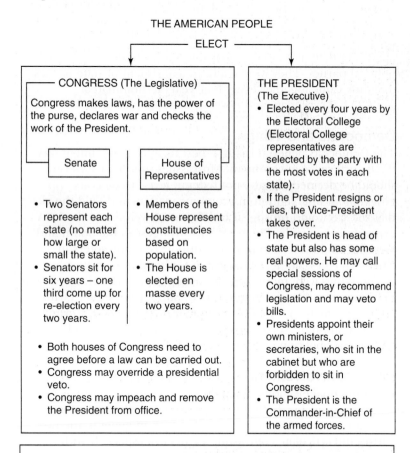

THE AMERICAN PEOPLE

── ELECT ──

CONGRESS (The Legislative)

Congress makes laws, has the power of the purse, declares war and checks the work of the President.

Senate | House of Representatives

- Two Senators represent each state (no matter how large or small the state).
- Senators sit for six years – one third come up for re-election every two years.
- Members of the House represent constituencies based on population.
- The House is elected en masse every two years.

- Both houses of Congress need to agree before a law can be carried out.
- Congress may override a presidential veto.
- Congress may impeach and remove the President from office.

THE PRESIDENT (The Executive)
- Elected every four years by the Electoral College (Electoral College representatives are selected by the party with the most votes in each state).
- If the President resigns or dies, the Vice-President takes over.
- The President is head of state but also has some real powers. He may call special sessions of Congress, may recommend legislation and may veto bills.
- Presidents appoint their own ministers, or secretaries, who sit in the cabinet but who are forbidden to sit in Congress.
- The President is the Commander-in-Chief of the armed forces.

THE SUPREME COURT (The Judiciary)
- This is the highest court. It approves the laws and decides whether they are Constitutional.
- The (usually nine) Supreme Court Judges are appointed by the President.
- The Senate ratifies the President's appointments.

Figure 1.1: The US Constitution

American democracy

By the 1820s almost all white males had the right to vote. The rise of democracy is often associated with President Andrew Jackson (1829–37), a successful soldier, politician and slave-holding landowner who claimed to represent the common man against the interests of privilege. In truth, Jackson benefited from, rather than created, the democratic tide. While there were limits to that tide – women and most blacks, for example, could not vote – the USA was far more democratic than Britain.

By the mid-nineteenth century the USA had two main political parties: the Democrats and the Whigs. President Jackson was very much the catalyst behind the development of the **second party system**. Many Americans loved him. Others hated him. His supporters called themselves Democrats. His opponents eventually were known as Whigs. The two parties, although operating nationally, were not as internally united as modern political parties. They were really an assortment of state parties that only came together every four years to nominate a presidential candidate and devise a national platform.

Democrats and Whigs

The Democrats believed that the best form of government was the least form of government. Most issues (not least slavery) should be decided at state, not federal, level. Democrats opposed government intervention in economic matters and held the view that the US would prosper if **tariffs** were lowered and the USA expanded westwards. The party was strongest in the South and West but could also count on the support of many voters in Northern cities, not least from Irish Catholics.

The Whigs were more likely to favour government intervention in economic and social matters. They supported higher tariffs and government-sponsored internal improvements (for example, railway building). Northern Whigs often supported 'good' causes such as the abolition of slavery.

Political involvement

In presidential elections, when efforts were made to win as much support as possible, both parties put forward **platforms** that evaded most controversial issues. However, in general, the two parties did articulate contrasting platforms, especially with regard to economic matters, which were of major concern to most Americans in the 1840s.

Political campaigns generated real excitement and high voter turn-outs. Both parties held barbecues and torchlight processions, and distributed a massive amount of campaign literature. Party-subsidised newspapers helped to shape political sentiment and raised tensions by indulging in scurrilous attacks on the enemy.

Throughout the 1840s most Americans committed themselves to one of the two parties. In many respects political allegiances were similar to present-day football allegiances. Indeed politics was the most popular spectator and participant 'sport' of the day: party activities offered excitement, entertainment and

Key question
How democratic was the United States?

Key terms

Second party system
The period from the mid-1830s to the mid-1850s when the Democrats and Whigs were the two main parties.

Tariff
Customs duty on imported goods.

Platforms
The publicly declared principles and intentions of a political party.

camaraderie. The political game was highly competitive: Whigs and Democrats looked forward to defeating the enemy. Political rallies drew large attendances and 'fans' often dressed for the occasion wearing the regalia of their party. Oddly, the main 'stars' – the presidential candidates – rarely participated much in the campaigns. Instead they retreated to their homes and let their supporters do the dirty work for them.

Presidential campaigns were by no means the only political 'events'. Elections were far more frequent at state and local level. Different states held elections in different months and in different years. In virtually every month of every year, Congressmen or state legislatures were elected somewhere in the USA.

The Democrat Party was usually the dominant party. Between 1840 and 1854 it held a majority of seats in both the House of Representatives and the Senate in five of the seven Congresses. Many Whig leaders believed the only way to win the presidency was to nominate military heroes as candidates and fight 'hurrah' campaigns in which the party made plenty of noise but said little about issues.

Limited government

Despite the fierce inter-party rivalry, government had a limited impact on the lives of most Americans. It was unusual for one party to control the presidency, both houses of Congress and the Supreme Court at the same time. It was thus difficult for the federal government to do very much. The fact that many matters were seen as state and not federal concerns was another limiting factor. So too was the notion, strongly held by the Democrats, that it was not government's responsibility to intervene much in social and economic matters.

The federal government was made up of only a handful of departments: State, Treasury, Interior, Navy, War and the Post Office. In 1860 there were 36,672 people on the federal government pay roll (excluding the armed forces). Over 30,000 of these were employed by the Post Office.

The vast majority of those who worked in the departments were political appointments: so, too, were the **postmasters**. Whig presidents appointed Whig civil servants (and postmasters): Democrats did the same. This **patronage** or 'spoils system' was an essential way of preserving and promoting party unity. The 'spoils' of office – jobs and government contracts – were what the game of politics was all about for some of those involved in it.

Presidents were more figureheads and distributors of patronage than active policy-makers. Congress, essentially a talking shop, rarely passed major legislation. Indeed it was rarely in session: it met in December and only sat until March. The actions of state legislatures had more influence on most Americans' day-to-day lives than the actions of the federal government. Apart from the postmaster, Americans rarely came across a federal official. Although states were responsible for matters such as education and public health, state governments did not impinge greatly on people's lives.

Key terms

Postmaster
The person in charge of a local post office.

Patronage
The giving of jobs or privileges to supporters.

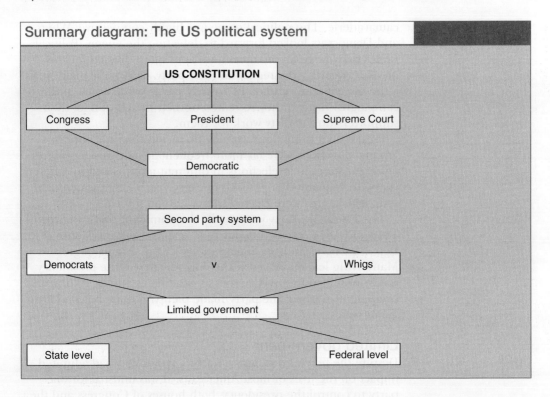

Summary diagram: The US political system

2 | US Social and Economic Development

In the 1830s a perceptive Frenchman, Alexander De Tocqueville, visited the USA and wrote a book recounting his experiences. What struck him was the fact that the country was far more equal than societies in Europe. He noted that there was no 'feudal' hierarchy: no sovereign, no court, no established aristocracy or church leaders. Instead there were opportunities for men of talent and ambition to rise to the top.

Historians today are suspicious of this early notion of the **'American Dream'**. Black slaves, Native Americans and women were far from equal. Moreover, there were great inequalities of wealth among white males. In 1860 the top five per cent of free adult males owned 53 per cent of the wealth. The bottom 50 per cent owned only one per cent. Family standing and inherited wealth were vital assets in terms of individual advancement in America as in most European societies.

Nevertheless, De Tocqueville's claim did have some basis. People were more likely to rise from 'rags' to 'riches' in the USA than in Europe.

Women's status

Mid-nineteenth century America assigned distinctly unequal roles to men and women. Women were seen, and saw themselves, as home-makers. Only 25 per cent of white women worked outside the home pre-marriage and fewer than five per cent did so while they were married. The notion that women's place was in the

Key question
Was the USA 'a society of equals'?

American Dream The idea that the American way of life offers the prospect of economic and social success to every individual.

Key term

Key terms

Cult of domesticity
The notion that women's place was in the home.

Abolitionism
The desire to end slavery.

Temperance
Opposition to the drinking of alcohol.

Key question
To what extent were Americans a 'people of plenty'?

home was disseminated by both the Church and the growing publishing industry.

Today, historians debate the extent to which the '**cult of domesticity**' was a setback for women. Many would claim it was. Women were denied the same social and political rights as men. They could not vote. In many states wives could not even own property.

Some historians have argued that the cult of domesticity actually gave women some power. They had responsibility for their children. (By 1850 the average white woman had five children.) Often seen as the guardians of morality, women tended to set family values and were greater church-goers than men. Middle-class women participated in many of the reform movements that were a feature of mid-nineteenth century American life, especially **abolitionism** and **temperance**.

A 'People of Plenty'

Historian David Potter described mid-nineteenth century Americans as a 'People of Plenty'. Prosperity and growth seem to be the two words that best describe America's economic development in the early nineteenth century. The country had enormous reserves of almost every commodity – fertile land, timber, minerals – and an excellent network of navigable rivers. In the period 1800–50 the USA's gross national product increased seven-fold and per capita income doubled.

Population growth

The USA's population grew rapidly, doubling every 25 years or so. In 1840 it stood at 17 million; by 1860 it had reached 31 million. Most of the growth came from natural increase: plenty of children were born and Americans lived longer than most people in the world. Population growth was also the result of immigration, especially from Ireland and Germany.

Western expansion

The population was mobile. Some Americans moved to find work in the towns. Others moved westwards to settle new land. In the early nineteenth century Americans had in-filled the area between the Appalachian Mountains and the Mississippi River. Between 1815 and 1850 the population west of the Appalachians grew three times as quickly as the population of the original 13 states. By 1850 one in two Americans lived west of the Appalachians. Many moved west – and west again. Abraham Lincoln's family was typical. Abraham's father was born in Virginia in 1778: in 1782 he was taken to Kentucky where Abraham was born in 1809. In 1816 the Lincoln family moved to Indiana. In 1831 Abraham moved farther west to Illinois.

In 1840 few Americans lived west of the Mississippi. The dry, treeless area beyond the river was referred to as the 'great desert' in atlases. However, in the 1840s Americans began crossing the Great Plains and the Rocky Mountains to settle in California and Oregon on the Pacific coast.

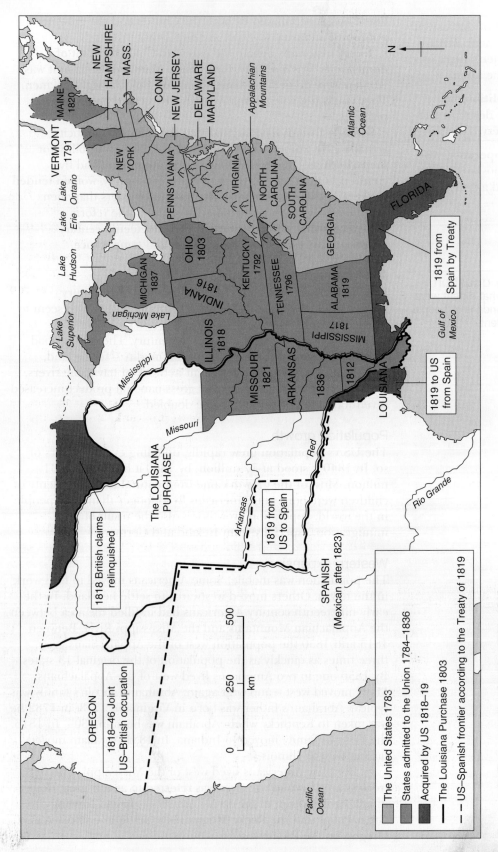

Figure 1.2: The expanding frontier 1783–1840

Agriculture

Most Americans were farmers. Small family farms still characterised agriculture, north and south, east and west. Between 1840 and 1860 food production increased four-fold. This was largely due to the opening up of new tracts of land in the west, and the development of more scientific techniques including fertilisation, crop rotation and the use of new machinery.

Transport

Massive changes in transport help to explain the agricultural – and industrial – changes that were underway. The development of steamboats revolutionised travel on the great rivers. By 1850 there were over 700 steamships operating on the Mississippi and its tributaries. The country also developed an impressive canal system. However, by 1850 canals were facing competition from railways. In 1840 the USA had over 3000 miles of track. By 1860 this had increased to over 30,000 miles – more track than the rest of the world combined.

Industrialisation

America's industrial 'revolution' very much mirrored that of Britain. There were important technological developments in textiles, coal, iron and steel, and in the use of steam power. New machines were introduced and constantly improved. The USA, fortunate in its enormous mineral wealth, could also count on British investment.

Urbanisation

Fewer than one in ten Americans lived in towns (defined as settlements with more than 2500 people) in 1820: one in five did so by 1860. Some cities experienced spectacular growth. Chicago had only 40 people in 1830: by 1860 it had 109,000. New York had over 800,000 inhabitants by 1860.

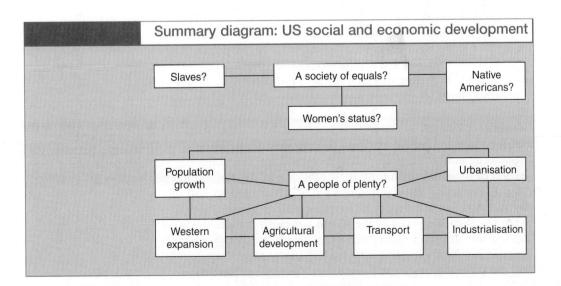

Summary diagram: US social and economic development

3 | Sectionalism

The United States had never been particularly united. For much of the early nineteenth century there were rivalries between the newer Western states and the older established Eastern states. Far more important, however, were the differences between North and South. Some historians have underplayed the differences, stressing instead the similarities between the two sections: the common language, the shared religion, the same legal, political and racial assumptions, and the celebration of the same history. Other historians, however, believe that there were deep divisions between North and South – divisions that helped to bring about war.

Key question
What were the main differences between North and South?

Economic differences

Historians once claimed that the Civil War was a conflict between a backward, **agrarian**, planter-dominated South and a modern, industrialised and **egalitarian** North. This view is far too sweeping. In reality, there was not one but many 'Souths' encompassing several distinct geographical regions. Eastern states such as Virginia were very different from Western states such as Texas. The lower (or Deep) South was different from the upper South. Accordingly, it is difficult to generalise about the 'Old' South.

There were also many 'Norths'. Moreover, in many respects, those 'Norths' were not dissimilar economically to the 'Souths'. The North was industrialising, not industrialised. Only four Northern manufacturing industries employed over 50,000 people. The North-West was still overwhelmingly rural.

Nor was the South economically backward. Many Southerners grew tobacco, sugar and particularly cotton. By the mid-nineteenth century cotton sales made up at least half of the USA's total exports. Trade in cotton ensured that white Southern society was prosperous and enterprising and that most Southerners had an economic interest in a good railway and telegraph network. Nor was the South totally lacking in industry. The Tredegar Iron Works in Richmond, Virginia, ranked fourth among the nation's producers of iron products by 1840.

The North was not more egalitarian than the South. In 1860 the wealthiest 10 per cent of Northerners owned 68 per cent of the wealth: these figures were almost identical in the South. The typical Northerner was a self-sufficient farmer, owning 50–500 acres of land. The same was true of the South. In 1860, 75 per cent of Southern families did not own slaves.

Key terms

Agrarian
Relating to land and farming.

Egalitarian
A society in which people are equal.

Planters
Men who owned plantations with 20 or more slaves.

Southern planters

Planters, who comprised less than five per cent of the white population, owned the South's best farmland and the major portion of its wealth, including most of its slaves. Historian Eugene Genovese believed that the planters led Southern politics and set the tone of social life, especially in states such as Virginia and South Carolina. However, in the North a minority of wealthy men wielded similar power. Rich Americans, North and South, found it easier to involve themselves in politics than the poor: they could find the time and money to pursue their 'hobby' or 'conviction'.

Key question
Was the South dominated by a reactionary planter class?

There was fluidity in Southern society. Sons of planters did not automatically become planters themselves. There were opportunities for self-made men to become planters, and then, perhaps, to involve themselves in politics. Of the eight governors of Virginia in the two decades before the Civil War, only one had been born a planter. Three had risen from relative obscurity. If planters involved themselves in politics (and by no means all did), they had to appeal to large electorates. Nor did they speak with one voice. Some were Whigs and some were Democrats.

North–South differences
Nevertheless, there were economic and social differences between North and South.

Industry
The North was more industrial (see Table 1.1). The Southern states, with about 35 per cent of the USA's population, produced only 10 per cent of the nation's manufactured output in the 1850s. The North had twice as much railway track as the South.

Table 1.1: Percentage of labour force in agriculture

	Northern States	Southern States
1800	68%	82%
1860	40%	81%

Urbanisation
The North was far more urban (see Table 1.2). In 1860 the Confederate states had only 20 towns over 5000 people. Even cities like Charleston and Richmond had populations of under 40,000. Only New Orleans with 175,000 inhabitants was comparable to Northern cities in size and diversity. Only one Southerner in 14 was a town dweller compared with one in four Northerners.

Table 1.2: Percentage of population living in towns of 2500 or more

	Northern States	Southern States
1820	10%	5%
1840	14%	6%
1850	26%	10%

Immigrants
Unlike the South, the North had a growing number of immigrants. Between 1830 and 1860 most of the five million immigrants to the USA settled in the North. Thus, one in six Northerners in 1860 was foreign-born compared with one in 30 Southerners.

Southern economic grievances

The two sections had different economic interests. The tariff (see page 6) was a source of constant grievance to most Southerners, who argued that it benefited Northern industrialists at the expense of Southern farmers. The South felt exploited in other ways. Southerners depended upon Northern credit to finance the growing of cotton, tobacco, sugar and rice: they relied upon Northerners to market these goods; and they were reliant on Northern vessels to transport them. Inevitably much of the profits from '**King Cotton**' ended up in Yankee pockets.

Southern honour

Historian Wyatt Brown (1985) claimed that Southerners were more concerned about their personal, family and sectional honour than Northerners. In Brown's view, Southern males were highly sensitive to personal insult, reacting violently to even trivial incidents, including resorting to duelling.

Values

Many Southerners, disliking what they saw in the North, had no wish to industrialise and urbanise. There was a general Southern belief that old agrarian ways and values were better than Yankee materialism. Southerners remained proudly and defiantly rooted in the past. Many held a 'romantic' view of the Southern way of life, seeing themselves as gracious and hospitable. Yankees, in contrast, were seen as ill-mannered, aggressive and hypocritical.

There were other differences. Northerners were generally better educated than Southerners and more responsive to new ideas. While Northerners espoused movements for reform, Southerners tended to condemn all radical 'isms', associating them with abolitionism and viewing them as a threat to old values and institutions (not least slavery). Not unnaturally, Northerners saw Southerners as backward and out of touch with 'modern' ideas and ideals.

The main difference between the sections, and the main reason for the growth of sectionalism, was slavery.

Key terms

King Cotton
Cotton was so important to the US economy that many Americans claimed that 'cotton was king'.

Plantation agriculture
Sugar, rice, tobacco and cotton were grown on Southern plantations.

4 | Slavery

The settlement of North America was an African as well as a European enterprise. Virtually all the Africans who 'settled' in the seventeenth and eighteenth centuries came as slaves. By 1808, when the African slave trade was declared illegal, there were over a million slaves in the USA. Slavery divided Americans. It continues to divide historians.

Key question
Why were Southerners so committed to slavery?

Slavery pre-1830

In 1776 slavery existed in all the 13 colonies. However, it was of major importance only in the South, largely because the Northern climate was not suited to **plantation agriculture**. In the last decades of the eighteenth century radical Protestants,

Summary diagram: Sectionalism

```
                    ┌──────────────────────────┐
                    │   North    v    South    │
                    └──────────────────────────┘
                          ┌──────────────┐
                          │ Similarities │
                          └──────────────┘
                          ┌──────────────┐
                          │  Differences │
                          └──────────────┘
    ┌────────────┐        ┌──────────────┐        ┌────────────────┐
    │  Economic  │        │    Social    │        │ Cultural values│
    └────────────┘        └──────────────┘        └────────────────┘
   ┌──────────────────────────────────┐
   │   North          │    South       │
   │ Industrialising  │  Agrarian      │
   │ Urbanising       │  Few towns     │
   │ Immigration      │  Few immigrants│
   └──────────────────────────────────┘
         ┌──────────────┐
         │   Slavery    │
         └──────────────┘
```

especially Quakers, condemned slavery as a moral evil. Others thought it inconsistent with enlightened ideas that stressed liberty, equality and free enterprise. Northern states abolished slavery, some at a stroke, others gradually. In 1787 Congress passed an Ordinance that kept slavery out of the North West Territory. In 1808 the US banned the slave trade with Africa. Even some Southerners regarded slavery as an evil (albeit a necessary one) and a few freed their slaves.

'King Cotton' ensured that slavery survived and throve. In 1790 only 9000 bales of cotton were produced in the USA. Eli Whitney's invention of a cotton engine (or 'gin') in 1793 revolutionised Southern agriculture. It enabled short-fibre cotton (the only cotton which easily grew in the South) to be quickly separated from its seed. Suddenly it became highly profitable to grow cotton and Southern farmers cashed in. By the 1830s the South was producing two million bales per year. 'King Cotton' soon outstripped all other plantation crops in economic importance. Such was the demand (mainly from Britain), and such were the profits, that the cotton belt spread westwards – to Kentucky, Tennessee, Alabama, Mississippi, Arkansas and Texas. Cotton production needed a large amount of unskilled labour. Slave labour was ideal. Cotton and slavery, therefore, were interlinked.

Most Southerners were committed to their **peculiar institution**. The Founding Fathers in 1787 had realised that they could not tamper with slavery in the South. While they had avoided using the word 'slave', they acknowledged slavery's existence. Slaves were accepted, for representation and taxation purposes, as three-

Key dates

The USA banned the slave trade with Africa: 1808

Eli Whitney, a Northerner, invented the cotton 'gin': 1793

Key term

Peculiar institution Southerners referred to slavery as their 'peculiar institution'.

fifths of a free person. Events in Haiti in the 1790s, where slaves had won their freedom, massacring most of the white population in the process, convinced most whites that slavery must be maintained as a means of social control.

Abolitionists

Most abolitionists in the first three decades of the nineteenth century supported gradual emancipation, with financial compensation for slave owners. They also believed that freed slaves should be encouraged to return to Africa. In 1822 the USA purchased Liberia, on the west coast of Africa, as a base for returning ex-slaves. However, this policy had little success. Only 10,000 blacks had returned to Africa by 1860; in the same period the United States' slave population increased by two million. There were never enough funds to free and then transport more than a fraction of the slaves. Moreover, most ex-slaves had no wish to move to Liberia.

Key question
How important was the abolitionist movement?

William Lloyd Garrison

In the early 1830s, a new and far more strident abolitionist movement developed. This was associated with William Lloyd Garrison who, in 1831, launched a new abolitionist journal, *The Liberator*. Convinced that slavery was a sin, Garrison demanded (without any notion of how it should be done) immediate abolition. For the next four decades he was to be one of the leading abolitionists.

Key date
William Garrison published *The Liberator*: 1831

William Lloyd Garrison. Garrison's supporters saw him as a dedicated idealist. His critics regarded him as a self-righteous bigot.

Formation of the
National Anti-Slavery
Society: 1833

The National Anti-Slavery Society

In 1833 a militant National Anti-Slavery Society was established. This organisation soon mushroomed: by 1838 it had 250,000 members. Most of its leaders were well educated and fairly wealthy. Women played a crucial role. So too did free blacks, some of whom, like Frederick Douglass (below), were ex-slaves. Helped by the new steam press, abolitionists churned out a mass of anti-slavery literature. They also organised frequent and massive petitions to Congress. To prevent North–South division, Congress introduced the 'gag rule' in 1836, which ensured that abolitionist petitions were not discussed.

Why did the abolitionist movement win support?

Historians have tried to explain why the abolitionist movement suddenly became so strong in the North in the 1830s. Some stress that it was part of a world-wide phenomenon, in which Britain in

Profile: Frederick Douglass 1818–95

1818	– Born: his mother was a slave; his white father was his mother's owner
1825	– Death of mother
1826	– Death of father
1826–33	– Learned to read and write while working as a household slave in Baltimore
1834	– Became a plantation field-hand
1835	– Escaped (posing as a sailor) to the North: worked as a labourer in New York before moving to Massachusetts
1839	– Joined the abolitionist movement
1841	– Gave his first speech to the Massachusetts Anti-Slavery Society. An immediate success, he was hired to conduct a regional speaking tour
1845	– Published a best-selling *Narrative* of his life
1846	– Embarked on a successful lecture tour of Britain
1847	– Founded his own abolitionist paper – *North Star*
1859	– Although a close friend of John Brown, he refused to join Brown's raid on Harper's Ferry (see pages 77–9): fled to Canada and then Britain after the raid's failure
1860	– Returned to the USA
1862–5	– Urged blacks to join the Union army
1889–91	– US Consul General to Haiti
1895	– Died

Douglass became the most famous and influential African American of his time. A leading campaigner for abolition, he was a great writer and also an inspiring speaker. 'I appear this evening as a thief and robber', Douglass told Northern audiences. 'I stole this head, these limbs, this body from my master and ran off with them.'

particular played an important role. British anti-slavery writings certainly had a receptive audience in the USA. (Britain abolished slavery throughout its colonies in 1833.)

Other historians stress American roots. Mid-nineteenth century America was a religious society and the Church had a powerful effect on most people's lives. Although Catholic Church membership was growing as a result of immigration, most Americans were Protestants: Baptists, Methodists, Unitarians, Presbyterians and Episcopalians. In the early nineteenth century, there was an upsurge in **evangelical** Protestantism known as the Second Great Awakening. Evangelical preachers fired up Americans to do battle against the sins of the world – not least slavery.

> **Evangelical**
> A passionate belief in Christianity and a desire to share that belief with others.
>
> *Key term*

Abolitionist problems in the North

The extent of the abolitionists' success must not be exaggerated. The movement had only limited appeal in the North. De Tocqueville commented: 'The prejudice of race appears to be stronger in the states that have abolished slavery than in those where it still exists.' Many Northerners, fearing a northern exodus of liberated slaves and fearful of the effect that the new crusade would have in the South, hated the abolitionists. Anti-slavery meetings (and abolitionist printing presses) were sometimes broken up by angry Northern mobs. In 1837 Elijah Lovejoy became the first abolitionist martyr when he was murdered by a (Northern) mob in Illinois.

The abolitionists also had limited political success. Failing to win the support of either the Whig or Democrat Party, abolitionists set up their own Liberty Party. In 1840 its presidential candidate won only 7000 votes. Not all abolitionists supported the Liberty Party's creation. Many preferred to work through the existing parties. Garrison tried to ignore the sordid business of politics altogether, refusing to vote under the US Constitution, which he regarded as a pro-slavery document.

Abolitionists were unable to agree about other strategies. Some wanted to initiate a slave revolt. Most, realising that a revolt would be suicidal for the slaves, favoured 'moral' force and hoped to win white support in the South. A plethora of different opinions, coupled with individual feuds, resulted in a major schism in the Anti-Slavery Society in 1840.

Abolitionist problems in the South

The abolitionists had no success whatsoever in winning Southern white support. They were not helped by the fact that in 1831, Nat Turner led a slave revolt in which 55 whites (mainly women and children) were killed before the insurrection was crushed. The revolt appalled Southerners who blamed abolitionists for inciting trouble among the slaves.

> **Nat Turner's slave revolt in Virginia: 1831**
>
> *Key date*

Abolitionist attacks goaded Southerners to extol the virtues of their peculiar institution. A clutch of Southern writers now argued that slavery was a positive good rather than a necessary evil. History, religion, anthropology and economics were all used to defend slavery. All the great civilisations in the past, it was claimed, had been based on slavery. The Bible seemed to sanction bondage. At no point did Christ actually condemn slavery. Blacks were depicted as an inferior species, incapable of taking responsibility for themselves. Protected by paternalistic slaveholders, they were better off than most working men in Northern factories or freed blacks in Haiti or Africa.

As well as vigorously defending slavery in print and in words, Southerners also took action against abolitionists. Abolitionist literature was excluded from most Southern states. In some states the penalty for circulating 'incendiary' literature among blacks was death. Those suspected of having abolitionist sympathies were driven out, often after being physically assaulted. The white South, slaveholders and non-slaveholders alike, was united in its resistance to abolitionism.

The abolitionist crusade, therefore, had little impact on the slaves: indeed it may have made their position worse, if only because many states placed new restrictions on slaves. Nevertheless, if the abolitionists did little in the short term to help the slaves, they did a great deal to heighten sectional animosity. They stirred the consciences of a growing number of Northerners and kept slavery in the forefront of public attention. Southerners, while exaggerating the extent of support for abolitionism, correctly sensed that more and more Northerners were opposed to slavery.

The nature of slavery

Historians continue to debate the nature of the peculiar institution. They have a considerable number of sources with which to work – plantation records, census returns, newspapers, diaries, travellers' accounts and political speeches. Unfortunately, there is limited evidence from the slaves themselves, few of whom were literate. The best accounts of what it was like to experience slavery were written by fugitive slaves, some of whom became leading abolitionists. Such men and women were probably not typical slaves. While there are large numbers of reminiscences resulting from interviews with ex-slaves, conducted in the 1930s, these accounts are flawed by the fact that those who provided their recollections had only experienced slavery as children.

Statistical evidence

The census returns of 1850 and 1860 provide a starting point for trying to understand the nature of slavery.

- In 1860 there were nearly four million slaves (compared to some eight million whites) in the 15 Southern states. They were concentrated mainly in the lower South. Slaves outnumbered whites in South Carolina.
- In 1850 one in three white Southern families owned slaves. By 1860, as a result of the rising cost of slaves, one family in four were slave owners. The decline in the number of slave owners worried some Southern politicians who believed that the South

would be more united if every white family owned a slave and thus had a vested interest in slavery.

- In 1860 50 per cent of slave owners owned no more than five slaves. Over 50 per cent of slaves lived on plantations with over 20 slaves. Thus the 'typical' slaveholder did not own the 'typical' slave.
- Most slaves were held by about 10,000 families.
- 55 per cent of slaves worked in cotton production, 10 per cent in tobacco and 10 per cent in sugar, rice and hemp, while 15 per cent were domestic servants.
- About 10 per cent of slaves lived in towns or worked in a variety of industries.

Free blacks

By 1860 there were about 250,000 free blacks in the South. Many of these were of mixed race and had been given their freedom by their white fathers. Southern free blacks had to carry documentation proving their freedom at all times or risk the danger of being enslaved. They had no political rights and their legal status was precarious. Job opportunities were also limited.

Some 200,000 blacks lived in the North. Many Northern whites were as racially prejudiced as Southerners. Northern blacks usually had the worst jobs and **segregation** was the norm in most aspects of life. Only three states allowed blacks to vote on terms of parity with whites in 1860. Some Northern states tried to exclude blacks altogether. However, a number of politicians in the decades before the Civil War worked to expand black rights. By 1861 Northern blacks had more rights than at any time in the previous 30 years.

Segregation
The system whereby blacks and whites are separated from each other (for example, in schools and housing) on grounds of race.

The impact of slavery on the Southern economy

Economists and politicians in the mid-nineteenth century debated whether slavery was economically profitable. Historians have continued the debate. Much depends on defining just who slavery was profitable for. Few historians claim that slavery was profitable for the slave. Slave owners obviously believed that it was profitable to buy slaves or they would not have done so. Slaveholding enabled planters to increase their cotton acreage and hence their profits.

Key question
Was slavery profitable?

Did slavery harm the Southern economy?

A more interesting debate is the extent to which the economy of the South gained or lost by slavery. In 1857 a Southerner, Hilton Rowan Helper published an influential book, *The Impending Crisis of the South*, in which he argued that slavery was responsible for the South's economic decline. Since the Civil War a number of historians (for example, Ulrich Phillips) have followed Helper's line. Arguably, slavery did not fully utilise the potential skills of the labour force. It helped to bring manual labour into disrepute among whites, thus helping to undermine the work ethic. It is also possible to claim that slaves were a poor investment and that Southern capital would have been better spent on investment in

Key question
How useful is this
source for historians
studying the nature of
slavery?

Sale of Slaves and Stock.

The Negroes and Stock listed below, are a Prime Lot, and belong to the ESTATE OF THE LATE LUTHER McGOWAN, and will be sold on Monday, Sept. 22nd, 1852, at the Fair Grounds, in Savannah, Georgia, at 1:00 P. M. The Negroes will be taken to the grounds two days previous to the Sale, so that they may be inspected by prospective buyers.

On account of the low prices listed below, they will be sold for cash only, and must be taken into custody within two hours after sale.

No.	Name.	Age	Remarks.	Price.
1	Lunesta	27	Prime Rice Planter,	$1,275.00
2	Violet	16	Housework and Nursemaid,	900.00
3	Lizzie	30	Rice, Unsound,	300.00
4	Minda	27	Cotton, Prime Woman,	1,200.00
5	Adam	28	Cotton, Prime Young Man,	1,100.00
6	Abel	41	Rice Hand, Eyesight Poor,	675.00
7	Tanney	22	Prime Cotton Hand,	950.00
8	Flementina	39	Good Cook. Stiff Knee,	400.00
9	Lanney	34	Prime Cottom Man,	1,000.00
10	Sally	10	Handy in Kitchen,	675.00
11	Maccabey	35	Prime Man, Fair Carpenter,	980.00
12	Dorcas Judy	25	Seamstress, Handy in House,	800.00
13	Happy	60	Blacksmith,	575.00
14	Mowden	15	Prime Cotton Boy,	700.00
15	Bills	21	Handy with Mules,	900.00
16	Theopolis	39	Rice Hand, Gets Fits,	575.00
17	Coolidge	29	Rice Hand and Blacksmith,	1,275.00
18	Bessie	69	Infirm, Sews,	250.00
19	Infant	1	Strong Likely Boy	400.00
20	Samson	41	Prime Man, Good with Stock,	975.00
21	Callie May	27	Prime Woman, Rice,	1,000.00
22	Honey	14	Prime Girl, Hearing Poor,	850.00
23	Angelina	16	Prime Girl, House or Field,	1,000.00
24	Virgil	21	Prime Field Hand,	1,100.00
25	Tom	40	Rice Hand, Lame Leg,	750.00
26	Noble	11	Handy Boy,	900.00
27	Judge Lesh	55	Prime Blacksmith,	800.00
28	Booster	43	Fair Mason, Unsound,	600.00
29	Big Kate	37	Housekeeper and Nurse,	950.00
30	Melie Ann	19	Housework, Smart Yellow Girl,	1,250.00
31	Deacon	26	Prime Rice Hand,	1,000.00
32	Coming	19	Prime Cotton Hand,	1,000.00
33	Mabel	47	Prime Cotton Hand,	800.00
34	Uncle Tim	60	Fair Hand with Mules,	600.00
35	Abe	27	Prime Cotton Hand,	1,000.00
36	Tennes	29	Prime Rice Hand and Coachman,	1,250.00

There will also be offered at this sale, twenty head of Horses and Mules with harness, along with thirty head of Prime Cattle. Slaves will be sold separate, or in lots, as best suits the purchaser. Sale will be held rain or shine.

Notice of slave sale, 1852.

manufacturing and transport. Slavery may have imposed a certain rigidity upon the Southern mind, ensuring that the South opposed industrialisation and remained dependent on cotton.

Did slavery benefit the Southern economy?

A clutch of recent historians, including Stampp, Fogel and Engerman, have argued (persuasively) that slavery was an efficient form of economic organisation which did not deter the growth of the Southern economy. Given that slave prices doubled in the 1850s, investors in slaves received returns similar to those who invested in industry. The fact that the South lagged behind the North in industrial development can be seen as a sign of its economic health. It was making so much money that it had no incentive to industrialise. From 1840 to 1860 the increase in per capita income in the South exceeded the rate of increase in the rest of the USA. This was largely due to cotton. Given that Southern plantations grew cotton more efficiently than any other area in the world, the South faced no immediate threat to its world dominance. Arguably, the planters were entrepreneurial businessmen, obsessed with economic advancement. Fogel and Engerman have claimed that Southern slave agriculture, as a result of specialisation, careful management and economies of scale, was 35 per cent more efficient than small-scale family farming.

The future of slavery

Some historians have argued that once cotton prices fell, as surely they must, then slavery would have withered away and died of its own accord. If this is correct, the blood-letting of the Civil War was unnecessary.

However, in 1860 there was still a world-wide demand for cotton and thus no valid economic reason for believing slavery was about to die out. Moreover, slavery was not simply an economic institution. It was also a system of social control. It kept blacks in their place and ensured white supremacy. Even the poorest, non-slaveholding whites felt they had a vested interest in preserving slavery: it kept them off the bottom of the social heap.

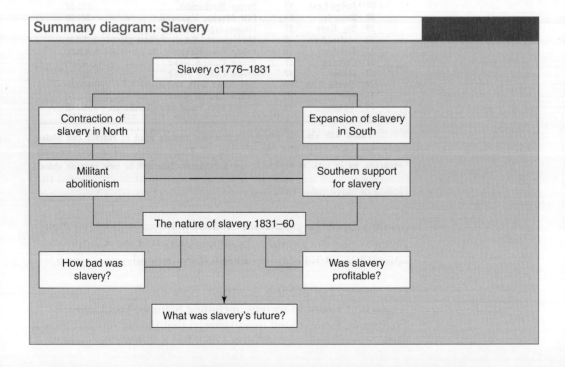

Summary diagram: Slavery

- Slavery c1776–1831
  - Contraction of slavery in North
  - Expansion of slavery in South
  - Militant abolitionism
  - Southern support for slavery
- The nature of slavery 1831–60
  - How bad was slavery?
  - Was slavery profitable?
- What was slavery's future?

Southerners feared that an end to slavery would result in economic collapse, social disintegration and race war. Thus slaveholders and non-slaveholders alike were committed to the peculiar institution: so committed that (ultimately) they were prepared to secede from the Union and wage a terrible war in an effort to maintain it. Given this commitment, it is difficult to see how slavery would have withered away without the Civil War.

5 | Key Debate

Over the last century there have been major debates about the following question.

> Was Southern slavery a system of ruthless exploitation or was it, on the contrary, a type of welfare state, offering protection for the slaves from the cradle to the grave?

In the early twentieth century Southern historian Ulrich Phillips argued that slavery was as benign and benevolent as slaveholders had always claimed it to be. Most slaves, thought Phillips, were content with their lot. Relationships between the slaves and their owners were marked by 'gentleness, kind-hearted friendship and mutual loyalty'.

In the 1950s Kenneth Stampp, while accepting that there were massive variations, claimed that slavery was harsh rather than benign. He saw little in the way of good relationships between owner and owned. In his view, the typical plantation was an area of persistent conflict between the master and the slaves who were, quite naturally, 'a troublesome property'. Stampp's thesis, which has been supported by a host of other historians, remains the prevailing view.

In 1974 Robert Fogel and Stanley Engerman produced *Time on the Cross*. Having fed a vast amount of source material into computers, they came up with a host of statistics which, they argued, showed that slave conditions were reasonably good. White planters were a 'rational' and humane capitalist class and slavery was a mild and efficient system of labour. Slaves, said Fogel and Engerman, were controlled with minimal force and enjoyed a standard of living comparable to that of Northern industrial workers. The response to *Time on the Cross* was overwhelmingly critical. Many historians attacked Fogel and Engerman's techniques and insisted that their conclusions did not possess the objective 'scientific' status that the authors claimed. Their findings, according to historians Sutch and Gutman, were 'confused, circular and so unsubtle as to be naive. Some of their conclusions can be disproved, while others remain unsupported conjectures, in some cases fanciful speculations.'

Slavery: The harsh view

- Slaves could be sold, separated from their families, punished, sexually exploited, and even killed without redress.
- Firm discipline seems to have been the norm. This was an age that believed to spare the rod was to spoil the child – and slave. On plantations, slaves worked in gangs supervised by a black driver and a white overseer, both of whom used the whip if workers fell behind the pace. 'Uppity' slaves were flogged, branded, mutilated or sold.
- Slaves usually worked longer hours than free Americans. Most slaveholders aimed to make a profit. They thus sought to extract the maximum amount of work for the minimum cost.
- Slaves' normal diet was monotonous (corn and pork were the main components) and resulted in many slaves having vitamin deficiencies.
- Most slaves lived in overcrowded log cabins.
- Slaves had few prospects of promotion.
- The slave family unit was far from sacrosanct. Possibly a quarter of slave marriages were broken by forced separation.
- By the 1850s few slaves were granted freedom. Between 1810 and 1860 all Southern states passed laws restricting the right of owners to free their slaves.
- The fact that there was no major revolt is not proof that slaves were content. A major revolt was impossible to organise. Slaves were a minority in most states. They were not allowed to own firearms or to congregate in large groups. A slave uprising would have been tantamount to mass suicide.
- It was virtually impossible for a family group to escape. Most individual fugitives were caught within days and severely punished. The '**underground railroad**', despite abolitionist propaganda and Southern fears, was far from extensive or well organised. Even those slaves who did make it to the North risked the possibility of being returned to their owners.
- The evidence suggests that most slaves hated slavery. Whenever they had the opportunity of freedom during the Civil War most took it.

Underground railroad
A network of anti-slavery houses that helped runaway slaves to escape to the North and to Canada.

Key term

Slavery: The benign view

- Slaves did not work much harder than most free Americans. Most did not work on Sundays and many had half a day's holiday on Saturdays.
- Floggings were rare, if only because slave owners had a vested interest in the maintenance of their property. Just as most Rolls Royce owners today take good care of their cars, so slave owners looked after their 'property'. (A slave was worth much the same as a modern day top-of-the-range car.) Most whites were restrained in their treatment of slaves by Christian morality and by their own standards of decency.
- Most owners preferred the carrot as a source of motivation to the stick. Slaves who worked hard were given extra holidays and better clothing and food.
- Given the standards of the day, slaves were reasonably well fed, clothed and housed.
- There was variety in the nature and organisation of slaves' work. By no means all toiled for long hours on cotton plantations. Within slavery there was a hierarchy, tantamount to a career structure. Hard-working – or lucky – slaves had a good chance of promotion. They could pick up a skill or become a domestic slave, slave driver or plantation overseer.
- By using strategies such as feigning illness or working slowly, slaves were able to modify and subvert the system.
- The slave population increased at much the same rate as white population growth.
- The slave family, far from being undermined by the slave system, was the basic unit of social organisation. Slaves usually chose their own partners. Slaves were often traded so that couples who were fond of each other could live together.
- The fact that there was no major slave revolt – Nat Turner's apart – suggests that slave conditions were not so bad.
- Only a few hundred slaves a year made any serious attempt to escape to freedom.
- Some slaves were granted, or made enough money to purchase, their freedom.

In Stampp's view, 'The only generalisation that can be made with relative confidence is that some masters were harsh and frugal; others were mild and generous and the rest ran the whole gamut in between.' Slaves who laboured in the rice-growing areas of the Deep South probably endured the worst conditions. Household servants generally had an easier life than field hands. Historian Paul Escott suggests that slaves on small farms had a worse lot than those on big plantations, if only because they spent much more time under the supervision of their owner and had no sense of belonging to a sizeable slave community.

Some key books in the debate

R.W. Fogel and S.L. Engerman, *Time on the Cross: The Economics of American Negro Slavery* (University Press of America, 1974).
P.J. Parish, *Slavery: History and Historians* (Icon Editions, 1989).
K.M. Stampp, *The Peculiar Institution: Slavery in the Ante-bellum South* (Eyre and Spottiswoode, 1956).

---

6 | Conclusion

By the mid-nineteenth century there were significant differences between North and South – differences that were growing as the North's industrial development outstripped that of the South. The North was changing: the South resisted change. By 1850 Southerners were conscious of their distinct 'Southernness'. North and South might speak the same language – but by the mid-nineteenth century (as historian James McPherson has pointed out) they were increasingly using this language to revile each other. Even the shared commitment to Protestantism had become a divisive rather than a unifying factor, with most of the major denominations splitting into hostile Southern and Northern branches over the question of slavery.

The fact that there was a widening disparity in numbers between North and South concerned Southerners. In 1790 the population of the Northern and Southern states had been about equal. By 1850 Northerners outnumbered Southerners by a ratio of more than three to two. Given that Northern states had more seats in the House of Representatives, Southerners were determined to maintain a position of equality in the Senate. This meant that westward expansion was a crucial issue.

Study Guide: AS Questions

In the style of OCR

Study the five sources on the impact of slavery in mid-nineteenth century America, and then answer **both** sub-questions. It is recommended that you spend two-thirds of your time in answering part **(b)**.

(a) **Study Sources A and C.**
Compare these sources as evidence for the economic impact of slavery. (30 marks)

(b) **Study all of the sources.**
Use your own knowledge to assess how far the sources support the interpretation that slavery was a kindly and profitable institution in mid-nineteenth century America. (70 marks)

Source A

From: G. Fitzhugh, Sociology for the South, *1854. The view of a Southerner who tries to defend slavery in a more intellectual way than most Southerners.*

There is no rivalry, no competition to get employment among slaves, as among free labourers. Nor is there a war between master and slave. The master's interest prevents his reducing the slave's allowance or wages in infancy or sickness, for he might lose the slave by so doing. His feeling for his slave never permits him to stint him in old age. The slaves are all well fed, well clad, have plenty of fuel, and are happy. They have no dread of the future – no fear of want. A state of dependence is the only condition in which reciprocal affection can exist among human beings – the only situation in which the war of competition ceases, and peace, amity and goodwill arise.

Source B

From: H.R. Helper, The Impending Crisis of the South, *1857. The view of a Southerner who claims that slavery was responsible for the economic decline of the South.*

Slavery, and nothing but slavery, has retarded the progress and prosperity of our portion of the Union; depopulated and impoverished our cities by forcing the more industrious and enterprising natives of the soil to emigrate to the free states; brought our domain under a sparse and inert population by preventing foreign immigration; made us a tributary to the North, and reduced us to the humiliating condition of mere provincial subjects in fact, though not in name.

Source C

From: F.L. Olmstead, The Cotton Kingdom: A Traveller's Observations on Cotton and Slavery in the American Slave States, *1861. The view of a Northerner who travelled widely in the South in 1859.*

Slavery withholds all encouragement from the labourer to improve his faculties and his skill; destroys his self-respect; misdirects and debases his ambition, and withholds all the natural motives that lead men to endeavour to increase their capacity of usefulness to their country and the world.

Source D

The estimated average slave prices for Georgia in selected years between 1828 and 1860. Note that there was very little inflation in these years.

1828 → $700
1837 → $1300
1839 → $1000
1840 → $700
1844 → $600
1848 → $900
1851 → $1050
1852 → $1200
1859 → $1650
1860 → $1800

Source E

From: R.B. Nye and J.E. Morpurgo, The Growth of the USA, *1965. Two modern historians argue that 1854 marked a turning point in Lincoln's public pronouncements on slavery.*

Not until 1854 did Lincoln publicly denounce slavery on moral grounds, condemning it as 'a monstrous injustice'. Not until then did he decide that the institution threatened the democratic tradition he believed in, that the alliance between cotton capitalism and industrial capitalism was close at hand. For Lincoln the slavery question was tied closely to the questions of Union and democracy. In every recorded speech from 1854 to 1861 he repeated the warning that slavery might become national, and that if it did, free America was doomed.

Exam tips

(a) Focus on and refer to the 'attitudes' shown in the two sources. Note that one was written by a Northerner and the other by a Southerner. What are the main points the two sources are making? Clearly Source A is positive about slavery while Source C is not very positive. Why might this be? Remember that the focus of your answer needs to be on comparison of 'economic impact'.

(b) You need to present a balanced answer that focuses on the question – 'was slavery a kindly and profitable institution' – and use your own knowledge in conjunction with the five sources. Try to classify the overall position of each source. Source A suggests that slavery was benign and profitable. Source B sees slavery as having negative economic effects on the South and Source C condemns slavery unreservedly. Source D implies that slaves were a reasonable investment, and Source E argues that Lincoln condemned slavery because it threatened America's democratic traditions. Rather than deal with each source separately, try to organise the issues thematically. Use the sources and your own knowledge to shed light on the value of the evidence. You might decide that slavery was not benign but was profitable (as Ulrich Phillips claimed). You might also argue that it was both benign and profitable or neither benign nor profitable. The important thing is that you use the five sources and that you have good evidence to support your case.

Study Guide: A2 Question

In the style of Edexcel

'Increasingly different, but equally successful.' How far do you agree with these judgements on the economies of the North and South of the USA in the period to 1850?   (30 marks)

Exam tips

The cross-references are intended to take you straight to the material that will help you to answer the question.

This essay question requires you to explore two judgements: whether the differences between the economies of North and South were increasing, and whether the economies were equally successful. You would be well advised to plan these two parts of the essay separately to ensure that both elements are properly explored.

The diagram on page 15 summarises the key differences and the material on pages 12–13 will help you to add to the summary. Note the need not to generalise too simply about North and South. The statistical evidence on pages 12–13 will help you to show the extent to which differences were increasing.

How far were these different economies equally successful? The success and growth of increasingly industrial North is easier to show. See pages 9–11 for evidence of prosperity and growth in the USA.

You will need to enter into a debate about the economy of the South:

- See pages 12 and 15 for evidence of Southern prosperity built on cotton.
- See pages 20–2 for a discussion of the impact of slavery on the Southern economy and whether the economic returns for investment in slaves indicated an economic success.

There is a real debate for you to enter into here. Be careful to keep the focus on the criteria you are using for 'economic success'.

You will need to reach an overall judgement. In doing so, be clear what criteria you are using to show 'economic success', and be careful not to assume without discussion that the failure of the South to industrialise at the pace of the North automatically indicates a weaker economy.

2 The Problem of Western Expansion 1846–54

POINTS TO CONSIDER
In the early 1840s the second party system seemed responsive to most voters' needs. Most Americans developed strong attachments to the Democrat or Whig Party. However, events between 1846 and 1854 undermined both the second party system and sectional harmony. Western expansion was the catalyst which set Southerners against Northerners and which threatened to tear the Union apart. This chapter will focus on:

- Missouri, Texas and Mexico
- The impact of the Mexican War
- The 1850 Compromise
- North–South problems 1850–3
- The problem of Kansas–Nebraska

Key dates

1820		Missouri Compromise
1836		Texas won independence from Mexico
1845		Texas joined the USA
1846	May	Start of Mexican War
	August	Wilmot Proviso
1848		Treaty of Guadalupe Hidalgo
1850		The 1850 Compromise
1854		Kansas–Nebraska Act

1 | Missouri, Texas and Mexico

Key question
Why was Western expansion a problem?

Western expansion had been a problem for the USA from the early nineteenth century. As new states applied to join the Union, there was one crucial question in the minds of most Americans: would the new state be free or slave?

The Missouri Compromise

Key date
The Missouri Compromise: 1820

By 1819 the original 13 states had grown to 22. Eleven states were free; 11 were slave. In 1819 Missouri applied to join the Union as a slave state. Given that this would tilt the balance against them, the free states opposed Missouri's admittance. The result was a series of furious debates, with Southern and Northern Congressmen lined up against each other. In 1820 a compromise was worked out. To balance the admittance of Missouri, a new free state of Maine was created. It was also agreed that henceforward there should be no slavery in the **Louisiana Purchase Territory**, north of latitude 36°30′ (see Figure 2.1). South of that line, slavery could exist. This 'Missouri Compromise' eased tension. Nevertheless the issues raised in 1819–20 alarmed many elder statesmen. 'This momentous question, like a fire bell in the night, awakened and filled me with terror', said former President Thomas Jefferson.

Texan independence

Americans had settled in Texas, then part of Mexico, from the 1820s. Most were Southerners and many had taken their slaves with them. In 1829 Mexico freed its slaves and the following year prohibited further American immigration into Texas. American Texans defied both laws and for some years the Mexican government was too weak to enforce its authority. By 1835 there were about 30,000 American immigrants in Texas (plus 5000 slaves) and only about 5000 Mexicans.

The efforts of the Mexican President, General Santa Anna, to enforce Mexican authority were resented by the American Texans and over the winter of 1835–6 they declared independence. Santa Anna marched north with a large army. A force of 187 Texans put up a spirited defence at the Alamo (a fortified **mission**) but this fell in March 1836. All the Texan defenders were killed. Although President Jackson sympathised with the Texans, he sent no official help. However, hundreds of Americans from the South and West rushed to the Texans' aid. In April 1836 an American-Texan army, led by Sam Houston, defeated the Mexicans at the battle of San Jacinto. Santa Anna was captured and forced to recognise the independence of Texas.

Texas and the USA

Although the Mexican government did not ratify Santa Anna's action, Texas was now effectively independent. Most Texans hoped to join the USA, a move that Southerners supported. However, many Northerners opposed the move, fearing that it would lead to the spread of slavery. So large was Texas that it could be divided into five new slave states, which would tilt the balance between free and slave states heavily in the South's favour. Given that Texas was a political hot potato, Jackson shelved the issue. So too did his successor Martin Van Buren. The result was that for a few years Texas was an independent republic, unrecognised by Mexico and rejected by the USA.

After 1836 there was continued agitation for annexation both from the Texans and from many Americans, particularly Southerners and Westerners. Texas became a major issue in the 1844 presidential election, fought between the Whig Henry Clay and the Democrat James Polk. Polk, a slaveholder from Tennessee, was elected president on a platform that promised the annexation of both Texas and Oregon – an area claimed by Britain. Outgoing (Southern) Whig President Tyler, anxious to

Key terms

Louisiana Purchase Territory
The huge area bought from France in 1803.

Mission
A religious settlement, set up by the Spanish to try to convert Native Americans to Christianity.

Key date

Texas won independence from Mexico: 1836

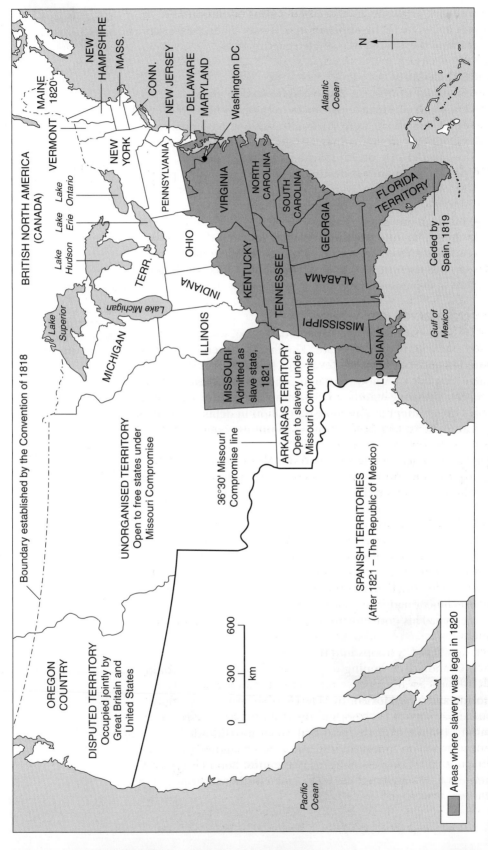

Figure 2.1: The Missouri Compromise

leave his mark on events, now secured a joint resolution of
Congress in favour of the annexation of Texas. Thus, Texas was
admitted into the Union, as a single state, in 1845.

Texas joined the USA:
1845

Key date

Manifest destiny

Polk, committed to Western expansion, wished to annex
California and New Mexico, provinces over which Mexico exerted
little control. Americans were starting to settle in both areas and
the Mexican population was small. Many Americans supported
expansion. In 1845 Democrat journalist John O'Sullivan
declared, 'it is our **manifest destiny** to overspread and to possess
the whole of the continent which Providence has given us for the
development of the great experiment of liberty and federated
self-government entrusted to us'.

Advocates of 'manifest destiny' invoked God and the glory of
democratic institutions to sanction expansion. Many Northern
Whigs saw this rhetoric as a smokescreen aimed at concealing the
evil intent of expanding slavery.

Manifest destiny
The USA's god-
given right to take
over North
America.

Key term

The outbreak of war

The USA's annexation of Texas angered Mexico, which still
claimed sovereignty over the state. The fact that there were
disputed boundaries between Texas and Mexico was a further
problem that the USA now inherited. There were other
difficulties. One long-standing US grievance was the failure of the
Mexican government to pay some $2 million in debts it owed to
American citizens, largely for damage to property destroyed in
periods of disorder in Mexico.

◄
Key question
Why did the USA go
to war with Mexico?

The barely concealed designs of Polk on California and New
Mexico did not help US–Mexican relations. Efforts to reach some
agreement were hindered by the situation in Mexico. Mexican
governments came and went with such rapidity that it was
difficult for the USA to know with whom to deal.

Polk, hoping to purchase the territory he coveted, sent John
Slidell as his special emissary to Mexico in 1845 with the
authority to offer $30 million for New Mexico and California.
Unfortunately, Slidell arrived in Mexico City at a time when a
new government had just come to power on a tide of anti-
Americanism. This government refused to have anything to do
with him.

Polk now sent US troops into the disputed border area north of
the Rio Grande river, hoping to provoke an incident that would
result in war – a war which would lead to US annexation of
California and New Mexico. In May 1846 Mexican troops duly
ambushed a party of US troops in the disputed area, killing or
wounding 16 men. Polk declared that Mexicans had 'shed
American blood on American soil' and asked Congress to declare
war (Figure 2.2). Congress obliged. While most Southerners and
Westerners fully supported the war, many Northerners saw it as a
Southern war of aggression.

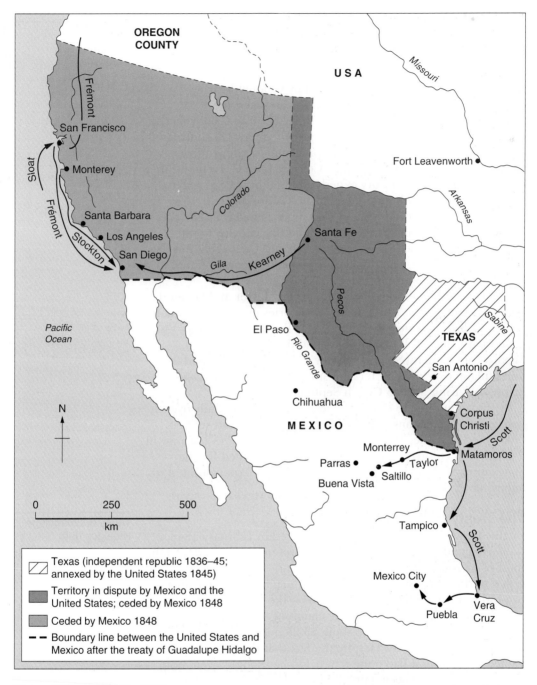

Figure 2.2: The Mexican War

The start of the
Mexican War: 1846

The Mexican War

Although the USA had a smaller army, it had twice as many
people and a much stronger industrial base than Mexico and thus
far greater military potential. Mexican forces were poorly led and
equipped. The USA's main advantages were:

• its superior artillery

- its pool of junior officers, most of whom had been well trained at **West Point**
- its enthusiastic (mainly Southern and Western) volunteers
- its naval supremacy.

West Point
The main US
military academy.

Key term

In the summer of 1846 US cavalry, led by Colonel Kearney, marched unopposed into Santa Fe and proclaimed the annexation of New Mexico. Kearney then set off to California. By the time he arrived the province was largely under US control. American settlers in California had proclaimed independence from Mexico. They were helped by Colonel John C. Frémont, in the region on an exploratory expedition, and by a US naval squadron, conveniently stationed off the California coast. Kearney's arrival in California in December ended what little Mexican resistance remained. Polk hoped that Mexico would accept defeat and the loss of New Mexico and California. But General Santa Anna, once again in control in Mexico, refused to surrender and the war continued.

The US war heroes were General Zachary Taylor and General Winfield Scott. Taylor won a series of victories over Santa Anna in 1846 and then defeated the Mexicans at the battle of Buena Vista in February 1847. Polk, meanwhile, had decided to strike at Mexico City. General Scott, with only 11,000 men, marched 260 miles inland over difficult terrain, storming several fortresses before capturing Mexico City in September 1847.

By the autumn of 1847 the Mexican War was essentially over. It had cost the Americans $100 million and 13,000 dead soldiers (2000 died in battle; 11,000 died of disease). The USA was now in a position to enforce peace. Some Southerners called for the annexation of all Mexico. However, many Northerners wanted to annex no territory whatsoever.

The Treaty of Guadalupe Hidalgo

By the Treaty of Guadalupe Hidalgo, signed in February 1848, California and New Mexico (including present-day Nevada, Utah, most of Arizona, and parts of Colorado and Wyoming) were ceded to the USA (see Figure 2.3). In return for this huge area – two-fifths of the USA's present territory – the US agreed to pay Mexico $15 million and to pay the claims of American citizens against Mexico, amounting to some $3.25 million. Polk was unhappy with the Treaty. Despite the fact that the USA had gained everything it had gone to war for, he thought even more territory could have been gained. Spurred on by Southerners, who saw the dizzy prospect of dozens of new slave states, Polk considered rejecting the Treaty. However, given Northern opinion and the fact that some Southerners balked at the notion of ruling Mexico's mixed Spanish and Indian population, he reluctantly accepted the Treaty, which was ratified by the Senate in May 1848.

Treaty of Guadalupe
Hidalgo: 1848

Key date

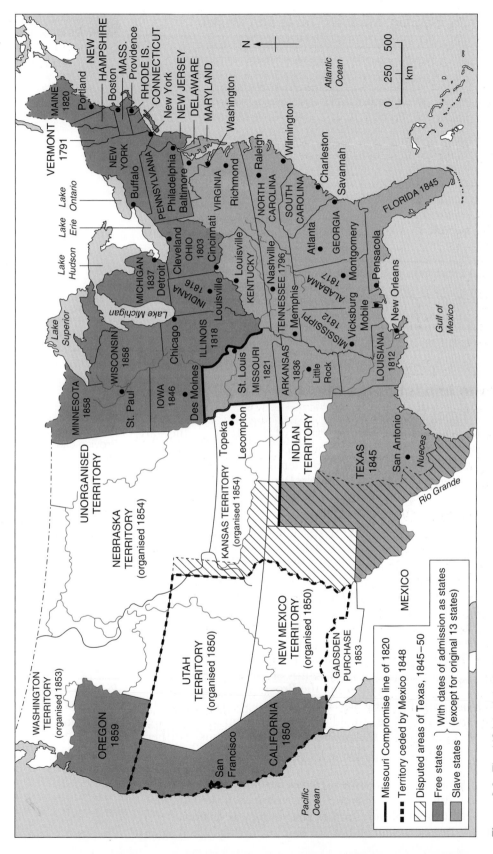

Figure 2.3: The USA in the 1850s

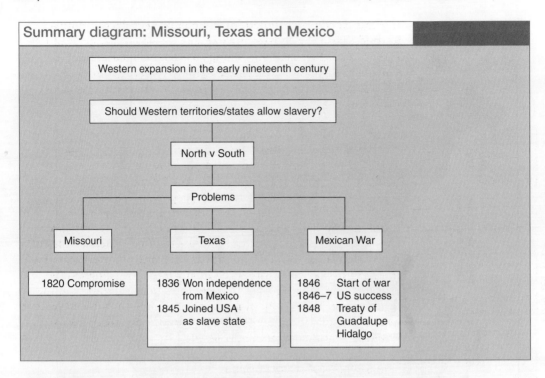

Summary diagram: Missouri, Texas and Mexico

Western expansion in the early nineteenth century

Should Western territories/states allow slavery?

North v South

Problems

Missouri — Texas — Mexican War

1820 Compromise

1836 Won independence from Mexico
1845 Joined USA as slave state

1846   Start of war
1846–7 US success
1848   Treaty of Guadalupe Hidalgo

2 | The Impact of the Mexican War 1846–50

The Wilmot Proviso

Americans anticipated winning territory from Mexico at the start of the war. Many politicians were worried because it was unclear whether states created from Mexican land would become slave or free. In August 1846 David Wilmot, a Democrat from Pennsylvania, proposed that slavery should be excluded from any territory gained from Mexico.

Wilmot was not an abolitionist. Like many Northern Democrats, he resented the fact that Polk seemed to be pursuing a pro-Southern policy. While happy to fight the Mexican War, Polk had reneged on his promise to take the whole of Oregon. Instead an agreement had been reached whereby Britain took the area north of the 49th parallel: the USA took southern Oregon. This made sense: the USA did well out of the deal and it would have been foolish to have fought both Mexico and Britain. But Northern Democrats felt that Polk's appeasement of Britain, coupled with his forceful action against Mexico, symbolised his pro-Southern bias. In supporting the **Proviso**, Northern Democrats hoped to keep blacks out of the new territories and ensure that white settlers would not face competition from slave planters. Concerned at the coming mid-term elections, Northern Democrats were warning Polk of their unease with the direction of his policies.

Most Southern Congressmen, Democrats and Whigs alike, were outraged. After a bitter debate, the Proviso passed the House of Representatives by 83 votes to 64. The voting was sectional: every Southern Democrat and all but two Southern Whigs voted against

Key question
Why did the Wilmot Proviso cause such a storm?

The Wilmot Proviso: August 1846

Key date

Proviso
A provision or condition. (The Wilmot Proviso was an amendment to a finance bill.)

Key term

it. Most Northerners voted for it. Senator Toombs of Georgia warned that if the Proviso became law, he would favour disunion rather than 'degradation'. Failing to pass the Senate, the Proviso did not become law. Nevertheless, for anti-slavery forces, the Proviso became a rallying cry. Many Northern state legislatures endorsed it. Most Southern states denounced it.

Key question
Why was the Calhoun Doctrine a threat to the Union?

The Calhoun Doctrine

Northerners believed that Congress had the power to exclude slavery from the **territories** and should exercise that power. Southerners, not surprisingly, challenged the doctrine of Congressional authority to regulate or prohibit slavery in the territories. John C. Calhoun, an elder statesman from South Carolina who had been largely responsible for the **Nullification Crisis** (1832), played a crucial role. In 1847 he issued a series of resolutions in which he claimed that citizens from every state had the right to take their 'property' to any territory. Congress, he asserted, had no authority to place restrictions on slavery in the territories. If the Northern majority continued to ride roughshod over the rights of the Southern minority, the Southern states would have little option but to secede.

The search for compromise

The problem of slavery expansion preoccupied the 30th Congress, which met in December 1847, to the exclusion of every other issue. Moderate politicians, aware that the issue could destroy the Union, tried to find a compromise. The preferred solution of some, including President Polk, was to continue the 36°30′ line across the continent. Slavery would be banned in any territory gained from Mexico north of this line but would be allowed south of the line. This proposal failed to win enough support to pass through Congress.

Popular sovereignty

A more successful compromise idea was the notion of **popular sovereignty**. This was associated with two Mid-western Democrats, Senator Lewis Cass and Senator Stephen Douglas. Consistent with democracy and self-government, popular sovereignty seemed to offer something to both sections. It met the South's wish for federal non-intervention and held out the prospect that slavery might be extended to some of the Mexican territories. It could also be presented to the North as an exclusion scheme because it was unlikely that settlers in the new territories would vote for the introduction of slavery.

There were problems with the concept of popular sovereignty. First, it went against previous practice. In the past, Congress had decided on what should happen in the territories. Did popular sovereignty mean that it no longer had that power? There were also practical difficulties. The main problem was when exactly a territory should decide on the slavery question. Northern Democrats envisaged the decision being made early – as soon as the first territorial assembly met. Southern Democrats, keen to ensure that slaves were allowed into territories, saw the decision being made

Key terms

Territories
Areas in the USA that had not yet become states and which were still under federal government control.

Nullification Crisis
In the late 1820s Calhoun had proclaimed the right of any state to over-rule or nullify any federal law deemed unconstitutional. When South Carolina disallowed two tariff acts, President Jackson threatened to use force. Unable to muster support from other Southern states, South Carolina pulled back from declaring secession.

Popular sovereignty
The notion that settlers, not Congress, should decide whether a territory should or should not allow slaves.

late, near the end of the territorial phase when settlers were seeking admission to the Union. In the interim, they envisaged that slavery would be recognised and protected. Despite this ambiguity, popular sovereignty was supported by many Democrats. It was opposed by a few Southerners who thought they had the right to take their 'property' anywhere they wanted, and by Northerners who believed that slavery should not be allowed to expand under any circumstances, not even if most settlers wished it to expand.

The 1848 election

Although Polk had presided over an administration that had won the greatest area of territory in US history, he gained little credit for the Mexican War. Worn out by constant opposition, he decided not to seek a second term. The Democrats thus had to choose a successor. The party rallied around a compromise candidate, Lewis Cass of Michigan. Cass and the Democrats supported popular sovereignty.

Key question
What were the main results of the 1848 presidential election?

The Whigs nominated Mexican war hero Zachary Taylor. Taylor had no previous political experience. Many leading Whigs were not altogether sure he was a Whig. The fact that he was a Louisiana slave owner did not endear him to abolitionists. Nevertheless, many Northern Whigs were prepared to endorse Taylor if only because he seemed a likely winner. To avoid a split between its Northern and Southern wings, the Whig Party had no national platform on slavery expansion. This meant that it could conduct a two-faced campaign, running as an anti-slavery party in the North and as a pro-Southern rights party in the South.

A new party, the Free Soil Party, was formed to fight the election. It included a number of Northern Democrats, especially from New York, who supported Martin Van Buren and who were alarmed at the Southern dominance of the Democrat Party. The new party also included 'Conscience' Whigs (who had no intention of campaigning for a Southern slave owner) and Liberty Party supporters. Van Buren was nominated as the Free Soil Party's presidential candidate. The party supported the Wilmot Proviso.

The election result

The election was a triumph for Taylor, who won 1,360,000 votes (47.5 per cent of the total) and 163 electoral college votes. Cass won 1,220,000 votes (42.5 per cent) and 127 electoral votes. Van Buren won 291,000 votes (10 per cent) but no electoral votes. Taylor's victory was not sectional. He carried eight of the 15 slave states and seven of the 15 free states. Even so, sectional issues influenced the result. Throughout the election, the expansion of slavery had been the crucial issue. The fact that the Free Soil Party won 10 per cent of the popular vote was some indication of Northern opinion.

Congressional tension

The Congress, which met in December 1848, was dominated by debates over slavery. Northern representatives, who controlled the House, reaffirmed the Wilmot Proviso and condemned slave trading in Washington DC. The same month that Congress met Calhoun issued his *Address to the People of the Southern States* – an effort to unite all Southern Congressmen behind the 'Southern cause'. The *Address* was very much a defence of slavery and an attack on Northern aggression. Calhoun's tactic, however, failed. At this stage, most Southern Whigs placed their trust in President Taylor. Only 48 members of Congress, about one-third of slave state members, were prepared to sign the *Address*.

California and New Mexico

Few Americans had thought that California or New Mexico would speedily apply for statehood if only because both areas seemed to have little to offer settlers. But the discovery of gold in California touched off the 1848–9 Gold Rush. Within months, there were 100,000 people in California, more than enough to enable the area to apply for statehood. New Mexico had fewer people. However, thousands of **Mormons** had settled around Salt Lake City in 1846–7. Now, as a result of the Mexican War, they found themselves under US jurisdiction.

President Taylor

While Zachary Taylor, was (and is) generally seen as a man of honesty and integrity, he was judged by most contemporaries (and historians alike) as a political amateur who was prone to over-simplify complex problems. Although he was a slave owner, he was determined to act in a way that, he hoped, benefited the national interest. Deliberately shunning the advice of Henry Clay of Kentucky, Taylor was far more influenced by New York Senator William Seward. Few Southern Whigs were happy with Seward's prominence.

Congress's sitting came to an end in March 1849. It would not meet again until December. Taylor determined to act decisively. Hoping that a quick solution to the California–New Mexico problem might reduce the potential for sectional strife, he encouraged settlers in the areas to frame constitutions and apply immediately for admission to the Union without first going through the process of establishing territorial governments. He was confident that people in both states would vote for free state constitutions. Taylor, who had no wish to see slavery abolished, believed that it would be best protected if Southerners refrained from rekindling the slavery issue in the territories. At the same time, he hoped his policy would acknowledge a position upon which all Southerners agreed: that is, that a state could bar or permit slavery as it chose.

In 1849 California duly ratified a constitution prohibiting ,slavery and applied for immediate admission to the Union. Taylor was also prepared to admit New Mexico, even though it had not enough people to apply for statehood. There was a further problem with New Mexico: it had a major boundary dispute with Texas. Southerners supported Texas's claim; Northerners – and Taylor – supported New Mexico. A clash between the state forces of Texas and the US army suddenly seemed imminent.

Southern resentment

Taylor's actions incensed Southerners, Democrats and Whigs alike. Having won the war against Mexico, most Southerners

Key term

Mormons
Members of a religious sect, founded in the 1820s by Joseph Smith. In 1846–7, Brigham Young established a Mormon 'state' in Utah, centred on Salt Lake City. Mormon men could have multiple wives; this made the sect unpopular with most Americans.

believed they were now being excluded from the territory gained. Many appreciated that the climate and terrain of the area made it inhospitable to slavery: there was no great rush to take slaves into New Mexico or California. Nevertheless, virtually all Southerners agreed that neither territory should be admitted to the Union as free states without substantial compensation to the South. Some Southerners went further. In October 1849 Mississippi issued a call to all slave states to send representatives to a convention to meet at Nashville in June 1850 to devise and adopt 'some mode of resistance to Northern aggression'.

Taylor's hopes of resolving the sectional strife were dashed. Bitter divisions were reflected in Congress, which met in December 1849. Fist fights on the floor of Congress became commonplace. The debates over slavery expansion were equally fierce. Southerners also raised the issues of fugitive slaves, claiming (rightly) that many Northern states were flouting the (1793) law and frustrating slaveholders' efforts to catch runaways and return them to the South. Northerners, on the other hand, objected to the fact that slavery was still allowed in Washington. The dispute between Texas and New Mexico added to the tension as more and more Southerners began to talk of secession.

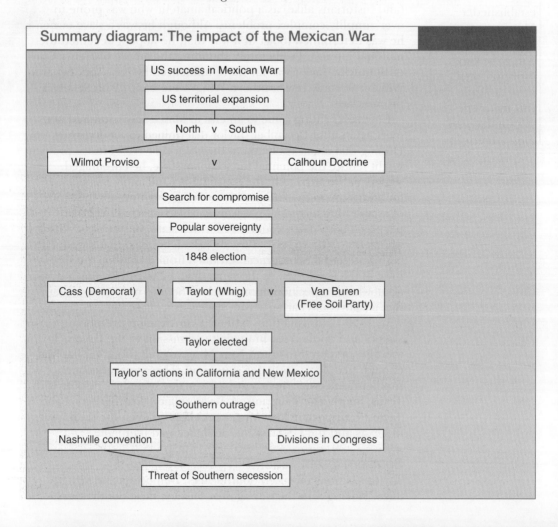

Summary diagram: The impact of the Mexican War

3 | The 1850 Compromise

Taylor was determined to make no concessions to the South. He was prepared to call (what he saw as) the Southern bluff and, if need be, be ready to lead an army into the South to prevent secession. However, many politicians from mid-Western states were worried by events and felt that the South had to be placated. Their leader was 73-year-old Henry Clay, who had served in Congress since 1812. With a reputation as a conciliator from previous crises, he seemed the ideal man to lead compromise efforts.

In January 1850 Clay offered the Senate a set of resolutions as a basis for a compromise.

- California was to be admitted as a free state.
- Utah (formerly the Mormon 'state' of Deseret) and New Mexico were to be organised as territories without any mention of, or restriction on, slavery.
- Slave-trading but not slavery itself should end in Washington.
- A more stringent Fugitive Slave Act should be passed to placate the South.
- In order to resolve the Texas–New Mexico dispute, Texas should surrender the disputed land to New Mexico. In return Congress would assume the $10 million public debt that Texas still owed.

The next few months were marked by a series of epic speeches as Clay's proposals, rolled into a single 'omnibus' bill, were debated in Congress. Most of the 'old guard' politicians, many making their last major appearance on the public stage, contributed to the debates. So too did a number of men who were just beginning what were to be prestigious political careers.

Senator Henry Clay. His 1850 Compromise helped to prevent a major crisis.

Senator John C. Calhoun, an ardent supporter of slavery. 'I hold that in the present state of civilisation', he said, 'the relation now existing in the slave-holding states between the two [races] is, instead of an evil, a good – a positive good'.

Clay defended his proposals in a four-hour speech in February 1850. He declared:

> I have seen many periods of great anxiety, of peril, and of danger in this country and I have never before risen to address any assemblage so oppressed, so appalled, and so anxious.

He warned the South against secession and assured the North that nature would check the spread of slavery more effectively than a thousand Wilmot Provisos.

Calhoun would have spoken but he was seriously ill. His speech was thus read by Senator Mason of Virginia on 4 March. (Within a month of the speech Calhoun was dead.) Calhoun declared that the North was responsible for the crisis: Northerners threatened slavery. If the threats continued, Southern states would have no option but to leave the Union.

On 7 March 69-year-old Daniel Webster, a leading Northern Whig, spoke in support of the Compromise. 'I wish to speak today', he declared, 'not as a Massachusetts man, not as a Northern man, but as an American'. Webster, aware that his speech would offend many of his constituents, hoped to offer an olive branch to the South. Moderates praised his devotion to the Union. But abolitionists bitterly denounced him for betraying the cause of freedom.

However eloquent, the conciliatory voices of Clay and Webster made few converts. With every call for compromise, some Northern or Southern speaker would rise and inflame passions.

Taylor soon made it clear that he opposed Clay's proposals. In his view, California should be admitted as a free state immediately while New Mexico should also come in with all possible speed. Southerners would have to accept their medicine.

The end of the crisis

In June 1850 delegates from nine slave states met at Nashville. The fact that six slave states did not send delegates was disconcerting to those 'fire-eaters' who supported secession. Even more worrying was the fact that the convention displayed little enthusiasm for secession. Moderates took control and isolated the extremists. Southern Whigs were still hopeful that some compromise could be arranged. The Nashville convention, therefore, had little impact.

President Taylor's death (of gastroenteritis) in July had a far greater impact. (Daniel Webster was not alone in believing there would have been a civil war if Taylor had lived.) Vice-President Millard Fillmore now became President. A New York Whig, Fillmore was sympathetic to the South. His break with the policies of his predecessor was immediately apparent. There were wholesale cabinet changes (Webster, for example, became Secretary of State) and Fillmore threw his weight behind the Compromise proposals. Nevertheless, on 31 July Clay's bill was defeated, mainly because most Northern Congressmen, anxious to escape the charge of bargaining with the South, voted against it.

Senator Douglas now demonstrated his political skill. Known as the 'Little Giant' (he was under 5 feet 4 inches tall), Douglas replaced Clay as leader of the Compromise cause. Stripping Clay's bill down to its component parts, he submitted each part as a separate bill. This strategy was successful. Southerners voted for those proposals they liked; Northerners did likewise. A few moderates, like Douglas himself, swung the balance. By September 1850, all the bits of the Compromise had passed:

- statehood for California
- territorial status for Utah and New Mexico, allowing popular sovereignty
- resolution of the Texas–New Mexico boundary dispute
- abolition of the slave trade in Washington
- a new Fugitive Slave Act.

Douglas and other political leaders hailed the Compromise as a settlement of the issues that threatened to divide the nation.

Compromise or armistice?

Historians continue to debate whether the 1850 Compromise was a success. David Potter questioned whether it was even a compromise. He thought it was more an armistice. Most Northern Congressmen had, after all, voted against the pro-slavery measures while most Southern Congressmen had voted against the anti-slavery measures. The Compromise had skirted, rather than settled, the controversy over slavery in the territories, providing no formula to guide the future.

Failure or success?

Many Northerners believed that Congress had cravenly surrendered to Southern threats. However, historians tend to the

view that the North gained more than the South from the
Compromise. The entry of California into the Union tilted the
balance in favour of the free states. The resolutions on New
Mexico and Utah were hollow victories for the South. The odds
were that these areas would also enter the Union as free states at
some time in the future. The Fugitive Slave Act was the North's
only major concession.

Most Americans seemed prepared to accept the Compromise.
Across the USA, there were mass meetings to celebrate its
passage. Southern secessionists' hopes foundered. Only half the
Nashville convention delegates turned up when it met again in
November. It was clear that the majority of Southerners still
supported the Union. In Southern state elections in 1851–2
unionist candidates defeated secessionists. The South had
decided against secession – for now. But ominously for the future,
many Southerners had come to accept Calhoun's doctrine that
secession was a valid constitutional remedy, applicable in
appropriate circumstances. The hope was that those
circumstances would not arise.

In December 1851 President Fillmore announced that the
Compromise was 'final and irrevocable'. Douglas resolved 'never
to make another speech on the slavery question … Let us cease
agitating, stop the debate and drop the subject'. Indeed, the
remainder of Fillmore's administration was a period of relative
tranquility. Nevertheless, some sectional problems did remain.

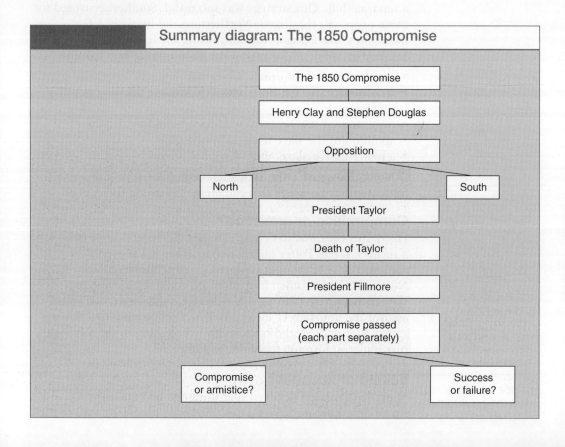

Summary diagram: The 1850 Compromise

Key question
How serious was sectional strife in the years 1850–3?

Key term

Posse
A group of men called out by a sheriff or marshal to aid in enforcing the law.

4 | North–South Problems 1850–3

The Fugitive Slave Act

While some Northerners accepted the Fugitive Slave Act as the price the North had to pay to save the Union, it contained a number of features that were distasteful to moderates and outrageous to abolitionists. For example, it authorised federal marshals to raise **posses** to pursue fugitives on Northern soil. Those who refused to join risked a $1000 fine. In addition, the law targeted not only recent runaways but also those who had fled the South decades earlier. Abolitionists were appalled. 'Let the President … drench our land of freedom in blood', proclaimed Congressman Joshua Giddings, 'but he will never make us obey the law'.

Efforts to catch and return fugitive slaves inflamed feelings. In 1854 a Boston mob broke into a courthouse and killed a guard in an abortive effort to rescue the fugitive slave Anthony Burns. Troops had to escort Burns to Boston harbour where a ship carried him back to slavery. The Burns affair was one of a number of well-publicised incidents. In response to the Act, vigilance committees sprang up in many Northern communities to help endangered blacks escape to Canada. During the 1850s nine Northern states passed personal liberty laws. By such techniques as forbidding the use of state jails to imprison alleged fugitives, these laws were intended to make it difficult to enforce federal law.

Southerners kept a watchful eye on proceedings, regarding the Fugitive Slave Act as a test of Northern goodwill. The fact that some free states went to great lengths to negate it caused huge resentment. However, it is likely that overt resistance to the Act was exaggerated by both Southerners and abolitionists. In most Northern states the law was enforced without much trouble.

The impact of *Uncle Tom's Cabin*

In 1851 Harriet Beecher Stowe began publishing *Uncle Tom's Cabin* in weekly instalments. The novel, which presented a fierce

Harriet Beecher Stowe, author of *Uncle Tom's Cabin*. When President Lincoln met Stowe in 1863 he is reported to have said: 'So you're the little woman who wrote the book that made this great war!'

attack on slavery, sold 300,000 copies in 1852 and a further two million copies in America over the next 10 years. Even those Northerners who did not read it were familiar with its theme because it was also turned into songs and plays. Stowe herself had little first hand knowledge of slavery: she relied upon her imagination and drew heavily on abolitionist literature when describing its brutalities. Although it is impossible to gauge its precise impact, the book undoubtedly aroused wide Northern sympathy for slaves and probably pushed some Northerners toward a more aggressively anti-slavery stance. In historian David Potter's view, Northerners' attitude to slavery was 'never quite the same after *Uncle Tom's Cabin*'.

The 1852 election

The Democrats, who had done well in the 1850 **mid-term elections**, were confident of victory in 1852. Many Irish and German immigrants were now entitled to vote and were expected to vote Democrat. Moreover, Van Buren and his supporters, who had formed the core of the Free Soil Party (see page 40), had now returned to the Democrat fold. The Democrats chose Franklin Pierce of New Hampshire as their presidential candidate. Handsome, charming but somewhat lightweight, Pierce's main asset was that he was acceptable to all factions of the party. 'We "Polked" 'em in "44"', boasted the Democrat press: 'we'll Pierce 'em in "52"'. The Democrats campaigned on a platform supporting the 1850 Compromise and popular sovereignty, and resisting 'agitation of the slavery question under whatever shape or colour the attempt may be made'.

The Whig Party was divided North against South, in terms of both agreeing to a platform and choosing a candidate. While most Northerners supported Mexican War hero General Winfield Scott (a Southerner), most Southern Whigs hoped to retain Fillmore (a Northerner). Scott was finally nominated on the 53rd ballot. In many ways he was a good choice. Although politically inexperienced, he was a man of integrity and ability and the Whigs had twice won elections by nominating military heroes. While the Whigs managed to agree on a leader, they could not agree on policies. Accordingly their platform said virtually nothing. Neither Northern nor Southern Whigs were happy with the outcome. Northerners disliked the (lack of) platform. Southerners were unhappy with the candidate, particularly as Scott seemed to have fallen under Seward's influence.

Pierce won the election with 1,601,274 votes (51 per cent). He carried 27 states (254 electoral college votes). Scott won 1,386,580 votes (44 per cent) but carried only four states (42 electoral votes). John Hale, the Free Soil Party candidate, won 156,000 votes (five per cent), carrying not a single state. Many Whigs were stunned by the defeat. In the six states of the Lower South, Scott won only 35 per cent of the popular vote: these same states had given Taylor 50 per cent in 1848. Whig Senator Alexander Stephens from Georgia moaned that 'the Whig Party is dead'. However, some leading Whigs, like Seward, were confident

Mid-term elections
The whole of the House of Representatives and a third of the Senate are re-elected every two years. This means that there are major elections half way through a president's term of office.

Key term

that they could heal the sectional wounds and that common hostility to the Democrats would revitalise the party.

President Pierce

Pierce was inaugurated President in March 1853. Although he lacked experience and was soon to prove himself weak and irresolute, he seemed to be in a strong position. The Democrats had large majorities in both Houses of Congress and the economy continued to boom. The Whig Party, seriously divided, was unable to mount much of a challenge and two of its best-known leaders, Webster and Clay, died in 1852. Pierce, hoping that the 1850 Compromise had settled the sectional conflict, intended to maintain the unity of his party by championing expansionist policies. Although a Northerner, he sympathised with, and was influenced by, the Southern wing of his party. Given the political situation, Southerners had good reason for hoping that the USA would expand into Central America and/or Cuba, thus allowing the opportunity for slavery also to expand.

The Gadsden Purchase

In 1853 Pierce gave James Gadsden the authority to negotiate the purchase of 250,000 square miles of Mexican territory. Gadsden eventually agreed to purchase 54,000 square miles. Southerners favoured the acquisition of this territory, not because of its slavery potential, but because it would assist the building of a Southern railway to the Pacific. Gadsden's treaty only gained Senate approval after an amendment slashed 9000 square miles from the proposed purchase.

Cuba

Key term

Filibuster
A military adventure, aimed at overthrowing a government.

Pierce encountered serious opposition when he tried to acquire Cuba, the last remnant of Spain's American empire. In 1851 an American-sponsored '**filibuster**' expedition to try to overthrow the Spanish Cuban government had failed miserably. In 1853–4 Mississippi's former senator John Quitman planned an even greater expedition. Several thousand American volunteers were recruited and contact made with Cuban rebels. In July 1853 Pierce met Quitman and, unofficially, encouraged him to go ahead with his plans. His aim may have been to scare Spain into selling the island to the USA. Pierce's main problem was Northern opinion: Northerners viewed filibustering as another example of Southern efforts to expand slavery. Pierce, alarmed by Northern reaction, forced Quitman to scuttle his expedition.

Still hoping to obtain Cuba, Pierce authorised Soule, the American minister in Spain, to offer up to $130 million for the island. Events, however, soon slipped out of Pierce's control. In October 1854 the American ministers to Britain (Buchanan), France (Mason) and Spain (Soule) met in Belgium and issued the Ostend Manifesto. This stated that Cuba 'is as necessary to the North American Republic as any of its present members'. If Spain refused to sell, then the USA would be 'justified in wresting it from Spain'. Unfortunately for Pierce, details of the Ostend

Manifesto were leaked and immediately denounced by Northern politicians. Pierce quickly repudiated the Manifesto and Soule resigned. The (unsuccessful) expansionist efforts angered Northerners who believed that the South aspired to establish a Latin American slave empire. Many Southerners did so aspire, and remained optimistic about their aspirations, throughout the 1850s.

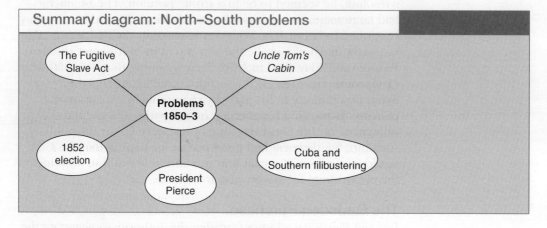

Summary diagram: North–South problems

The Fugitive Slave Act

Uncle Tom's Cabin

Problems 1850–3

1852 election

Cuba and Southern filibustering

President Pierce

5 | The Problem of Kansas–Nebraska

Nebraska, part of the Louisiana Purchase, was still unsettled by Americans in the early 1850s. Until Congress organised the area into a territory, land could not be surveyed and put up for sale. While Northerners were keen to see Nebraska developed, Southerners were less enthusiastic. Nebraska lay north of latitude 36°30′ and, by the terms of the Missouri Compromise, new states in the area would enter the Union as free states. Southern politicians, therefore, made every effort to delay granting territorial status to Nebraska.

Key question
Why did the Kansas–Nebraska Act cause such a storm?

Douglas's motives
In January 1854 Senator Douglas, Chairman of the Senate Committee on Territories, introduced the Kansas–Nebraska bill into Congress. Douglas, one of the main architects of the 1850 Compromise, was a man of talent, energy and (presidential) ambition. He had pushed – unsuccessfully – for Nebraska becoming a territory since 1844. In order to get a Nebraska bill enacted Douglas knew he needed the support of some Southern senators. He also knew that those Southerners were likely to drive a hard bargain. Indeed Southerners were only likely to vote for Douglas's bill if they felt they had a chance of expanding slavery in the area: this meant that the 1820 Missouri Compromise ban (see pages 31–2) would have to be bypassed in order to get the bill through Congress.

Douglas's original bill, while avoiding all mention of the Missouri Compromise, was designed to appeal to the South. The entire area of Nebraska was to be organised into a single territory. The states eventually formed from it were to be received into the

The Kansas–Nebraska Act: 1854

Key date

Union 'with or without slavery as their constitution may prescribe at the time of their admission'. The bill, which substituted popular sovereignty for the Missouri Compromise, gave Southerners some hope of establishing slavery in Nebraska.

But Douglas's bill did not satisfy Southern senators. A number, including Senator Atchison of Missouri, made it clear to Douglas that if he wanted Nebraska to become a territory, his bill must specifically repeal the ban on slavery there. An amendment to that effect was introduced and Douglas reluctantly agreed to it. He also accepted another change. The new Kansas–Nebraska bill divided the Nebraska territory into two: Kansas, the area immediately west of Missouri; and Nebraska, the area west of Iowa and Minnesota. There was little chance of slavery taking hold in Nebraska: the climate was too cold for plantation agriculture. But it did seem possible it might spread to Kansas (see Figure 2.3 on page 37).

Douglas, a dedicated patriot who had no wish to heighten sectional tension, was confident that his bill would cause no great strain. Although in theory slavery could now expand northwards it was unlikely that it would do so. Douglas, a great believer in popular sovereignty, saw no problem in letting the people of Kansas–Nebraska decide their own fate. He was confident that they would not vote for slavery. A supporter of manifest destiny (see page 34), he did not want the settlement of the West to be stalled by sectional controversy. Such controversy could prevent the building of a Northern trans-continental railway that would have to run through Kansas–Nebraska.

Douglas had other motives. He believed there was political capital to be gained from his Kansas–Nebraska measure. It should enhance his reputation in Illinois, where many people (not least himself) stood to benefit financially from a trans-continental railway leading west from Chicago. Settlement of the Nebraska issue would also enhance his presidential ambitions.

'A hell of a storm'

Douglas believed he had succeeded in winning over the South without conceding much in return. However, he seriously miscalculated. His bill, far from healing tension, created a 'hell of a storm'. It was proof to many Northerners that the **Slave Power conspiracy** was still at work. Abolitionists had a field day. One of the most effective pieces of abolitionist propaganda was a tract, written by Salmon Chase, entitled *The Appeal of the Independent Democrats in Congress to the People of the United States*, published in January 1854. 'We arraign this bill as a gross violation of a sacred pledge; as a criminal betrayal of precious rights; as part and parcel of an atrocious plot to exclude from the vast unoccupied region immigrants from the Old World and free labourers from our own states and convert it into a dreary region of despotism, inhabited by masters and slaves.'

The following extract from a sermon by abolitionist preacher Theodore Parker, delivered in February 1854, is another example

Slave Power conspiracy
A Northern notion that Southerners were plotting to expand slavery. Those who believed in the conspiracy were never very specific about who exactly was conspiring.

Profile: Stephen Douglas 1813–61

1813	Born in Vermont
1833	Settled in Illinois, where he practised law
1843	Elected to the House of Representatives as a Democrat
1847	Became a Senator for Illinois
1850	Helped to pass the Compromise
1852	Re-elected Senator
1854	Introduced the Kansas–Nebraska bill
1857	Denounced the Lecompton Constitution and broke with President Buchanan
1858	Campaigned for re-election to the Senate: he and Lincoln took part in a series of famous debates: Douglas was re-elected
1860	Nominated as Democratic candidate for the presidency
1861 April	Following the attack on Fort Sumter, he pledged support for the Union
June	Died of typhoid fever

Douglas was committed to popular sovereignty. Energetic and eloquent, the 'Little Giant' had presidential ambitions. These ambitions were not helped by the Kansas–Nebraska Act. In 1854 he was depicted as a traitor to the North. 'I could travel from Boston to Chicago by the light of my own effigy', said Douglas, referring to the fact that models of him were burned across the Northern states.

of the North's response to Douglas's measure: 'The Slave Power has long been seeking to extend its jurisdiction. It has eminently succeeded. It fills all the chief offices of the nation; the Presidents are Slave Presidents; the Supreme Court is of Slave Judges, every one … In all that depends on the political action of America, the Slave Power carries the day.'

Initially most Southerners had been apathetic about the Kansas–Nebraska bill. But the ferocity of Northern attacks led to a Southern counter-attack. Passage of the bill suddenly became a symbol of Southern honour. The result was a great struggle in Congress. Northern Free-Soilers, Democrats and Whigs joined forces in opposition to it. Southern Whigs and Democrats united in supporting the bill. Pierce's administration, unwilling to risk losing the South, agreed to make it a test of party loyalty, thus ensuring that some Northern Democrats would support the measure. After months of bitter debate, the bill passed through both houses of Congress and became law in May 1854. It had sectionalised Congress: 90 per cent of Southerners voted for it; 64 per cent of Northerners voted against it. The Northern Democrats splintered: 44 in the House voted for it; 43 voted against it.

In the summer of 1854 Douglas, delighted that both Kansas and Nebraska could now set up territorial governments, was still confident that the sectional storm would be short-lived and that the Democrats would retain their strength in the North. In truth, Douglas had little cause for optimism. By failing to predict the extent of Northern outrage generated by his Act, he weakened his party, damaged his own presidential ambitions and revived North–South rivalry.

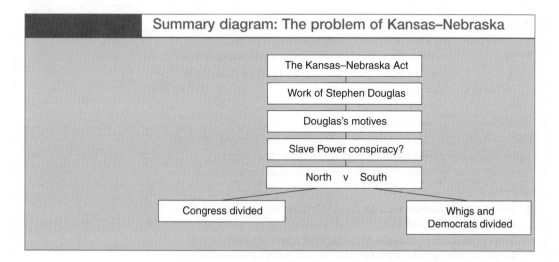

Summary diagram: The problem of Kansas–Nebraska

The Kansas–Nebraska Act

Work of Stephen Douglas

Douglas's motives

Slave Power conspiracy?

North v South

Congress divided

Whigs and Democrats divided

Study Guide: AS Questions

In the style of OCR

Study the five sources on the threat of secession in 1850, and then answer **both** sub-questions. It is recommended that you spend two-thirds of your time in answering part **(b)**.

(a) **Study Sources B and C.**
    Compare these sources as evidence for the seriousness of the crisis of 1850. (30 marks)

(b) **Study all of the sources.**
    Use your own knowledge to assess how far the sources support the interpretation that sectional tensions in the period 1848–61 were largely caused by the threat of secession. (70 marks)

Source A

From: Henry Clay, in resolutions laid before the Senate, January 1850. Clay, a veteran senator and known as 'the great pacificator', sets down his proposals for reducing sectional tensions.

1. The entry of California into the Union as a free state at the earliest possible date.
2. The organisation of New Mexico and Utah for statehood, leaving their legislatures free to decide on the future of slavery.
3. Texas to give up any parts of New Mexico unlawfully seized; the federal government to assume responsibility for the debts incurred by the Texan government before independence.
4. The slave trade in the District of Columbia to be abolished.
5. A new, stricter fugitive slave law to be introduced, allowing the more rapid recovery of escaped slaves.

Source B

From: Daniel Webster, in a speech to political supporters, January 1850. Webster, a former secretary of state and opposed to both slavery and the disintegration of the Union, comments on the crisis of 1850.

All this agitation, I think will subside without serious result, but still it is mischievous and creates heart burnings. But the Union is not in danger.

Source C

Henry Clay, in a speech to the Senate, February 1850. Clay speaks in support of his proposals.

We are told now, and it is rung throughout this entire country, that the Union is threatened with subversion and destruction. Well, the first question which naturally rises is, supposing the Union to be dissolved – having all the causes of grievance which are complained of – how far will a dissolution furnish a remedy for those grievances? If the Union is to be dissolved for any existing causes, it will be dissolved because slavery is threatened to be abolished in the District of Columbia and because fugitive slaves are not returned, as in my opinion they ought to be … Mr President, I am directly opposed to any purpose of secession, of separation. I am for staying within the Union, and defying any portion of this Union to expel or drive me out of the Union.

Source D

John C. Calhoun, in a speech to the Senate, March 1850. Senator Calhoun, a champion of states' rights and slaveholding, suggests how the Union might be saved.

I have, senators, believed from the first that the agitation of the subject of slavery would, if not prevented by some timely and effective measure, end in disunion. The agitation has been permitted to proceed with almost no attempt to resist it, until it has reached a point when it can no longer be disguised or denied that the Union is in danger. How can the Union be saved? There is but one way by which it can be, and that is by adopting such measures as will satisfy the States belonging to the Southern section, that they can remain in the Union consistently with their honour and their safety. But can this be done? Yes, easily; not by the weaker party, for it can of itself do nothing – not even protect itself – but by the stronger. The North has only to will it to accomplish it – to do justice by conceding to the South an equal right in the acquired territory, and to do her duty by causing the stipulations relative to fugitive slaves to be faithfully fulfilled – to cease the agitation of the slave question.

Source E

From: M.F. Holt, The Political Crisis of the 1850s, 1978. A modern historian argues that Republican politicians exploited sectional differences to gain power.

To say that Republican politicians stirred up and exploited sectional grievances in order to build a winning party is a simple description of fact. It is not meant to imply that winning was their only objective or meant to be a value judgement about the sincerity or insincerity of their personal hatred of black slavery. The anti-slavery pedigree of Republican leaders, however, was in a sense irrelevant to the triumph of the Republican party. Much more important was the campaign they ran to obtain power: their skill in politicising the issues at hand in such a way as to convince Northern voters that control of the Federal government by an exclusive Northern party was necessary to resist slave power aggressions.

Exam tips

(a) The best answers will offer a comparative analysis of both sources. Webster and Clay were leading senators, and both supported compromise. Webster has a different perspective to Clay in January 1850. Might this be due to the timing of the speeches? Had the situation changed between January and February? How important are the different audiences? Webster was speaking to supporters. Clay was speaking in the Senate.

(b) Three of the sources allude directly to the possibility of secession. Sources B and C both discuss the extent of the danger and Source D clearly states the danger to the Union. Although Source A does not mention secession directly, it can be inferred that the proposals are designed to avert this threat. Source E, on the other hand, suggests that Republican politicians exploited sectional tension by playing on voters' fears concerning secession. There is also evidence in the sources that points to other factors. Several issues are mentioned in Source A, including boundary disputes, the organisation of territories and, of course, slavery and related problems. Several of these issues are raised again in Source D. Agitation is mentioned in Sources B and E. The best answers:

- may challenge the question
- will have a reasonable balance between the sources and wider knowledge, and will show an appreciation of the limitations of the sources
- will show an understanding of the link between issues causing sectional tension and the threat of secession, and will be able to demonstrate and evaluate the importance of that threat both from the sources and from contextual knowledge.

Study Guide: A2 Question

In the style of Edexcel

'Misjudgements by politicians explain why the issue of western expansion divided North and South so sharply in the years 1820–54.' How far do you agree with this opinion? (30 marks)

Exam tips

The cross-references are intended to take you straight to the material that will help you to answer the question.

You might well be tempted to see this question as an invitation to narrate the disagreements that arose in the period. That will gain you few marks. The question requires you to focus on why expansion was so divisive, why compromises were unable to provide permanent solutions, and whether politicians mishandled the conflicts that arose.

Was the problem so intractable that it was almost impossible for politicians to prevent tensions erupting into open division? You can show the divisions between Northerners and Southerners over the issue of slavery (pages 14–26) and use the struggle over Missouri (pages 31–2) to show the way in which expansion became inextricably linked with the issue of slavery.

As you plan your essay, examine the key points at which divisions surfaced later in the period, taking care to keep the focus on the issues and difficulties created by expansion at each stage – and whether there is evidence of mishandling of the situation by politicians.

- The issue of Texas (pages 32 and 34) and the Wilmot Proviso (pages 38–9) – note the sectional bitterness that developed over this, and explain why.
- The issue of California and New Mexico (pages 41–2) and the tensions provoked by Taylor's policies. Why did a crisis develop (pages 43–5)?
- The tensions revealed in the 1850 Compromise and the inadequacy of the compromise 'providing no formula to guide the future' (pages 45–6). However, what evidence is there of Douglas's political skill here?
- The problem of Kansas–Nebraska (pages 50–3). Why did Douglas's bill create 'a hell of a storm'? How far had tensions over slavery deepened as a result of other factors in the years 1850–4?

In coming to a conclusion you will first need to weigh up the significance of political misjudgements in relation to other factors. Were real political skills evident during the period that reduced the tensions? Did political ineptitude account for the severity of the crises? What part did the increasing tension over slavery itself play? Were politicians powerless in the face of the divisions over slavery and its expansion?

3 The Rise of the Republican Party

1 | The Collapse of the Second Party System

The 1854 mid-term elections

In the 1854 mid-term elections the Democrats, apparently blamed for sponsoring the Kansas–Nebraska Act (see page 50), lost all but 23 of their (previously 91) free state seats in Congress. (In the South the Democrats retained all but four of the 67 seats held.) Prior to 1854 the Whigs would have benefited from Democratic unpopularity in the North. By 1854, however, the Whig Party was no longer a major force in many free states.

The Whig collapse has often been seen as a direct result of the Kansas–Nebraska Act, which set Southern against Northern Whigs. However, while divisions over slavery certainly played a part in the Whig collapse, other factors were also vital. Interestingly, Whig decline began well before the debates over

Key question
Why did the second party system collapse?

Kansas–Nebraska. State and local elections in 1853 were a disaster for Northern Whigs. The main problem confronting Northern politicians at local level in the early 1850s was not the slavery question. Anti-immigration and anti-Catholicism were much more important issues.

Catholic immigrants

Between 1845 and 1854 some three million immigrants entered the USA. Over one million of these were Irish Catholics, escaping the horrors of the **potato famine**. German immigrants, many of whom were Catholic, outnumbered the Irish. Few Germans who came to America were escaping persecution (as historians once thought): most simply wanted to better themselves and many had sufficient funds to buy land. The Irish, with fewer resources, tended to settle in North-eastern cities. Native-born Americans accused the Irish of pulling down wage levels and taking jobs from native-born workers. They also associated Irish immigrants with increased crime and welfare costs.

Fear of a papal plot to subvert the USA was deep-rooted among native-born Americans, most of whom were strongly Protestant. Many were horrified by the growth of Catholicism: between 1850 and 1854 the number of Catholic bishops, priests and churches almost doubled. The growing political power of Catholic voters, particularly in cities such as New York and Boston, was also resented by native-born Americans. Protestants claimed that the Irish voted en masse as their political bosses, or their priests, told them. This was seen as a threat to democracy and the very basis of what it meant to be American.

Whig failure

Given that most Irish and Germans voted Democrat, that party was unlikely to support anti-immigrant or anti-Catholic measures. The Whigs also failed to respond to **nativist** concerns. Indeed, in the 1852 election the Whigs were actively pro-Catholic in an effort to capture the growing immigrant vote. The strategy failed: few Irish were persuaded to vote Whig while some traditional Whig voters stayed at home rather than vote for a party which seemed to be trying to appease Catholics. Thus, by the early 1850s many Northerners had become alienated from the Whigs and Democrats and began to look to new parties to represent their views. This happened first at state and local level. Disintegration of loyalty to the old parties in 1853 had little to do with sectional conflict between North and South; indeed it occurred during a temporary lull in that conflict.

The Know Nothings

Concern about immigration and Catholicism resulted in the rise of the Know Nothing movement. This was an offshoot of the Order of the Star-Spangled Banner, a nativist society formed in New York in 1849. In the early 1850s the Know Nothing movement mushroomed. As membership grew, an elaborate local, state and national structure was created. Know Nothings, who

Key terms

Potato famine
In 1845–6 the Irish potato crop was hit by blight – a fungus which destroyed the crop. The result was a serious famine. Millions of Irish people died or emigrated to Britain or the USA.

Nativism
Suspicion of immigrants.

pledged to vote for no-one except native-born Protestants, learned rituals and passwords as they were initiated to different degrees of membership. When asked questions about the order, they were supposed to reply, 'I know nothing', thereby giving the movement its name.

The Know Nothing order first entered politics by throwing its support behind suitable candidates from the existing parties. It had so much success that by 1854 the movement took on the characteristics of a political party, selecting its own candidates – often choosing men who had little previous political experience. Most Know Nothings wanted checks on immigration and a 21-year probationary period before immigrants could become full American citizens.

Northerners joined the movement for a variety of other reasons.

- Most supported its anti-Catholic stance.
- Some approved of the fact that it was **anti-establishment** and promised to return power to the people.
- The unpopularity of the Kansas–Nebraska Act, associated with the Democrats, also helped the Know Nothings. So many Whigs joined the Know Nothing order that leading Democrats initially thought it was an arm of the Whig Party. They soon discovered that their own supporters were also streaming into the order.

Anti-establishment Opposed to the opinions of those in power.

Key term

By 1854 the Know Nothings had over one million members and began to wield real political power. In 1854 the movement won 63 per cent of the vote in Massachusetts. In 1855 it won control of three more New England states. It even began to win large-scale support, mainly from ex-Whigs, in the South. By 1855 the Know Nothing order, now calling itself the American Party, held open conventions on a state and national level.

The Republican Party

The Northern electorate was not just concerned with anti-immigrant and anti-Catholic issues. The Kansas–Nebraska Act awakened the spectre of the Slave Power (see page 51) and many Northerners were keen to give support to parties opposed to slavery expansion. In 1854 several anti-slavery coalitions were formed under a variety of names. The Republican name finally caught on.

By 1854–5 it was not clear whether the Know Nothings or Republicans would pick up the tattered Whig mantle in the North. In general, the Republicans were strongest in the Mid-west; the Know Nothings were strongest in New England. However, in most free states the two parties were not necessarily in competition; indeed they often tried to avoid a contest in order to defeat the Democrats. Many Northerners hated both Catholicism and the Slave Power.

Given the Democrat reverses in the North in 1854, it was clear that there would be an anti-Democrat majority in the Congress which met in December 1855. Whether the anti-Democrat

Congressmen were more concerned with immigration or slavery expansion remained to be seen. At this stage many Republicans were Know Nothings and vice versa. For those 'pure' Republicans who were opposed to nativism, the 1854 elections were a major setback. Given Know Nothing strength, the rise of the Republican Party was far from inevitable. Indeed, most political observers expected the Know Nothings to be the main opponents of the Democrats in 1856. Given its concerns, the Republican Party could never be more than a Northern party. In contrast, the Know Nothings drew support from both North and South.

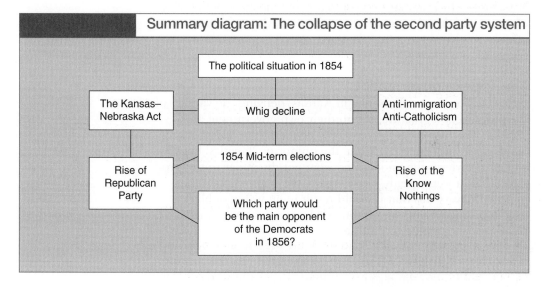

Summary diagram: The collapse of the second party system

- The political situation in 1854
- The Kansas–Nebraska Act
- Whig decline
- Anti-immigration Anti-Catholicism
- 1854 Mid-term elections
- Rise of Republican Party
- Rise of the Know Nothings
- Which party would be the main opponent of the Democrats in 1856?

Key question
How did events in Kansas help the Republicans?

2 | The Situation in Kansas 1854–6

After 1854 settlers began to move into Kansas. Their main concern was land and water rights. However, for politicians far more was at stake. Northerners thought that if slavery expanded into Kansas it might expand anywhere. Southerners feared that a free Kansas would be another nail in the slavery coffin. In the Senate, William Seward of New York threw down the gauntlet to the South: 'We will engage in competition for the virgin soil of Kansas and God give the victory to the side which is stronger in numbers as it is in right.' Senator Atchison of Missouri took up the challenge. 'We are playing for a mighty stake; if we win we carry slavery to the Pacific Ocean; if we fail, we lose Missouri, Arkansas and Texas and all the territories; the game must be played boldly.'

A number of Northerners and Southerners tried to influence events in Kansas. The Massachusetts Emigrant Aid Company, for example, sponsored over 1500 Northerners to settle in Kansas in 1854–5. However, pro-slavers seemed to be in the stronger position, given the proximity of Kansas to Missouri. Senator Atchison formed the Platte County Defensive Association which was pledged to ensure that Kansas became a slave state.

Elections in Kansas

In March 1855 Kansas elected its first territorial legislature which would decide on the subject of slavery; the elections were thus seen as crucial. 'There are 1100 coming over from Platte County to vote and if that ain't enough we can send 5000 – enough to kill every God-damned abolitionist in the Territory', declared Atchison. The fact that hundreds of pro-slavery Missourians did cross into Kansas to vote was probably a tactical mistake. In March 1855 the pro-slavers would probably have won anyway. The Missourians simply cast doubt on the pro-slavery victory. The legislature, which met at Lecompton, proceeded to pass a series of tough pro-slavery laws. (For example, it became a **capital offence** to give aid to a fugitive slave.) Northern opinion was outraged.

Capital offence
A crime punishable by death.

Key term

The Topeka government

'Free-state' or 'free-soil' settlers in Kansas, denying the validity of the pro-slavery legislature, set up their own government at Topeka. The free-staters were deeply divided, especially between 'moderates' and 'fanatics'. While the (minority) 'fanatics' held abolitionist views, the 'moderates' were not dissimilar to the pro-slavers. Most were openly racist: one of the main reasons they opposed slavery was that it would result in an influx of blacks. The Topeka government, dominated by moderates, banned blacks, slave or free, from Kansas.

'Bleeding Kansas' 1856

In May 1856 a pro-slavery posse, trying to arrest free-state leaders, 'sacked' Lawrence, a free-state centre, burning some buildings. This event was blown up out of all proportion by Northern journalists. According to the first reports dozens of free-staters were killed in the 'attack'. In reality there were no casualties (except a member of the pro-slave 'army' who died when a burning building collapsed on him).

The Lawrence raid sparked off more serious violence. The man largely responsible for this was John Brown, a fervent abolitionist. At Pottawatomie Creek, he and several of his sons murdered five pro-slavery settlers. Northern newspapers, suppressing the facts, claimed that Brown had acted in righteous self-defence. Overnight, as a result of a vicious crime, he became a Northern hero. In Kansas, his actions led to an increase in tension and a series of tit-for-tat killings. The Northern press again exaggerated the situation, describing it as civil war.

With events seemingly drifting out of control, Pierce appointed a new governor, John Geary, who managed to patch up a truce between the warring factions. Nevertheless, events in Kansas, and the distorted reporting of them, helped to boost Republican fortunes. 'Bleeding Kansas' became a rallying cry for Northerners opposed to what they perceived to be the Slave Power at work.

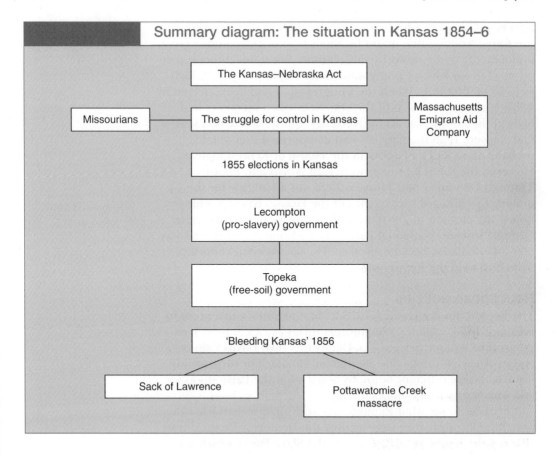

Summary diagram: The situation in Kansas 1854–6

The Kansas–Nebraska Act

Missourians — The struggle for control in Kansas — Massachusetts Emigrant Aid Company

1855 elections in Kansas

Lecompton (pro-slavery) government

Topeka (free-soil) government

'Bleeding Kansas' 1856

Sack of Lawrence

Pottawatomie Creek massacre

Key question
Why did the Republicans emerge as the Democrats' main rivals?

3 | The Emergence of the Republicans

American Party problems

The American Party – the party of the Know Nothings – was the main anti-Democrat party in both the North and South in 1855. (In the South it was essentially the Whig party under a new name.) Ironically, success in the South was to be a major reason for the American Party's undoing. The Know Nothing order had won massive support in the North in 1854–5 because it had been able to exploit both anti-slavery and nativist issues. However, by 1856 the American Party, if it was to be a national party, had no option but to drop its anti-Kansas–Nebraska position. By so doing, it lost Northern support.

Other factors damaged the party.

- The decline of immigration in the mid-1850s resulted in a decline of nativism.
- The failure of Know Nothing-dominated legislatures to make good their campaign promises enabled critics to claim that the movement did nothing.
- Some Americans hated the secretive side of the movement.
- The very success of the American Party helped to tarnish its image as an authentic people's party: it attracted to it many of the 'old guard' politicians – the very people the Know Nothing order had been set up to help purge.

Events in Congress, which met in December 1855, indicated that the Know Nothing tide might be about to ebb. Democrats were undoubtedly in the minority in Congress. But it was difficult then (as now) to say which Congressmen were Republican and which were Know Nothing. When the Congressmen had been elected in 1854–5, about two-thirds of the anti-Nebraskan members had been affiliated with the Know Nothings. Since then over a year had elapsed. If all the nativists had co-operated they would probably have had a majority in the House of Representatives. However, the Know Nothings were split North and South. Through December and January there was a struggle for the powerful position of speakership of the House. Know Nothings hoped the election might reunite their Northern and Southern factions. Instead, Nathanial Banks, an ex-Know Nothing who was now a Republican, became speaker. The speakership contest helped to weld the Republicans into a more coherent party.

Republican policies

The Republican Party, which held its first national convention in February 1856, included abolitionists (like Charles Sumner), ex-Whigs (like William Seward), ex-Democrats (like David Wilmot) and ex-Know Nothings (like Nathanial Banks). Not surprisingly historians have different opinions about what the Party stood for and why Northerners supported it.

It is easier to say what Republicans were against than what they were for. Obviously they were against the Democrat Party. Almost all were also united in opposition to the Slave Power which was seen as conspiring against Northern interests. However, Republican leaders were not consistent in defining who was conspiring. Was it all or just some planters, all slaveholders or all Southerners? Republicans also had different views about the nature of the conspiracy. Many were convinced it sought to re-establish slavery in the North. There is no doubt that Republican fears were grossly exaggerated. Nevertheless, the idea of a Slave Power conspiracy was an **article of faith** of most Republicans.

Moral antipathy to slavery was certainly a moving force behind the Republican Party. However, while almost all Republicans were opposed to slavery expansion, many did not support immediate abolition. Many viewed with horror the prospect of thousands of emancipated slaves pouring northwards and relatively few believed in black equality.

Early twentieth century historians such as Charles Beard thought that the Republican Party represented the forces of emerging capitalism and that its main concern was the promotion of industrialisation: its supporters wanted a high tariff, a centralised banking system and federal aid to internal improvements. Few historians now accept this thesis. Industrialisation does not seem to have been a major concern of Republican voters in the 1850s, most of whom were farmers. The party itself was divided on many economic issues.

Article of faith
A main belief.

Key term

SOUTHERN CHIVALRY — ARGUMENT versus CLUB'S.

A Northern cartoon condemning Preston Brooks for his caning of Senator Charles Sumner. The cartoon shows Southern Senators enjoying the sight and preventing intervention by Sumner's friends. (This did not actually happen.)

Republican leaders were also divided on nativist issues. Some wanted to appeal to both anti-slavery and anti-Catholic forces and reach a compromise with – or steal the clothing of – the Know Nothings. Others wanted no concessions to nativism.

'Bleeding Sumner'

A single event in Congress in May 1856 may have been even more important in helping Republican fortunes than the situation in Kansas. Following a speech in which Senator Sumner attacked Southern Senator Butler, Congressman Preston Brooks entered the Senate, found Sumner at his desk and proceeded to beat him, shattering his cane in the process. (Sumner's supporters claimed that his injuries were so severe that he was unable to return to the Senate for over two years; his opponents claimed he was 'milking' his martyrdom for all it was worth.) 'Bleeding Sumner' seems to have outraged Northerners more than 'bleeding Kansas'. Here was clear evidence of the Slave Power at work, using brute force to silence free speech.

While Sumner became a Northern martyr, Brooks became a Southern hero. Resigning from Congress, Brooks stood for re-election and won easily. Scores of Southerners sent him new canes to replace the one he had broken when beating Sumner.

4 | The 1856 Presidential Election
American v North American Parties

Key question
Why was the 1856 presidential election so important?

Millard Fillmore, American Party candidate in 1856.

The American Party held its national convention in February 1856. After a call to repeal the Kansas–Nebraska Act was defeated, 73 Northern delegates left the organisation and formed a splinter 'North American' Party. The American Party went on to select ex-President Fillmore as its presidential candidate. This proved to be a serious mistake. Fillmore, more an old-fashioned Whig than a Know Nothing, was known to have pro-Southern sympathies (as President in 1850 he had signed the Fugitive Slave Law) and thus had limited appeal in the North. North American Party members planned to meet in June to nominate their own candidate.

John C. Frémont

Potential Republican presidential candidates included Samuel Chase and William Seward. Chase, however, seemed too abolitionist while Seward, who had denounced the Know Nothings, was unlikely to win nativist support. Republican leaders decided that the party's best choice would be John C. Frémont. Born in the South, Frémont had had a colourful career as a Western explorer. He was also a national hero: many saw him (wrongly) as the 'Conqueror of California' in 1846 (see page 36). (While he had assumed leadership of some American settlers in California, he had achieved very little, except getting in the way of the official US forces.) Relatively young (he was 43 in 1856), he had limited political experience. An ex-Know Nothing, he had been a (Democrat) Senator for California for just 17 days.

A Southern-born, ex-Know Nothing and ex-Democrat was a strange choice for Republican candidate. But the romance

John C. Frémont, the Republican candidate.

surrounding Frémont's career was likely to make him popular. His lack of political experience meant he had few enemies. Those who knew Frémont were aware that he was rash and egoistical. However, these flaws in character could easily be concealed from the voters. Confident that Frémont was an excellent candidate, the Republicans' main fear was that the North Americans, whose convention met a few days before their own, might nominate him first. Skullduggery on the part of Nathanial Banks saved the day. Banks allowed his name to be put forward as the North American candidate, ensuring that Frémont was not nominated.

Banks' scheme worked to perfection. In June 1856 the Republican convention nominated Frémont. Banks now withdrew in Frémont's favour and urged North Americans to vote for Frémont. The North Americans had little choice but to endorse the man who was now patently the Republican nominee.

The Republican platform was radical. Congress, it declared, had 'both the right and the imperative duty ... to prohibit in the Territories those twin relics of barbarism – **Polygamy** and Slavery'. (The polygamy reference was an unequivocal, and popular, attack on Mormon practices in Utah.) The platform also supported the notion of a Northern Pacific railroad. The Republican slogan was clear: 'Free Soil, Free Labour, Free Men, Frémont.'

The Democrats in 1856

The Democrats agreed that Pierce was so unpopular that he faced almost certain defeat. Douglas, the most dynamic Democrat, was tarnished (in the North) by events in Kansas. He eventually agreed to withdraw his name in the interests of the party, and the

Key term

Polygamy
The practice of having more than one wife.

Democrat candidate
James Buchanan.

Democrats nominated James Buchanan. Although lacking charisma, Buchanan seemed 'safe'. He had spent four decades in public service. A Northerner, he was nevertheless acceptable to the South. Given that his native state was Pennsylvania, regarded as the key **battleground state**, he was probably the Democrats' strongest candidate. The Democratic platform upheld the 1850 Compromise (see page 43) and endorsed popular sovereignty.

Battleground state
A state whose voters might well determine the outcome of the presidential election.

Key term

The campaign
The 1856 campaign generated great excitement. In the North, the contest was essentially between Buchanan and Frémont. In the South, it was between Buchanan and Fillmore. For the first time since 1849–50 there was widespread fear for the safety of the Union. Frémont had no support in the South. If he won, it was conceivable that many Southern states would secede from the Union. Senator Toombs of Georgia declared that: 'The election of Frémont would be the end of the Union and ought to be.' Republicans stressed the fact that Frémont was young and vibrant; Buchanan, by contrast, was portrayed as an old fogey and a lackey of the South. The Democrats claimed that they were the party of stability, peace and Union, and attacked the Republicans for being rabid abolitionists who aimed to elevate blacks to equality with whites.

The 1856 result
In November Fillmore obtained 871,731 votes (21.6 per cent) and eight electoral college votes. Frémont won 1,340,537 votes (33.1 per cent in total: 45 per cent of the Northern vote, but only 1196 votes in the South) and won 114 electoral votes. Buchanan, with

Key date

Buchanan won
presidential election:
1856

1,832,955 votes (45.3 per cent) and 174 electoral votes, became President. He won all but one Southern state plus Pennsylvania, New Jersey, Indiana, Illinois and California. Frémont won the rest of the free states. In the North, native-born Protestants, skilled workers and small farmers overwhelmingly voted Republican.

The Democrats had cause for celebration. They had seen off the Fillmore challenge in the South and retained their traditional supporters – Catholics and Midwestern farmers – in the North. Northern Democrats increased the number of seats they held in the House to 53, although they were still outnumbered by 75 Southern Democrats and 92 Republicans.

Some Republicans were disappointed by the result. However, when they had time to consider what had happened, there was good cause for optimism. From 1854 the Republicans and Know Nothings had battled for control of the anti-Democrat forces in the North. The 1856 election showed that the Republicans had destroyed the American Party, a remarkable performance given the situation in early 1856. The election indicated that Northerners perceived the Slave Power to be a greater threat than the Catholic Church. The Republicans had actually come close to capturing the presidency. If the party had carried Pennsylvania and Illinois, Frémont would have become president. Optimistic Republican pundits, confident that they could win over the remaining anti-Democrat groups in the North, were soon predicting victory in 1860. However, that victory was far from certain. Although the Democrat vote in the North had declined, it had not disappeared. Nor in 1856 was there any guarantee that Northerners would continue to vote Republican. The Party was far from united. It was possible that it would collapse as quickly as it had risen.

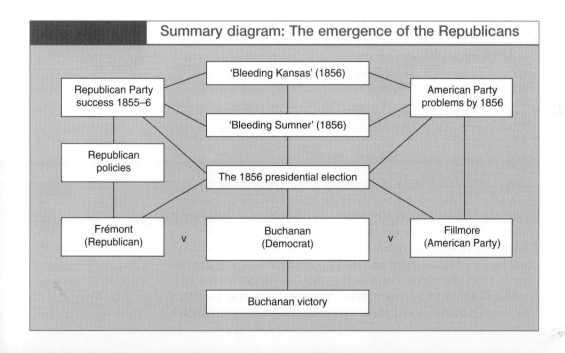

Summary diagram: The emergence of the Republicans

5 | The Presidency of James Buchanan 1857–8

Key question
How successful was
Buchanan in 1857–8?

At the start of 1857 many Americans, not least new President James Buchanan, were optimistic about the future. Buchanan's success in 1856 had prevented a major schism. If the problem of Kansas could be solved, then sectional tension was likely to ease. No other territory, at least in the immediate future, was likely to be so contentious. Buchanan's position seemed strong. Both Houses of Congress and the Supreme Court were dominated by Democrats.

By the end of 1857, historian Kenneth Stampp has claimed that North and South had probably reached 'the political point of no return'. The events of 1857, according to Stampp, were decisive in preventing a peaceful resolution to sectional strife. Buchanan, in Stampp's view, must shoulder much of the blame – pursuing policies which pushed most Northerners into the Republican camp and which contributed to the fragmentation of the Democrat Party.

A loyal Democrat, Buchanan had served in both the House and Senate, in the Cabinet, and as US minister in Russia and Britain. He was not a great orator. His skills were thought to lie more in the area of compromise.

Ideologically attached to the South and aware that he needed Southern support to ensure a majority in Congress, Buchanan chose a pro-Southern cabinet. (Four of his cabinet members were slave owners.) From the start, many Northerners feared that he was a tool of the Slave Power. His actions soon confirmed this fear.

The Dred Scott case

Key question
Why was the Dred
Scott case important?

Dred Scott was a slave who had accompanied his master (an army surgeon) first to Illinois, then to the Wisconsin territory, before returning to Missouri. In the 1840s, with the help of anti-slavery lawyers, Scott went before the Missouri courts, claiming he was free on the grounds that he had resided in a free state and in a free territory. The Scott case proved to be long and drawn out. Different courts gave different verdicts. Eventually the case reached the Supreme Court. There were three main questions.

Key date
The Dred Scott
verdict: 1857

- Did Scott have the right to sue in federal courts?
- Was he free as a result of having lived in the free state of Illinois?
- Was he free as a result of having lived in the Wisconsin territory, where slavery had been outlawed by the Missouri Compromise?

By March 1857 the Supreme Court was ready to give judgement. Buchanan referred to the case in his **inaugural address**. Claiming (not quite truthfully) that he knew nothing of the Supreme Court's decision, he said he was ready to 'cheerfully submit' to its verdict and urged all good citizens to do likewise. Two days later the Supreme Court's decision was made public. The Court was composed of nine Justices: five were Southerners;

Key term
Inaugural address
A new president's
first speech, made
after he has been
sworn in as
president.

four were Northerners. Under the leadership of 79-year-old Chief Justice Roger Taney, the Court decided (by seven votes to two) that:

- Scott could not sue for his freedom. Black Americans, whether slave or free, did not have the same rights as white citizens.
- Scott's stay in Illinois did not make him free.
- Scott's stay in Wisconsin made no difference. The 1820 Missouri Compromise ban on slavery in territories north of 36°30′ was illegal. All US citizens had the right to take their 'property' into the territories.

Northern reaction

Northerners were horrified. The Dred Scott decision seemed further proof of the Slave Power at work. Republicans claimed that the whispered conversations between Taney and Buchanan on inauguration day proved that the President had been aware of the Court's decision when he asked Americans to accept it. The Northern press launched a fierce onslaught on the Supreme Court and some editors talked openly of defying the law. However, the judgement was easier to denounce than defy. In part, it simply annulled a law which had already been repealed by the Kansas–Nebraska Act (page 51). The Court's decision even had little effect on Scott. Thanks to Northern sympathisers, he soon purchased his freedom.

Nevertheless, the verdict was important. Rather than settling the uncertainty about slavery in the territories, the decision provoked further sectional antagonism. It was seen by some Northerners as an attempt to outlaw the Republican Party, which was committed to slavery's exclusion from the territories. The judgement even seemed to undermine the concept of popular sovereignty – that territorial legislatures could prohibit slavery if they chose.

The Panic of 1857

In 1857 US industry was hit by depression, resulting in mass Northern unemployment. Buchanan, believing the government should not involve itself in economic matters, did nothing. Inevitably he and his party were blamed by Northerners for their seeming indifference. Republican economic proposals – internal improvement measures and higher protective tariffs – were blocked by Democrats in Congress. The depression, albeit short-lived (it was over by 1859), helped the Republicans in the 1858 mid-term elections.

Problems in Kansas

Key question
Why were events in Kansas so important nationally?

In Kansas, Buchanan faced a situation which seemed to offer some hope. Although there were still two governments, the official pro-slave at Lecompton and the unofficial free state at Topeka, Governor Geary had restored order in the territory. It was obvious to Geary, and to other independent observers, that free-staters now had a clear majority in Kansas. Given his declared commitment to popular sovereignty, all that Buchanan needed to do was ensure that the will of the majority prevailed. A fair solution of the Kansas problem would deprive the Republicans of one of their most effective issues.

Geary, who had arrived in Kansas heartily despising abolitionists, had by 1857 turned against the Lecompton government. Resigning in March 1857, he warned Buchanan that he should not support the pro-slavers. Buchanan now appointed Robert Walker, an experienced Southern politician, in Geary's place. Walker only accepted the job after being given firm assurances from Buchanan that he would support fair elections.

Arriving in Kansas in May, Walker realised almost immediately that most settlers opposed slavery. He also believed that most supported the Democrat Party. Accordingly, he decided that his aim should be to bring Kansas into the Union as a free, Democrat-voting state. Realising the aim, however, was never likely to be easy. In February 1857 the Lecompton government had authorised the election (in June) of a convention to draw up a constitution that would set the territory on the road to statehood. Free-staters, suspecting that any election organised by the pro-slavers would be rigged, refused to get involved, despite Walker's urgings. In the event only 2200 of the registered 9000 people entitled to vote did so. The pro-slavers thus won all the convention seats.

The pro-slavers' success, while making a mockery of popular sovereignty, raised the expectations of Southerners who realised that the creation of a new slave state was now a real possibility. Meanwhile, elections for a new territorial legislature in Kansas were held in October.

By now Walker had managed to convince free-staters that they should participate, assuring them that he would do all he could to see that the elections were fairly conducted. When the pro-slavers won, free-staters immediately charged the pro-slavers with fraudulence. Walker, true to his word, investigated the charges. They were easily confirmed. Hundreds of fictitious people had been recorded as voting for the pro-slavers. One village, for example, with 30 eligible voters returned more than 1600 pro-slavery votes. Walker overturned enough fraudulent results to give the free-staters a majority in the legislature.

The Lecompton constitution

The constitutional convention was now the last refuge of the pro-slavers. Few thought that the convention represented majority opinion in Kansas. Yet it proceeded to draft a pro-slavery Lecompton constitution. While agreeing to allow a referendum on its proposals, it offered voters something of a spurious choice:

- they had to accept the pro-slavery constitution as it was
- they could accept another constitution which banned the future importation of slaves but guaranteed the rights of slaveholders already in Kansas.

Walker denounced the convention's actions as a 'vile fraud' and urged Buchanan to repudiate the Lecompton constitution.

Until now, Buchanan had supported Walker. However, some influential Southerners insisted on making the Lecompton constitution a test of the South's ability to find equality within the Union. The ultimatum – 'Lecompton or disunion' – rang out in Southern newspapers. Buchanan knew he could not afford to lose Southern support. However, it seems that he decided to reject Walker's advice, not so much because he was browbeaten by his Southern advisers, but more because he thought it was the right thing to do. He seems to have genuinely believed that anti-slavery forces were to blame for all the troubles in Kansas.

In November, Walker left Kansas, met Buchanan in Washington, and insisted that the Lecompton constitution did not fulfil the promise of popular sovereignty. Failing to change Buchanan's mind, Walker resigned in December. That same month Kansas voted on the Lecompton constitution. In fact, most free-staters abstained in protest. The pro-slave returns showed 6143 for the constitution with slavery and 569 for it without slavery. In December, in his annual message to Congress, Buchanan endorsed the actions of the Lecompton convention, claiming that the question of slavery had been 'fairly and explicitly referred to the people'.

Buchanan versus Douglas

Buchanan's decision to support the Lecompton constitution was a huge blunder. By the end of 1857 everyone knew that most people in Kansas were opposed to slavery. Even some Southerners were embarrassed by the fraud perpetrated by the pro-slavers. Had Buchanan accepted Walker's advice, he might not have lost much Southern support. By accepting the Lecompton constitution, he gave the Republicans massive political ammunition. Here was more proof of the Slave Power conspiracy at work. More importantly, he enraged Northern Democrats, like Senator Douglas, who were committed to popular sovereignty. In an impassioned speech in the Senate, Douglas attacked both Buchanan and the Lecompton constitution. Southern Democrats immediately denounced Douglas as a traitor. The Democrat Party, like almost every other American institution, was now split North and South.

A titanic Congressional contest followed with Douglas siding with the Republicans. Using all the powers of patronage at his disposal, Buchanan tried to ensure that Northern Democrats voted for the Lecompton constitution. His threats had some effect: the Senate passed the constitution (by 33 to 25 votes). The real battle was in the House of Representatives. Despite all the **patronage pressure**, enough Northern Democrats opposed Buchanan, ensuring that the Lecompton constitution was defeated by 120 votes to 112.

Buchanan, recognising that he had lost, accepted that Kansas should vote again on the Lecompton constitution. The new elections took place in August 1858. Conducted as fairly as possible, they resulted in a free-state victory: 11,300 voted against the Lecompton constitution while only 1788 voted for it. Kansas now set about drawing up a new free-state constitution. It finally joined the Union in January 1861 as a free state.

Key date

The Lecompton – pro-slavery – constitution was supported by Buchanan: 1857

Key term

Patronage pressure Using the offer of government jobs and offices effectively to bribe Congressmen.

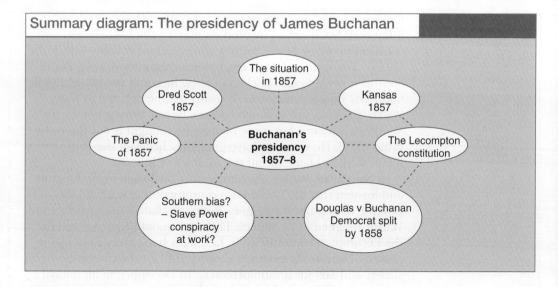

Summary diagram: The presidency of James Buchanan

6 | The 1858 Congressional Elections

Key question
What issues divided
Lincoln and Douglas?

The 1858 mid-term elections came at a bad time for the Northern Democrats, with the party split between those who supported Buchanan and those who supported Douglas. Given that Douglas had to stand for re-election in 1858, national attention focused on the Illinois campaign. The fourth largest state in the USA, its voters might determine the outcome of the 1860 presidential election. The Republicans chose Abraham Lincoln to run against Douglas.

Abraham Lincoln

Lincoln in many ways epitomised the American Dream. Born in a log cabin, he had little formal schooling. Able and ambitious (and determined to escape from farming, which he hated), he won the first of four terms as an Illinois state legislator in 1834. A loyal Whig (his hero was Henry Clay), politics became his passion. In 1846 he was elected to the House of Representatives, where he spoke in opposition to the Mexican War. Defeated in 1848, he returned to Illinois, resumed his successful law practice and for a few years took less interest in politics.

The Kansas–Nebraska Act brought him back into politics. He hoped at first that the Act, which he described as a 'great moral wrong', would bring new life to the Whigs. Although he had excellent contacts with Republican leaders, he did not join the Republican Party until 1856. Once committed, he threw himself into the Republican cause with vigour. Previously, his main political concern had been economic matters. Now his speeches became more anti-slavery and anti-Slave Power. Although he had not much of a national reputation in 1858, he was well known in Illinois. Douglas respected his ability, commenting: 'I shall have my hands full. He is the strong man of the party – full of wit, facts, dates – and the best stump speaker with his droll ways and dry jokes, in the West. He is as honest as he is shrewd.'

Profile: Abraham Lincoln 1809–65

1809 – Born in Kentucky

1831 – Moved to Illinois and over the next few years experienced a host of jobs: store clerk, postmaster and surveyor

1832 – Volunteered to fight against hostile Indians in the Black Hawk War but saw no action

1834 – Elected as a state legislator in Illinois

1837 – Moved to Springfield, Illinois's state capital, and became a lawyer

1842 – Married Mary Todd, daughter of a Kentucky slaveholder

1846 – Elected to the House of Representatives

1856 – Joined the Republican Party

1858 – Challenged Douglas for election as senator for Illinois

1860 – Elected president

1861 – Inaugurated president

1862 – Issued the Emancipation Proclamation (see page 200)

1864 – Re-elected president

1865 – Assassinated

Lincoln was complex and enigmatic. On the one hand he was a calculating politician, often non-committal and evasive. On the other, he was a humane, witty man who never seemed to worry much about his own bruised ego. Historians continue to debate whether he was moderate, radical or conservative. He was certainly cautious, preferring to think over problems slowly and deliberately before reaching a decision. This was true on the slavery issue. He had always been opposed to slavery, believing it to be immoral and against the Declaration of Independence's assertion that 'all men are created equal'. But realising that it was a divisive issue, he had kept quiet on the subject for much of his early political career and had often been critical of abolitionists. He had shown no personal animosity towards Southern slave owners, indeed he had married one.

When he was chosen by the Republicans to run against Douglas in 1858 he determined to remind Illinois voters of the gulf separating him from his opponent. In his acceptance speech in June 1858, Lincoln declared:

> A House divided against itself cannot stand. I believe this government cannot endure permanently half slave and half free. I do not expect the Union to be dissolved – I do not expect the house to fall – but I do expect it will cease to be divided. It will become all one thing or all the other.

The Lincoln–Douglas debates

Key date

Mid-term elections: Lincoln–Douglas debate: 1858

Douglas agreed to meet Lincoln for seven open-air, face-to-face debates. These debates have become part of American political folklore. They ran from August to October 1858 and drew vast crowds. Visually the two men were a strange pair: Lincoln, a gawky 6 feet 4 inches tall; Douglas a foot shorter. Both were gifted speakers.

The seven debates were confined almost exclusively to three topics – race, slavery and slavery expansion. The two men had been arguing the nuances of their respective positions for years so little was said that was new or unexpected. By today's standards, Lincoln and Douglas do not seem far apart. This is perhaps not surprising: both men were moderates as far as their parties were concerned and both were fighting for the middle ground. Both considered blacks to be inferior to whites. Lincoln declared: 'I am not, nor ever have been in favour of bringing about in any way the social and political equality of the white and black races – that I am not nor ever have been in favour of making voters or jurors of negroes, nor of qualifying them to hold office, nor to intermarry with white people.'

Even the difference between Lincoln's free-soil doctrine (see page 62) and Douglas's popular sovereignty, in terms of practical impact, was limited: neither man doubted that popular sovereignty would keep slavery out of the territories.

However, the two did differ in one key respect. Douglas never once said in public that slavery was a moral evil. Lincoln may not have believed in racial equality but he did believe that blacks and whites shared a common humanity: 'If slavery is not wrong', he said, 'then nothing is wrong.' He did not expect slavery to wither and die immediately. He did not suppose that 'the ultimate extinction would occur in less than a hundred years at the least', but he was convinced that 'ultimate extinction' should be the goal. If slavery did not expand, he believed it would eventually die.

The Illinois result

Lincoln won some 125,000 popular votes to Douglas's 121,000. However, Douglas's supporters kept control of the Illinois legislature which re-elected Douglas as Senator. This was a significant triumph for Douglas, solidifying his leadership of the Northern Democrats, and ensuring he would be in a strong position to battle for the presidential candidacy in 1860. However, during the debates with Lincoln, Douglas had said much that alienated Southerners, not least his stressing of the **Freeport Doctrine**. Although Lincoln had lost, at least he had emerged from the Illinois election as a Republican spokesman of national stature, battling Douglas on even terms and clarifying the issues dividing Republicans from Northern Democrats.

The 1858 results

The 1858 elections were a disaster for the Northern Democrats. The Republicans, helped by the collapse of the American Party, won control of the House. The Republican share of the vote in the crucial states of Pennsylvania, Indiana, Illinois and New Jersey rose from 35 per cent in 1856 to 52 per cent in 1858. If the voting pattern was repeated in 1860 the Republicans would win the presidency.

Freeport Doctrine
A view that voters in a territory could exclude slavery by refusing to enact laws that gave legal protection to owning slaves, thus effectively invalidating the Dred Scott ruling.

Key term

Summary diagram: The 1858 Congressional elections

```
                    ┌──────────────┐
┌──────────────┐    │  The 1858    │    ┌──────────────┐
│ The situation │───│  mid-term    │───│ The situation │
│  in Illinois  │    │  elections   │    │  nationally   │
└──────────────┘    └──────────────┘    └──────────────┘
        │                                        │
┌──────────────┐                                 │
│ Lincoln v Douglas │                            │
└──────────────┘                                 │
        │                                        │
┌──────────────┐                          ┌──────────────┐
│ Douglas success │──────  BUT  ──────────│  Republican   │
│    – just     │                         │   triumph     │
└──────────────┘                          │   in North    │
                                          └──────────────┘
```

7 | John Brown's Raid

Key question
How significant was John Brown's raid on Harper's Ferry?

Key date
John Brown's raid on the federal arsenal at Harper's Ferry: 1859

Key terms

Arsenal
A place where military supplies are stored or made.

State militia
All able-bodied men of military age (in most states) could be called up to fight in an emergency.

John Brown had risen to fame – or infamy – in Kansas (page 62). Now in his late fifties, Brown was still determined to do something decisive for the anti-slavery cause. Some thought he was mad. (There was a history of insanity in his family.) However, many abolitionists believed that Brown was a man of integrity and moral conviction. The fact that he was able to win financial support from hard-headed Northern businessmen is testimony to both his charismatic personality and the intensity of abolitionist sentiment.

On the night of 16 October 1859 Brown and 18 men (including three of his sons) left their base in Maryland and rode to the federal **arsenal** at Harper's Ferry. Brown's aim was to seize weapons, retreat to the Appalachian mountains and from there spark a great slave revolt. The fact that it was impossible to inform the slaves in advance of his intentions was a major – but by no means the only – flaw in Brown's plan. In retrospect what is remarkable is that the raid was kept secret. Brown's main financial backers – the 'Secret Six' – although not certain of his precise goal, were aware of his broad intentions. Politicians who had heard rumours of Brown's intentions refused to take them seriously.

Brown captured the arsenal with remarkable ease. A few slaves were induced or compelled to join Brown and a number of hostages were taken. Then things began to go wrong. A train pulled into Harper's Ferry, shots were fired by one of Brown's men, and the first person to die was a black baggage master. Rather than escape to the hills, Brown took refuge in the fire-engine house at the arsenal. His position soon became desperate. Virginia and Maryland **state militia** units and a detachment of troops, led by Colonel Robert E. Lee, quickly converged on the town. A 36-hour siege followed with Brown threatening to kill the hostages and Lee attempting, in vain, to persuade Brown to give himself up. On 18 October, Lee ordered the fire-engine house to

John Brown reminded many Northern admirers of an Old Testament prophet. Southerners considered him a devil.

be stormed. In the ensuing struggle Brown was wounded and captured along with six of his men. Ten of his 'army' were killed (including two of his sons). Seven other people also died.

The results of the raid

Brown was tried for treason. Refusing a plea of insanity, he determined to die a martyr's death; by so doing helping the anti-slavery cause rather more than his raid had done. He was quickly found guilty and sentenced to death. He was executed on 2 December 1859. In his last letter he wrote: 'I, John Brown am now quite certain that the crimes of this guilty land will never be purged away but with Blood.'

Brown's raid was a crucial event. Most Southerners were appalled at what had happened. Their worst fears had been realised. An abolitionist had tried to stir up a slave revolt. Aware that Brown had considerable financial support, they suspected that most Northerners sympathised with his action. Some Northerners did see Brown as a hero. Church bells were rung across the North on the day of his execution. But by no means all Northerners approved of Brown's raid. Northern Democrats condemned Brown out of hand. Many leading Republicans dissociated themselves from the raid, depicting it as 'fatally wrong' and 'utterly repugnant'.

Key terms

Slave patrol
Armed men who rode round slave areas, especially at night, to ensure that there was no disorder.

Free homesteads
The Republicans hoped to provide 160 acres of land to farmers who settled in the West.

Black Republicans
A term used by Southerners to describe Republicans who were seen as being sympathetic to slaves.

Few Southerners were reassured. Most saw Republicans and abolitionists (like Brown) as one and the same. 'The Harper's Ferry invasion has advanced the cause of disunion more than any other event that has happened since the formation of its government', said one Richmond newspaper.

Sectional tension 1859–60

Over the winter of 1859–60 there were rumours of slave insurrection in many Southern states. Local vigilante committees were set up and **slave patrols** strengthened. Dozens of slaves, suspected of planning revolt, arson or mass poisoning, were rounded up and some were lynched. Southern state governments purchased additional weapons and Southern militia units drilled rather more than previously.

When Congress met in December 1859, both Houses divided along sectional lines. Northern and Southern politicians exchanged insults and accusations and some came to Congress armed. Southerners opposed all Republican measures: **free homesteads**, higher tariffs and a Pacific railroad. Northerners blocked all pro-Southern proposals, such as the purchase of Cuba.

By 1860 Northerners and Southerners carried inflammatory rhetoric to new heights of passion. Northerners feared a conspiracy by the Slave Power. Southerners feared the growing strength of the '**Black Republicans**'. Buchanan, who had sought to avoid controversy, had failed. Far from easing tension, his policies had helped to exacerbate the sectional rift. His presidency must thus be regarded as one of the great failures of leadership in US history.

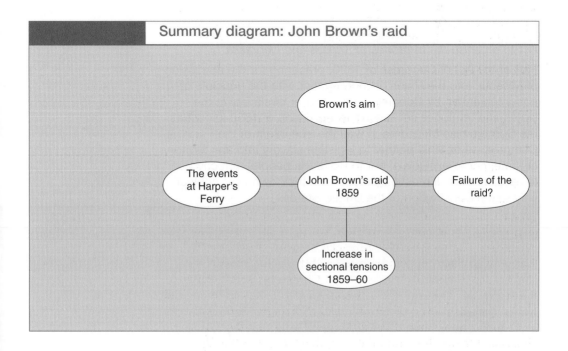

Summary diagram: John Brown's raid

- Brown's aim
- The events at Harper's Ferry
- John Brown's raid 1859
- Failure of the raid?
- Increase in sectional tensions 1859–60

Study Guide: AS Questions

In the style of OCR

Study the five sources on slavery and secession in the 1850s, and then answer **both** sub-questions. It is recommended that you spend two-thirds of your time in answering part **(b)**.

(a) **Study Sources C and D.**
   Compare these sources as evidence for differing views on slavery in the territories.   (30 marks)
(b) **Study all of the sources.**
   Use your own knowledge to assess how far the sources support the interpretation that the Kansas–Nebraska Act made it impossible to stop the extension of slavery into the territories after 1854.   (70 marks)

Source A

From: an appeal of independent Democrats, January 1854.
A group of senators and congressmen appeal for public action to prevent the passage of the Kansas–Nebraska bill.

Do not submit to become agents in extending legalised oppression over a vast territory still exempt from these terrible evils. We implore Christians and Christian ministers to act. Their divine religion requires them to see every man as a brother. Whatever apologies may be offered for the toleration of slavery in the states, none can be offered for its extension into the territories where it does not exist. Let all protest loudly, by whatever way may seem suitable, against this enormous crime.

Source B

From: the Kansas–Nebraska Act, May 1854. Congress passes the Act to organise the territories of Kansas and Nebraska.

Part of the Act of Congress of 1820, preparing for the admission of Missouri into the Union, is inconsistent with the principle of non-intervention by Congress in the matter of slavery in the states and territories set out in the legislation of 1850 known as the Compromise Measures. It was the true intent of the Compromise of 1850 neither to legislate slavery into any territory or state, nor to exclude it, but to leave the people perfectly free to regulate their domestic institutions in their own way, subject only to the Constitution of the United States.

Source C

From: the third Lincoln–Douglas debate at Jonesboro, Illinois, September 1858. Lincoln replies to Douglas on the issue of slavery in the territories.

The Supreme Court has decided in the case of Dred Scott that any Congressional prohibition of slavery in the territories is unconstitutional. It has also decided that the Constitution of the USA expressly recognises slaves as property, and that no person shall be deprived of his property. Hence the court reaches the conclusion that to pass an Act of Congress by which a man who owned a slave on one side of a line would be deprived of him if he took him across the other side is to pass an Act that deprives him of his property. I understand that Senator Douglas agrees most firmly with that decision. The difficulty is this: how is it possible for any power to exclude slavery from the territories unless it defies that decision? The proposition that slavery cannot enter a new country without police regulation is false.

Source D

From: The Charleston Mercury, February 1860. A Southern newspaper argues that Northern political interference has prevented slavery from entering the new territories.

What has been the policy pursued in Kansas? Has the territory had a fair chance of becoming a slave state? Has the principle of equal protection to slave property been carried out by the government there? On the contrary, has not every device been used to hinder the South and to expel or prohibit her sons from colonising there? In our opinion, had the principle of equal protection to Southern men and property been rigorously observed, Kansas would undoubtedly have come into the Union as a slave state.

Source E

From: J.F. Rhodes, Lectures on the American Civil War, *1913. An American historian of the post-Civil War generation comments on the significance of the 1860 presidential election.*

Through the election of Lincoln as president, the majority of the Northern people declared that slavery was wrong and should not be extended. The sectional character of the contest is obvious: Lincoln did not receive a single vote in 10 out of the 11 states that afterwards seceded and made up the Southern Confederacy. As soon as the election result was known, South Carolina led off with a prompt reply. The crowd that thronged the streets of its capital, Charleston, felt that they had an undoubted grievance and that their sole remedy now was secession.

Exam tips

(a) Both Sources C and D argue that the case for the extension of slavery was handled wrongly, but from very different perspectives. Source D, a Southern source, argues that every attempt was made to prevent slave owners from colonising the territories. Lincoln, in contrast, argued that the Dred Scott decision made it impossible to prevent the extension of slavery. Was he correct? How might Douglas have responded to Lincoln in the third debate at Jonesboro in 1858?

(b) Although there is much in the sources that points to the view given in the question, no set response is required and you must examine the given claim, even if you then reject it. You should show an appreciation of the importance of the different circumstances from which the sources originated. The role of the Kansas–Nebraska Act is vital when assessing the extension of slavery into the territories. Strike a reasonable balance between analysing the sources and using your own knowledge to put forward an informed and reasoned judgement. Your own knowledge will need to be secure as the sources say very little about what actually happened in the territories after 1854. Slavery did not actually expand, despite the fears expressed in Sources A and C. Why did slavery make no headway? Do Sources D and E provide a reasonable explanation?

In the style of OCR

Assess the reasons why the Republican Party emerged as the main rival of the Democrats in the 1856 presidential election?

(50 marks)

Exam tips

The cross-references are intended to take you straight to the material that will help you to answer the question.

You will need to assess the significance of the following:

- Why did the second party system collapse (pages 58–61)?
- Why did the Know Nothings and the Republican Party emerge (pages 59–61)?
- Why did the Know Nothing order (later the American Party) lose support (pages 63–4)?
- Why did events (particularly in Kansas in 1856) help the Republicans (pages 61–2)?
- Why did the Republicans do well in the 1856 campaign (pages 63–9)?

Study Guide: A2 Question

In the style of Edexcel

'The most significant event heightening tension between North and South in the years 1850–7.' How far do you agree with this view of the Dred Scott judgement?   (30 marks)

Exam tips

The cross-references are intended to take you straight to the material that will help you to answer the question.

The key to success in dealing with essay questions is to be clear about the question focus and to be careful to select precisely the material you need to answer the question. This question is about the impact of events. You must come to a judgement about the significance of the one stated in the question relative to other events that had an impact on North–South tension. And you must not stray outside the period of the question.

Below is a list of events that contributed to heightening tension. What impact did they have? How will you show this impact? How will you organise this material either to argue that one or more of them was more significant than the Dred Scott judgement, or to construct an argument agreeing with the statement?

- The 1850 Compromise (pages 43–6).
- The Fugitive Slave Act (pages 47–8).
- The publishing of *Uncle Tom's Cabin* (pages 47–8).
- The 1852 election (pages 48–9).
- The Ostend Manifesto (pages 49–50).
- The introduction of the Kansas–Nebraska Bill (pages 50–3).
- 'Bleeding Kansas' (page 62).
- 'Bleeding Sumner' (page 65).
- The 1856 election (pages 66–9).
- The Dred Scott judgement (pages 70–1).
- The 1857 depression (page 71).
- The Lecompton constitution (pages 72–3).

Could some of these be grouped into a single paragraph? Did some do no more than reinforce the trend of animosity and division? Which events had such serious implications that the situation after them was different from the previous situation? If you think about the implications and consequences of events in this way, your essay will have more focus, and you will find it easier to reach a conclusion.

4 The 1860 Election, Secession and Civil War

POINTS TO CONSIDER

In early 1860 'fire-eaters' who claimed that the South would be better off going its own way were still a minority. However, by February 1861 seven Southern states had seceded from the Union and formed the Confederacy. By April 1861 the Confederacy was at war with the Union. To explain how and why this happened, this chapter will focus on the following:

- The 1860 presidential election
- Secession
- The creation of the Confederacy
- The search for compromise
- The problem of Fort Sumter

Key dates

1860	November	Lincoln elected president
	December	South Carolina seceded
1861	January	Mississippi, Florida, Alabama, Georgia and Louisiana seceded
	February	Texas seceded
	February	Confederacy established
	March	Lincoln inaugurated president
	April	Confederate forces opened fire on Fort Sumter
	April–June	Virginia, Arkansas, North Carolina and Tennessee seceded

1 | The 1860 Presidential Election

Key question
Why did Lincoln win the 1860 election?

The events of the 1850s had brought a growing number of Southerners to the conclusion that the North had deserted the true principles of the Union. In Southern eyes, it was the North, not the South, that was 'peculiar'. It was the North that had urbanised, industrialised and absorbed large numbers of immigrants while the South had remained agricultural, Anglo-Saxon and loyal to its roots. Southerners suspected that most Northerners held abolitionist views and the prospect of a Republican triumph in 1860 filled them with outrage and dread. It was not merely that a Republican victory might threaten slavery. More fundamentally, Southerners believed that the North was treating the South as its inferior. The most conspicuous badge of sectional inferiority was the Republican intention of prohibiting slavery in the territories. Submission to the Republicans, declared Mississippi Senator Jefferson Davis, 'would be intolerable to a proud people'. If a Republican did become president, then plenty of Southerners were prepared to consider the possibility of secession. The stakes in the 1860 election, therefore, were alarmingly high.

The Democratic convention

If the Republicans were to be defeated in 1860 it seemed essential that the rifts within the Democrat Party should be healed. Douglas, determined to run for president, made some efforts to build bridges to the South in 1859–60. Rationally he was the South's best hope: he was the only Democrat who was likely to carry some free states – and to win the election the Democrats had to win some free states. But Douglas's stand against the Lecompton constitution (page 73) alienated him from most Southerners.

Events at the Democrat convention, which met in April 1860 at Charleston, South Carolina, showed that the party, never mind the country, was a house divided against itself. From Douglas's point of view, Charleston, situated in the most fire-eating of the Southern states, was an unfortunate choice for the convention. Townspeople, many of whom crowded into the convention hall, made clear their opposition to Douglas.

In spite of this opposition, Douglas's aspiration to gain the nomination was far from hopeless. The fact that delegates to the convention were appointed according to the size of a state's population ensured that Northern Democrats outnumbered Southerners. They were aware they faced political extinction at home unless they ended the party's perceived pro-Southern policies. When Northern Democrats blocked a proposal which would have pledged the party to protect the rights of slaveholders in the territories, some 50 delegates from the **lower South** walked out of the convention. Unable to reach consensus on policy, the Democrats found it equally impossible to nominate a candidate. Although Douglas had the support of more than half the delegates, he failed to win the two-thirds majority which Democrat candidates were expected to achieve. After 57 ballots the Democrat convention agreed to reconvene at Baltimore in June.

Democratic division

When some of the Southern delegates who had left the Charleston convention tried to take up their seats at Baltimore, the convention, dominated by Douglas's supporters, preferred to take pro-Douglas delegates from the lower South. This led to another mass Southern walk-out. With so many Southern delegates gone, Douglas easily won the nomination of the official convention.

Lower South
The Deep Southern states: Alabama, Louisiana, Georgia, Texas, Florida, South Carolina and Mississippi.

Key term

Key question
Did Democratic division make Republican success inevitable?

The Southern delegates now set up their own convention and nominated the current Vice-President John Breckinridge of Kentucky on a platform that called for the federal government to protect slavery in the territories.

Although Breckinridge was supported by Cass, Pierce and Buchanan (the last three Democratic presidential candidates – all Northerners) and by eight of the ten Northern Democrat Senators, it was clear that the Democrat Party had split along sectional lines. The fact that Southerners, unable to control the Democrat Party, had petulantly 'seceded' from it, was something of a dress rehearsal – an indication of the South's likely action in November should the Republicans triumph.

The Democratic split is often seen as ensuring Republican success. However, even without the split, the Republican Party, which simply had to carry the North, was odds-on favourite to win. The Democrat schism may actually have weakened, rather than strengthened, the Republicans, if only because Douglas could now campaign in the North without having to try to maintain a united national Democrat Party. Given that he had cut his links with the South, it was possible that Northerners would be more likely to vote for him.

The Republican convention

The Republican convention met in May at Chicago in the **Wigwam**. The delegates found it easier to agree on a platform than a candidate. In 1856 the Republicans had been largely a single-issue, free-soil party. To win in 1860 the party needed to broaden its appeal. The 1860 platform, therefore, called for:

- higher protective tariffs
- free 160-acre homesteads for western settlers
- a northern trans-continental railway.

While opposed to any extension of slavery, the platform specifically promised that the party had no intention of interfering with slavery where it already existed and it condemned John Brown's raid as 'the gravest of crimes'.

Lincoln becomes the Republican candidate

Seward, Governor of New York for four years and a Senator for 12 years, was favourite to win the Republican presidential nomination. However, the fact that he had been a major figure in public life for so long meant that he had many enemies. Although he was actually a pragmatic politician who disdained extremism, he was seen as holding radical views on slavery. Moreover, he had a long record of hostility to nativism. His nomination, therefore, might make ex-Know Nothings think twice about voting Republican. There were a number of other potential candidates. These included Edward Bates of Missouri, Salmon Chase of Ohio and Simon Cameron of Pennsylvania.

Seward's main opponent turned out to be Abraham Lincoln. Lincoln had several things in his favour.

Key term

Wigwam
A huge wooden building that could hold over 10,000 people.

Key question
Why did the Republicans choose Lincoln?

- He came from the key state of Illinois.
- He had gained a national reputation as a result of his debates with Douglas in 1858.
- While denying he held any presidential ambitions, in 1859–60 he had made dozens of speeches across the North, gaining friends and making himself known.
- Given that it was difficult to attach an ideological label to him, he was able to appear to be all things to all men.
- His lack of administrative experience helped his reputation for honesty and integrity.
- Lincoln's ambitions were helped by the convention being held at Chicago (in Illinois). His skilful campaign managers were thus able to pack the Wigwam with his supporters.

On the first ballot, Seward won 173 votes: a majority – but not the 233 votes needed for an absolute majority. Lincoln won 102 votes, well behind Seward but more than twice the votes of anyone else. With the race now clearly between Seward and Lincoln, other candidates began to drop out. Most of their votes drifted to Lincoln. The second ballot was very close. By the third ballot there was an irresistible momentum in Lincoln's favour, helped in part by the sheer noise in the Wigwam. Lincoln's campaign managers almost certainly made secret deals with delegates from Pennsylvania and Indiana, probably to the effect that Lincoln would appoint Cameron (from Pennsylvania) and Caleb Smith (from Indiana) to his cabinet. These deals helped Lincoln to win the Republican nomination on the third ballot.

The Constitutional Unionist Party
The – new – Constitutional Unionist Party also mounted a challenge for the presidency. Composed mainly of ex-Whigs, its main strength lay in the upper South. The party nominated John Bell of Tennessee as its presidential candidate. Its platform was the shortest in US political history: 'The Constitution of the Country, the Union of the States and the Enforcement of the Laws of the United States.' Essentially the party wanted to remove the slavery question from the political arena, thus relieving sectional strife.

The campaign
In the North the main fight was between Lincoln and Douglas. Bell and Breckinridge fought it out in the South. Douglas was the only candidate who actively involved himself in the campaign. At some personal risk, he campaigned in the South, warning Southerners of the dangerous consequences of secession.

Throughout the campaign, Lincoln remained in Springfield, answering correspondence, conferring with Republican chiefs, but saying nothing. Perhaps he should have made some effort to reassure Southerners that he was not a major threat to their section. However, he could hardly go out of his way to appease the South: this would have done his cause no good in the North. Moreover, it is difficult to see what he could have said to allay

Southern fears, given that the very existence of his party was offensive to Southerners.

Although Lincoln, Bell and Breckinridge kept silent this did not prevent their supporters campaigning for them. Republicans, flooding the North with campaign literature, held torchlight processions and carried wooden rails, embodying the notion that Lincoln was the common man who had once split wood for rails. Republican propaganda concentrated on the Slave Power conspiracy.

Southern Democrats stereotyped all Northerners as 'Black Republicans' set on abolishing slavery. A few fire-eaters apart, most of Breckinridge's supporters did not draw attention to the fact that they might support secession if Lincoln triumphed.

In some states the three anti-Republican parties tried to unite. These efforts at 'fusion' were too little and too late and were bedevilled by the bitter feuds that existed between the supporters of Breckinridge, Douglas and Bell.

Key date

Lincoln elected president: November 1860

The election results

In November 81 per cent of the electorate voted. Bell won 593,000 votes – 39 per cent of the Southern vote but only five per cent of the free-state vote – carrying the states of Virginia, Kentucky and Tennessee. Breckinridge, with 843,000 votes (45 per cent of the Southern vote but only five per cent of the free states) won 11 of the 15 slave states. Douglas obtained 1,383,000 votes – mainly from the North – but won only two states, Missouri and New Jersey. Lincoln won 1,866,000 votes – 40 per cent of the total vote. Although he got no votes at all in 10 Southern states, he won 54 per cent of the Northern vote and, except for New Jersey, carried all the free states. With a majority of 180 to 123 in the electoral college, he became the new president. Even if the opposition had combined against him in every free state, Lincoln would still have triumphed because he won a majority of votes in virtually every Northern state.

Breckinridge, the most popular Southern candidate, won less than half the vote in the slave states as a whole. Not that this made any difference. Lincoln would have won the election if the South had voted solidly for Breckinridge or for anyone else. All Lincoln's votes were strategically positioned in the North. It was in the North where Lincoln had to be challenged. Douglas came close in Illinois, Indiana and California: if Douglas had carried these states Lincoln would not have won the election.

Why did Northerners vote Republican?

Northerners voted for Lincoln because he seemed to represent their section. A vote for Lincoln was a vote against the Slave Power. While not wishing to get rid of slavery immediately, most Northerners had no wish to see it expand. Slavery and the Slave Power, however, were not the only concerns of Northerners. Nativism had not disappeared with the demise of the Know Nothings. Although the Republicans took an ambiguous stand on nativist issues, anti-Catholic Northerners had little option but to vote Republican, if only because the Democrat Party remained the home of Irish and German Catholics. Many Northerners approved the Republican economic proposals. The corruption issue was also important. In June 1860 a House investigative committee, dominated by Republicans, had found fraud and corruption at every level of Buchanan's government. This had tarnished the Democrat Party. 'Honest Abe' Lincoln, by contrast, had a reputation for integrity.

Summary diagram: The 1860 presidential election

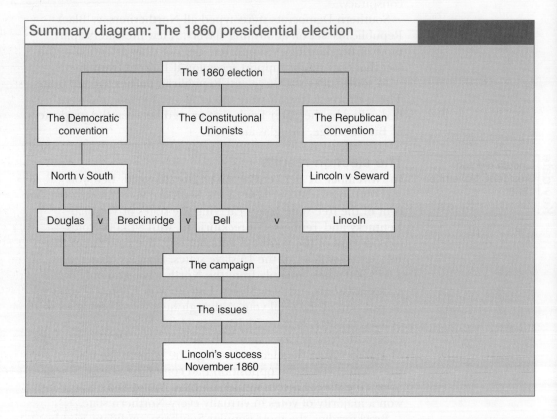

2 | Secession

Lincoln's victory was the green light that secessionists had been waiting for. This need not have been so. Rationally, there were excellent reasons why the Southern states should not secede from the Union.

- Lincoln's election posed no immediate threat. He had promised he would not interfere with slavery in those states where it existed.
- Even if Lincoln harboured secret ambitions to abolish slavery, there was little he could do: his party did not control Congress or the Supreme Court, and presidential power was strictly limited by the Constitution.
- Secession would mean abandoning an enforceable Fugitive Slave Act: slaves would be able to flee to the North.

Key questions
Why and how did the lower South states secede?

Should the Southern states have seceded?

- Finally, and most importantly, secession might lead to civil war, which would threaten slavery far more than Lincoln's election.

Few Southerners regarded things so calmly. A Northern anti-slavery party, with no pretence of support in the South, had captured the presidency. Given that few Southerners had ever seen any of Lincoln's supporters, much less the man himself, they tended to believe the worst: he was depicted as a rabid abolitionist who would encourage slave insurrections. He would certainly stop slavery expansion. Southerners feared they would be encircled by a swelling majority of free states and that, ultimately, slavery would be voted out of existence.

For more than a generation Southerners had seen themselves as the aggrieved innocents in an unequal struggle that unleashed more and more Northern aggressions on Southern rights. They believed they had been denied their fair share of the Western territories and unfairly taxed through high tariffs to subsidise Northern industry. Honour demanded that a stand be taken against the latest outrage, the election of Lincoln.

Across the South there was a strange mixture of moods – hysteria, despondency and elation. Fire-eaters, who had agitated for years for the cause of Southern independence, capitalised on the mood. Long on the fringe of Southern politics, they now found themselves supported by 'mainstream' politicians.

Problems for the secessionists

Secession was not inevitable. There was still much Unionist sympathy in the South. Nor was there any great Southern organisation that might organise a secessionist movement. Southerners were loyal to their state rather than to the 'South'. There had never been a Southern nation. Nor was the South united. Virtually every state was rife with tensions, often between small, self-sufficient farmers and the great planters. Non-slaveholding farmers composed the largest single bloc in the electorate. Although tied to the planters by a mutual commitment to white supremacy, these farmers often resented the planters' pretensions to speak for them.

There was not even unity on the best political strategy to adopt. While some believed that Lincoln's election was grounds enough for secession, others thought it best to wait until he took hostile action against the South. 'Immediate' secessionists knew that if they forced the issue, they might destroy the unity they were seeking to create; but if they waited for unity, they might never act.

How to force the issue was another problem. If individual states acted alone, there was the danger that they would receive no support from other states, as South Carolina had found in the 1832 Nullification Crisis (page 39). Yet trying to organise a mass move for secession might ensure nothing happened – as in 1849–50 (page 45).

South Carolina secedes

Events moved with a rapidity that few had foreseen. On 10 November South Carolina's state legislature called for elections to a special convention to meet on 17 December to decide whether the state would secede. This move created a chain reaction. Alabama, Mississippi, Georgia, Louisiana and Florida all put similar convention procedures underway. In Texas, Governor Sam Houston, who opposed disunion, delayed proceedings but only by a few weeks.

Individual states committed themselves, initially, to individual action. However, it was clear that Southerners were equally committed to joint action. There was liaison between the Southern states at various levels but particularly between Southern Congressmen. When Congress met in early December, 30 representatives from nine Southern states declared: 'The argument is exhausted … We are satisfied the honour, safety and independence of the Southern people are to be found only in a Southern Confederacy – a result to be obtained only by separate state secession.'

Separate state secession was not long in coming. On 20 December the South Carolina convention voted 169 to 0 for secession. The state defended its action, claiming it now 'resumed her separate and equal place among nations', and blaming the North for attacking slavery. 'For twenty-five years this agitation has been steadily increasing, until it has now secured to its aid the power of the common Government … A geographical line has been drawn across the Union, and all the States north of that line have united in the election of a man to the high office of President of the United States whose opinions and purposes are hostile to Slavery.'

South Carolina sent commissioners to other Southern states to propose a meeting, in Montgomery, Alabama on 4 February 1861, to create a new government.

Key dates

South Carolina seceded: December 1860

Mississippi, Florida, Alabama, Georgia, Louisiana and Texas seceded: January–February 1861

Secession spreads

Over the winter of 1860–1 the election of delegates for conventions that would decide on secession took place in six other lower South states in an atmosphere of great excitement and tension. Voters generally had a choice between 'immediate secessionists' and 'cooperationists'. While the standpoint of the immediate secessionists was clear, the cooperationists represented a wide spectrum of opinion. Some were genuine secessionists but believed the time was not yet right to secede; others were unionists, opposed to secession. Historians find it hard to determine the exact distribution of voters along this spectrum. The situation is even more confused because some candidates, running as independents, committed themselves to no position.

- In Mississippi there were 12,000 votes for candidates whose positions were not specified and whose views remain unknown. 12,218 voted for cooperationist candidates. 16,800 voted for immediate secession. On 9 January 1861 the Mississippi convention supported secession by 85 votes to 15.

- On 10 January a Florida convention voted 62 to seven for secession – but cooperationists won over 35 per cent of the vote.
- Alabama voted to secede by 61 votes to 39 on 11 January. The secessionists won 35,600 votes, the cooperationists 28,100 votes.
- Secessionist candidates in Georgia won 44,152 votes, cooperationists 41,632. The Georgia convention voted to secede on 19 January by 208 votes to 89.
- In Louisiana secessionists won 20,214 votes, the cooperationists 18,451. On 26 January the Louisiana convention voted to secede by 113 votes to 17.
- Despite the opposition of Governor Houston, a Texas convention voted (on 1 February) for secession by 166 votes to eight. Texas then had a referendum to ratify the convention's action. Secession was approved by 44,317 votes to 13,020.

A Slave Power conspiracy?

Republicans, including Lincoln, saw events in the South as a continuation of the Slave Power conspiracy. They claimed that a few planters had conned the electorate into voting for secession, to which most Southerners were not really committed.

The debate about whether secession was led by a small aristocratic clique or was a genuinely democratic act has continued. Slaveholders certainly dominated politics in many lower South states. Apart from Texas, no state held a **referendum** on the secession issue. Areas with few slaves tended to vote against disunion. Conversely, secession sentiment was strongest wherever the percentage of slaves was highest. According to historian David Potter, 'To a much greater degree than the slaveholders desired, secession had become a slave owners' movement.' Potter believed that a secessionist minority, with a clear purpose, seized the momentum and, at a time of excitement and confusion, won mass support.

Potter conceded that the secessionists acted democratically and in an 'open and straightforward' manner. By no means all the secessionists were great planters. (Nor did all great planters support secession.) Many non-slaveholders supported secession. While it is true that secessionists opposed efforts by cooperationists to submit the secession ordinances to a popular referendum, this would probably have been superfluous. The Southern electorate had made its position clear in the convention elections. There was no conspiracy to thwart the will of the majority. Moreover, many cooperationists were quite prepared to support secession.

Key term

Referendum
A vote on a specific issue.

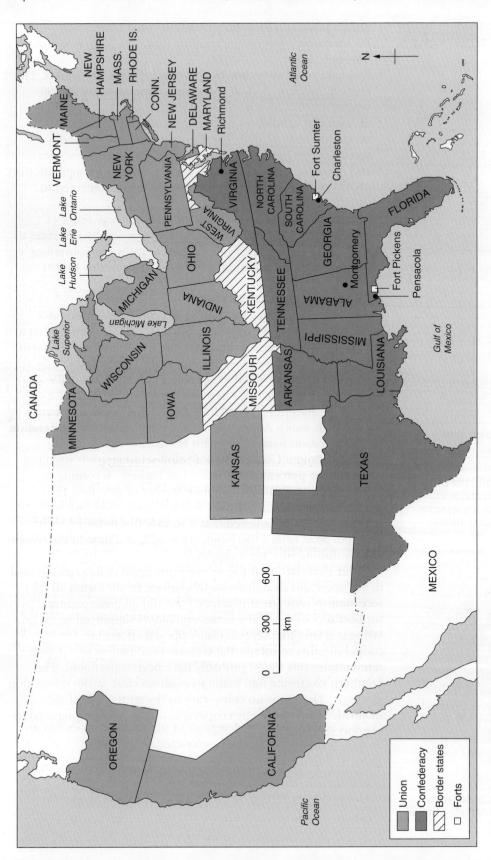

Figure 4.1: The Confederate and Union states

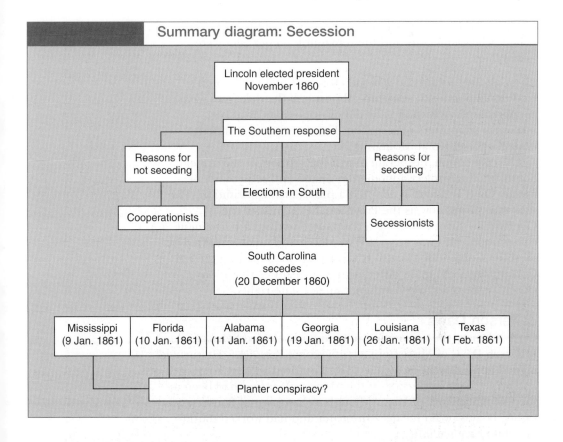

Summary diagram: Secession

Lincoln elected president
November 1860

↓

The Southern response

- Reasons for not seceding
- Reasons for seceding

Elections in South

- Cooperationists
- Secessionists

South Carolina
secedes
(20 December 1860)

| Mississippi (9 Jan. 1861) | Florida (10 Jan. 1861) | Alabama (11 Jan. 1861) | Georgia (19 Jan. 1861) | Louisiana (26 Jan. 1861) | Texas (1 Feb. 1861) |

Planter conspiracy?

3 | The Creation of the Confederacy

Key question
Why did the upper South states not join the Confederacy in February 1861?

Few Americans expected war in early 1861. Most Northerners believed that the seceded states were bluffing or thought that an extremist minority had seized power against the wishes of the majority. Either way, the seceded states would soon be back in the Union: the Southern bluff would be called or the Unionist majority would assert itself. In contrast, most Southerners thought that the North would not fight to preserve the Union. **Border state** Americans were confident that a compromise could be arranged which would bring the seceded states back into the Union. These hopes and expectations were not to be realised. By April 1861 the United States were no longer united; they were at war. Was this the fault of blundering politicians? Or was the rift between North and South so great that war was inevitable?

Key term

Border states
The states between the North and the Deep South (for example, Kentucky, Maryland, Tennessee, Delaware and Missouri). These states supported slavery but were not committed to secession.

The Confederacy

On 4 February 1861, 50 delegates of the seceded states met at Montgomery to launch the Confederate government.

- Chosen by the secession conventions, most of the delegates were lawyers or well-to-do planters.
- Of the 50, 49 were slave owners and 21 owned at least 20 slaves.

Key date

The Confederacy established: February 1861

- Almost all had extensive political experience. Sixty per cent had been Democrats and the remaining 40 per cent were ex-Whigs.

All-in-all they comprised a broad cross-section of the South's traditional political leadership. Almost half the delegates were cooperationists who had been either opponents or at best lukewarm supporters of secession. Fire-eaters were distinctly under-represented at Montgomery.

The convention, desperate to win the support of the upper South, tried to project a moderate, united and self-confident image. On 8 February it adopted a provisional constitution. The next day, sitting now as the Provisional Congress of the Confederate States, it set up a committee to draft a permanent constitution. This was approved in March and quickly ratified by all seven Confederate states. It was closely modelled on the US Constitution. The main differences were features that more closely protected slavery and guaranteed state rights.

Jefferson Davis

On 9 February the convention unanimously elected Senator Jefferson Davis of Mississippi as provisional President. He seemed a good appointment (see page 118). Educated at West Point, he had served with distinction in the Mexican War and had been a successful Secretary of War. Although a champion of Southern rights, he was by no means a fire-eater and had worked hard to maintain national unity.

Alexander Stephens, from Georgia, became vice-president. As a leading anti-secessionist, he seemed the logical choice to attract and weld cooperationists to the new government. Davis's cabinet was made up of men from each Confederate state.

On 18 February Davis took the oath of office as President. In his inaugural speech he asked only that the Confederacy be left alone. Although he expected the North to oppose secession, he was confident that the Confederacy would survive. His main concern was the fact that no states from the upper South had yet joined the Confederacy. The seven original Confederate states comprised only 10 per cent of the USA's population and had only five per cent of its industrial capacity.

Confederate legislation

The Provisional Congress quickly got down to business:

- It passed major pieces of financial legislation.
- It adopted the Stars and Bars as the national flag.
- It set about raising an army.

The upper South

In January 1861 the state legislatures of Arkansas, Virginia, Missouri, Tennessee and North Carolina all called elections for conventions to decide on secession. The results of these elections proved that the upper South was far less secessionist-inclined than the lower South. In Virginia only 32 immediate secessionists won seats in a convention with 152 members. Tennessee and North Carolina had referendums, which opposed conventions being held. Arkansas voted for a convention but most of the delegates voted to reject secession. Secessionists made no headway in Maryland, Delaware, Missouri or Kentucky.

A number of reasons have been put forward to explain why the upper South states did not vote immediately for secession.

- Importantly these states had a smaller stake in slavery than the lower South. Less than 30 per cent of the upper South's population was black. Nearly half of Maryland's blacks were already free.
- Many non-slaveholders questioned how well their interests would be served in a planter-dominated Confederacy.
- The upper South had close ties with the North and thus more reason to fear the economic consequences of secession.
- If war came the upper South would be the most likely battleground.

In many respects the upper South voting came as no surprise: the majority of its voters had supported Bell and Douglas in 1860, not Breckinridge. Nevertheless, many people in the upper South had a deep distrust of Lincoln. The legislatures of Virginia and Tennessee made it clear that they would oppose any attempt to force the seceding states back into the Union. If it came to the crunch, there would be many in the upper South who would put their Southern affiliations before their American loyalties.

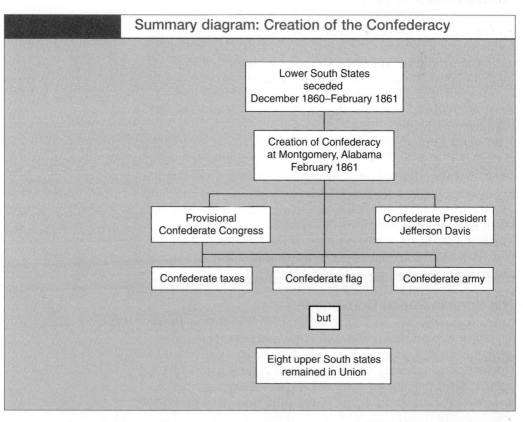

Summary diagram: Creation of the Confederacy

Lower South States seceded December 1860–February 1861

Creation of Confederacy at Montgomery, Alabama February 1861

Provisional Confederate Congress

Confederate President Jefferson Davis

Confederate taxes

Confederate flag

Confederate army

but

Eight upper South states remained in Union

4 | The Search for Compromise

Key question
Could a compromise have been found in 1860–1?

Lincoln did not take over as president until March 1861. In the meantime Buchanan continued as president. Blaming the Republicans for the crisis, he did little to stem the tide of disunion. His main concern was not to provoke war. He thus took no action as federal institutions across the South – forts, custom houses and post offices – were taken over by the Confederate states. However, he determined not to recall the federal garrisons at Fort Sumter and Fort Pickens. This was to have major repercussions. Buchanan has been criticised for not doing more to seek a compromise. In fairness, it is difficult to see what he could have done, given that Republicans did not trust him and the lower South was set upon leaving the Union.

Congressional efforts

Congress met in December. Most Congressmen from the Confederate states did not attend and those who did soon left. However, there were many Congressmen, particularly Northern Democrats and representatives from the upper South, who hoped to work out a compromise. Both the House and the Senate set up committees to explore plans of conciliation. The House Committee, with 33 members, proved to be too cumbersome. The Senate Committee of 13, on which Kentucky unionist John Crittenden played a significant role, was more effective. It recommended a package of compromise proposals (which came out under Crittenden's name).

- The main idea was to extend the Missouri Compromise line to the Pacific, giving the South some hope of slavery expansion. Slavery would be recognised south of 36°30′ in all present territories, as well as those 'hereafter acquired'.
- The Crittenden proposals recommended a constitutional amendment guaranteeing that there would be no interference with slavery in those states where it already existed.
- Congress would be forbidden to abolish slavery in Washington and would not be allowed to interfere with the inter-state slave trade.

Republicans, whose strength in Congress had grown significantly with the withdrawal of Southern delegates, rejected the proposals, which seemed to smack more of surrender than compromise. 'Given the momentum of secession and the fundamental set of Republicanism', observed David Potter, 'it is probably safe to say that compromise was impossible from the start'.

The Virginia Peace Convention

In February 1861 a Peace Convention met in Washington, at the request of Virginia, to see if it could find measures that would bring the seceded states back into the Union. It was attended by 133 delegates, including some of the most famous names in US politics. The Confederate states did not send delegates. After three weeks of deliberation, the Convention supported proposals similar to those of Crittenden. These proposals were ignored by Congress.

Key question
Was Lincoln prepared to compromise?

Lincoln's position

Up to 1860 slavery had been the main issue dividing North from South. That had now been replaced by secession. There were some, like newspaper editor Horace Greeley, who thought that the 'erring' Confederate states should be allowed to 'go in peace'. However, most Northerners were unwilling to accept the dismemberment of the USA. The great experiment in self-government must not collapse. 'The doctrine of secession is anarchy', declared a Cincinnati newspaper. 'If the minority have the right to break up the Government at pleasure, because they have not had their way, there is an end of all government.'

Few Republicans, however, demanded the swift despatch of troops to suppress the 'rebellion'. There was an appreciation that precipitous action might have a disastrous impact on the upper South. The best bet seemed to be to watch, wait and avoid provocation, hoping that the lower South would see sense and return to the Union.

Lincoln continued to maintain a strict silence. However, in a letter written on 1 February 1861 to William Seward (soon to be his Secretary of State), Lincoln made it clear that he was ready to compromise with the South on a number of issues such as the fugitive slave law, slavery in Washington, and 'whatever springs of necessity from the fact that the institution is amongst us'. He was even prepared to make some concessions with regard to New Mexico, given that the 1850 Compromise specifically allowed settlers there to decide on the issue. However, Lincoln's general position with regard to slavery expansion was clear.

> I say now ... as I have all the while said, that on the territorial question – that is, the question of extending slavery under the national auspices – I am inflexible. I am for no compromise which assists or permits the extension of the institution on soil owned by the nation.

Lincoln believed that he had won the 1860 election on principles fairly stated and was determined not to concede too much to the South. 'If we surrender it is the end of us', he said. Like many Republicans, he exaggerated the strength of Union feeling in the South; he thought, mistakenly, that secession was a plot by a small group of wealthy planters. His hope that inactivity might allow Southern Unionists a chance to rally and overthrow the extremists was naive. In truth, this probably made little difference. Even with hindsight, it is difficult to see what Lincoln could have done before he became president that would have dramatically changed matters.

Lincoln's cabinet

Lincoln's seven-man cabinet was more a cabinet of all factions than of all talents. Some of its members were radical, others conservative. Some represented the East, others the West. (Lincoln would have liked to appoint a 'real' Southerner but there was no obvious candidate.) Some were ex-Whigs, others ex-Democrats. Four had been competitors for the 1860 Republican nomination. Not one had been friendly with Lincoln pre-1861; he knew little about them and they knew even less about him.

- Seward, the best-known Republican in the country, became Secretary of State. Once considered a radical but now increasingly conservative, he expected, and was expected, to be the power behind the throne.
- Salmon Chase, Secretary of the Treasury, was seen as the main radical spokesman in the cabinet.
- Gideon Welles became Secretary of the Navy.
- The appointments of Caleb Smith, from Indiana, as Secretary of the Interior and Simon Cameron, from Pennsylvania, as Secretary of War were seen as 'debt' appointments in return for support for Lincoln's presidential nomination.
- Attorney General Edward Bates and Postmaster General Montgomery Blair completed the cabinet.

Some doubted that Lincoln would have the personality to control such an unlikely 'team'. However, Lincoln trusted to his political skill to make the separate elements pull together.

Lincoln arrives in Washington

Lincoln set out from Springfield to Washington in February 1861. Instead of travelling directly to the capital, he stopped at various towns to show himself and to make set speeches. This was probably a mistake: there was relatively little he thought he could say before his inauguration and thus he said little – to the disappointment of many who heard him.

Nearing Baltimore, Lincoln was warned of an assassination plot. Heeding the advice of his security advisers, he abandoned his planned journey and slipped into Washington anonymously, 'like a thief in the night' according to his critics. This cast doubts about his courage and firmness to face the crisis ahead. In addition, neither his Western accent nor his social awkwardness inspired much confidence.

The next few days were a nightmare. Lincoln met mobs of office seekers and endless delegations, as well as Congressmen and members of his cabinet. Meanwhile, he worked hard on his inauguration speech. The speech was looked over by several people, including Seward, who persuaded Lincoln to soften a few phrases.

Lincoln's inauguration

On 4 March 1861 Lincoln became president. His inaugural speech was conciliatory but firm. He said that he would not interfere with slavery where it already existed. Nor would he take immediate action to reclaim federal property or appoint federal officials in the South. However, he made it clear that, in his view, the Union was unbreakable and that secession was illegal. He thus

Lincoln was inaugurated president: March 1861

Key date

intended to 'hold, occupy and possess' federal property within the seceded states. He ended by saying:

> In your hands, my dissatisfied fellow countrymen, and not in mine, is the momentous issue of civil war. The government will not assail you. You can have no conflict without being yourselves the aggressors. You have no oath registered in heaven to destroy the government, while I shall have the most solemn one to 'preserve, protect, and defend' it ... We are not enemies, but friends. We must not be enemies. Though passion may have strained, it must not break, our bonds of affection.

Some Democrat newspapers claimed that Lincoln's speech was rambling and unscholarly. However, most Republicans liked his firm tone. Border state Unionists and many Northern Democrats approved of his attempts at conciliation. Unfortunately, the speech had no effect whatsoever in the Confederate states.

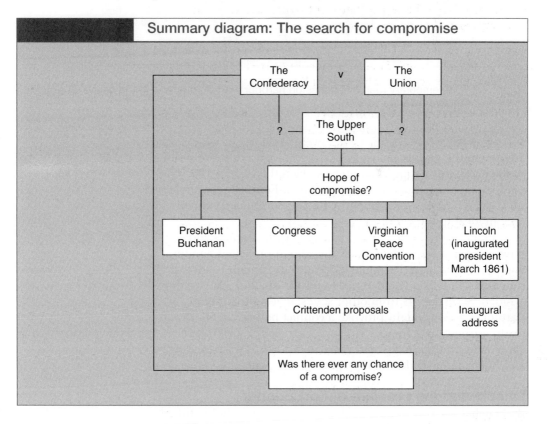

Summary diagram: The search for compromise

5 | The Problem of Fort Sumter

Over the winter the Confederacy had taken over most of the (virtually unmanned) forts and arsenals in the South. There were two exceptions: Fort Pickens and Fort Sumter. Both forts were on islands. Pickens, off Pensacola, Florida, was well out of range of shore batteries and could easily be reinforced by the federal navy.

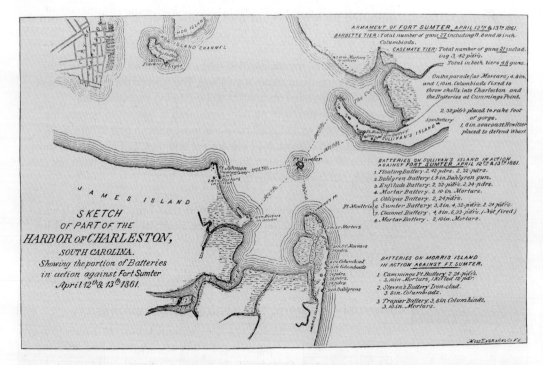

Figure 4.2: Contemporary map of Charleston harbour. Fort Sumter was in the centre, surrounded by Confederate cannon.

Sumter, in the middle of Charleston harbour, was a more serious problem. Union troops in Sumter numbered less than 100. They were led by Major Robert Anderson, an ex-Kentucky slaveholder who, while having some sympathy for the South, determined to remain loyal to the Union.

In January 1861 Buchanan sent a ship with supplies and reinforcements for Anderson. As the ship approached Sumter, South Carolina batteries opened fire and its captain hastily retreated. Anderson decided not to return fire and war was thus avoided. Secessionists from other states, fearing that South Carolina's actions might provoke a conflict before the South was ready, warned the state to cool down. A truce (of sorts) was agreed. South Carolina would make no efforts to seize the fort and Buchanan would send no further aid to Sumter.

Lincoln and the problem of Fort Sumter

By March 1861 Fort Sumter had become the symbol of national sovereignty for both sides. If the Confederacy was to lay claim to the full rights of a sovereign nation it could hardly allow a 'foreign' fort in the middle of one of its main harbours. Lincoln had made it clear in his inaugural speech that he intended to hold on to what remained of federal property in the South. Retention of Sumter was thus a test of his credibility.

Lincoln had spoken as he did at his inauguration, believing that time was on his side. But within hours of his speech, he learned that the Sumter garrison only had enough supplies of food left for four to six weeks. Lincoln, aware that any attempt to supply Sumter might spark war, sought the advice of his general-in-chief, 74-year-old Winfield Scott. Sumter's evacuation, Scott informed Lincoln, was 'almost inevitable': it could not be held without a large fleet and 25,000 soldiers, neither of which the USA possessed. On 15 March Lincoln brought the matter before his cabinet. Most favoured withdrawal. Lincoln put off making an immediate decision. In the meantime he sent trusted observers to Charleston to assess the situation.

Seward was the chief spokesman for the policy of masterly inactivity. If the upper South was not stampeded into joining the Confederacy by a coercive act, Seward argued, the 'rebel' states would be forced to rejoin the Union. Fearing that conflict between the federal government and the Confederacy might unite the entire South, he urged Lincoln to make some effort to appease the Confederacy. While Lincoln prevaricated, Seward, on his own initiative, sent assurances to Confederate leaders that Sumter would be abandoned.

At the end of March, following a report from Scott advising that both Sumter and Pickens should be abandoned, Lincoln called another cabinet meeting to discuss the crisis. By now, the fact-finding mission to Charleston had returned and reported finding no support for the Union whatsoever; the hope that Unionist sentiment would prevail was thus gone. Moreover, Northern newspapers were now demanding that Sumter be held. Heedful of Northern opinion, most of the cabinet favoured re-supplying Sumter and protecting Pickens.

Key question
Did Lincoln deliberately manoeuvre the Confederacy into war?

Lincoln acts

Lincoln determined to send ships to re-provision, but not reinforce, both forts. Seward, who had thought Sumter's evacuation a foregone conclusion, had miscalculated. He now suggested that Lincoln should delegate power to him, evacuate Sumter, and provoke a war against France and Spain which might help re-unite to the nation. Lincoln made it clear that he had no intention of delegating power, of abandoning Sumter or of fighting more than one war at a time.

On 4 April Lincoln informed Anderson that a relief expedition would soon be coming and that he should try to hold out. Two days later he sent a letter to South Carolina's governor telling him that he intended to re-supply Sumter. A small naval expedition (three ships and some 500 men) finally left for Charleston on 9 April.

It has been claimed that Lincoln deliberately manoeuvred the Confederacy into firing the first shots. More likely, he was simply trying to keep as many options open as possible. He hoped to preserve peace, but was willing to risk, and possibly expected, war. By attempting to re-supply Sumter, he was lobbing the ball into Jefferson Davis's court. The Confederate leader now had to decide what to do. If he gave the orders to fire on unarmed boats carrying food for hungry men, he would clearly be in the wrong.

A contemporary engraving showing Fort Sumter under attack.

This would unite Northern opinion and possibly keep the upper South loyal.

On 9 April Davis's cabinet met. Most members thought that the time had come to lance the Sumter boil. The fact that the Union flag was still flying on the fort was an affront to Southern honour. Moreover, a crisis might bring the upper South into the Confederacy. Thus Davis issued orders that Sumter must be taken before it was re-supplied. General Beauregard, commander of Confederate forces in Charleston, was to demand that Anderson evacuate the fort. If Anderson refused, then Beauregard's orders were to 'reduce' Sumter.

The first shots of the war

On 11 April Beauregard demanded Sumter's immediate surrender. Anderson, who had once been Beauregard's tutor and then colleague at West Point, refused. He pointed out that lack of food would force him to surrender in a few days anyway. Negotiations dragged on for several hours but got nowhere. And so, at 4.30 a.m. on 12 April, the opening shots of the Civil War were fired. For the next 33 hours the defenders of Sumter exchanged artillery fire with Confederate land batteries. Some 5000 rounds were fired: 3500 by Confederate forces, 1500 by Sumter's defenders. Extraordinarily there were no deaths. The relief expedition arrived too late, and was too small, to affect proceedings. On 13 April, with fires raging through the fort, Anderson surrendered. His troops were allowed to march out, with colours flying, and were evacuated to Washington.

Confederate forces opened fire on Fort Sumter: 12 April 1861

Key date

This contemporary photograph shows Confederate forces occupying Fort Sumter immediately after its surrender. Note the Confederate flag, the 'stars and bars', flying from the makeshift flagpole.

The attack on Sumter electrified the North. In New York, a city which had previously tended to be pro-Southern, 250,000 people turned out for a Union rally. 'There can be no neutrals in this war, only patriots – or traitors', thundered Senator Douglas. On 15 April Lincoln issued a **Call to Arms**. Few expected a long conflict. Lincoln asked for 75,000 men for 90 days; Davis called for 100,000 men. Such was the enthusiasm that both sides were inundated with troops. Lincoln insisted that he was dealing with a rebellion and that this was not a war. Nevertheless, on 19 April he ordered a blockade of the Confederacy. This implied that the conflict was more a war than a rebellion. It is rare that a country blockades itself.

Secession: the second wave

Given that Lincoln called on all Union states to send men to put down the rebellion, the upper South states had to commit themselves. Virginia's decision was crucial. Its industrial capacity was as great as the seven original Confederate states combined. If it opted to remain in the Union, the Confederacy was unlikely to survive for long. In fact, most Virginians sympathised with the

Key term

Call to Arms
A presidential order calling up troops and putting the USA on a war-footing.

Key date

Virginia, Arkansas, North Carolina and Tennessee joined the Confederacy:
April–June 1861

Confederacy. A state convention voted by 88 votes to 55 to support its Southern 'brothers'. A referendum in May ratified this decision, with Virginians voting by 128,884 votes to 32,134 to secede. Richmond, Virginia's capital, now became the Confederate capital. In May Arkansas and North Carolina joined the Confederacy. In June Tennessee voted by 104,913 votes to 47,238 to secede.

However, support for the Confederacy in the upper South was far from total. West Virginia now seceded from Virginia and remained in the Union. East Tennessee was pro-Unionist. More importantly, four slave states – Delaware, Maryland, Missouri and Kentucky – did not secede.

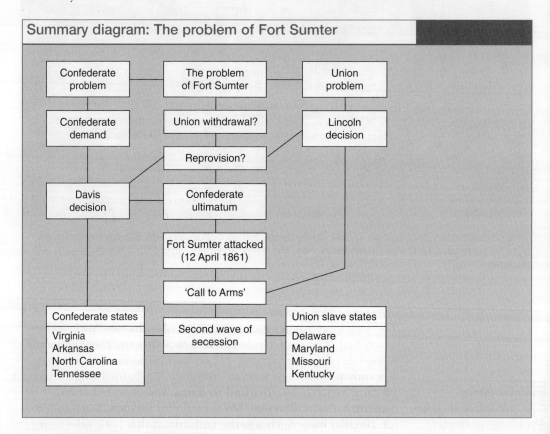

Summary diagram: The problem of Fort Sumter

6 | Key Debate

In March 1865 Lincoln, in his second inaugural address, presented a succinct explanation of how and why the war came:

On the occasion corresponding this four years ago all thoughts were anxiously directed to an impending civil war … .

One eighth of the whole population was coloured slaves, not distributed generally over the Union, but localised in the southern part of it. These slaves constituted a peculiar and powerful interest. All knew that this interest was somehow the cause of the war. To strengthen, perpetuate, and extend this interest was the object for which the insurgents would rend the Union even by war, while the government claimed no right to do more than to restrict the territorial enlargement of it.

For 50 years after the war, few Northern historians dissented from this view. However, Jefferson Davis insisted in his memoirs that the Southern states had fought solely 'for the defence of an inherent, unalienable right … to withdraw from a Union which they had, as sovereign communities, voluntarily entered … The existence of African servitude was in no way the cause of the conflict, but only an incident.' This explanation was accepted by many Southerners who continued to view the conflict as a war of Northern aggression.

The progressive interpretation

In the 1920s 'progressive' historians (such as Charles Beard) believed that clashes between interest groups and classes underpinned most events in history. The war, in the eyes of the 'progressives', was a contest, not between slavery and freedom, but between plantation agriculture and **industrialising capitalism**. According to Beard, economic issues (such as the tariff and government subsidies to transportation and manufacturing) were what really divided the power-brokers – Northern manufacturers and Southern planters. The Confederacy could thus be seen as fighting for the preservation of a stable, **agrarian civilisation** in the face of the grasping ambitions of Northern businessmen. Perhaps it was no coincidence that this interpretation emerged at much the same period that *Gone With the Wind* became one of the most popular literary and cinematic successes of all time.

The revisionist interpretation

By the 1940s another interpretation, usually called 'revisionism', dominated the work of historians. Revisionists denied that sectional conflicts between North and South, whether over slavery, state rights, or industry versus agriculture, were genuinely divisive. The differences between North and South, wrote Avery Craven, a leading revisionist, were 'no greater than those existing at different times between East and West'. In the revisionist view, far more united than divided the two sections. Revisionists insisted that the sectional quarrels could have been accommodated peacefully. Far from being irrepressible, the war was brought on by extremists on both sides – rabble-rousing abolitionists and fire-eaters – who whipped up emotions and hatreds. The passions they aroused got out of hand because politicians, lacking the skill of previous generations, failed to find a compromise. The result was a tragic, unnecessary war.

The importance of slavery

Historians have now come full circle. The progressive and revisionist schools are presently dormant if not dead. The view

Key terms

Industrialising capitalism
A society in which industry and big business are developing.

Agrarian civilisation
An advanced and sophisticated society based on farming.

Gone With the Wind
This novel, written by Margaret Mitchell (a Southerner), was published in 1936. It sold over 10 million copies and was soon made into a successful film. Both book and film suggested that the pre-war South was a civilised society.

that slavery was 'somehow' the cause of the war is almost universally accepted. Slavery defined the South, permeating almost every aspect of its life. The market value of the South's four million slaves in 1860 was $3 billion – more than the value of land and cotton. Slavery, moreover, was more than an economic system. It was a means of maintaining racial control and white supremacy. While only a quarter of Southern whites owned slaves in 1860, the vast majority of non-slaveholding whites supported slavery.

The rise of militant abolitionism in the North increased tension. Although the abolitionists did not get far with their message of racial equality, the belief that slavery was unjust and obsolete entered mainstream Northern politics. Slavery was seen as impoverishing poor and middling whites who could not compete with slave planters.

It was the issue of slavery expansion, not the existence of slavery itself, that polarised the nation. Most of the crises that threatened the bonds of Union arose over this matter. Convinced that a Slave Power conspiracy was at work, Northerners came to support the Republican Party, which was pledged to stop slavery expansion. For many Southerners the election of Lincoln was the last straw – an affront to their honour. While the Confederacy might claim its justification to be the protection of state rights, in truth, it was one state right – the right to preserve slavery – that impelled the Confederate states' separation.

The importance of nationalism

In 1861 Lincoln was pledged to preserve the Union, not end slavery. Most Northerners fought to save the Union. The Confederate states fought for the right to **self-determination**. Thus **nationalism** became the central issue. Pre-1860 most Southerners saw themselves as loyal Americans: fire-eaters were a distinct minority. The creation of the Confederacy was a refuge to which many Southerners felt driven, not a national destiny that they eagerly embraced. The Civil War did more to produce Southern nationalism than Southern nationalism did to produce war. In so far as there was a sense of Southernness in 1861, it had arisen because of slavery.

Who was to blame?

With hindsight, it is clear that Southerners got things wrong. Slavery was not in immediate peril in 1860–1. Given that the Republicans did not have a majority in Congress, there was little Lincoln could do to threaten slavery. Indeed, he was prepared to make some concessions to the South. From November 1860 to April 1861 Lincoln acted reasonably and rationally.

The same cannot be said for Southerners and their leaders. The South did not have to secede. The maintenance of slavery did not require the creation of an independent Southern nation. For much of the pre-war period most Southerners regarded the fire-eaters as quasi-lunatics. Unfortunately, in the emotionally charged atmosphere of 1860–1, lunatic ideas – not so much the

Key terms

Self-determination
The right of a population to decide its own government.

Nationalism
Loyalty and commitment to a country.

lunatics themselves – took over the South. Secession was a reckless decision. Some Southerners at the time realised that it would mean war – and that war would probably result in Confederate defeat and the end of slavery. Governor Houston of Texas observed: 'Our people are going to war to perpetuate slavery and the first gun fired in the war will be the knell of slavery.' The North, so much stronger in terms of population and industrial strength, was always likely to win a civil war. The fact that this was not obvious to most Southerners is symptomatic of the hysteria that swept the South in 1860–1. Southerners picked the quarrel. They fired the first shots. And they suffered the consequences.

Some key books in the debate
Gary S. Boritt (ed.), *Why the Civil War Came* (OUP, 1996).
David M. Potter, *The Impending Crisis 1846–61* (Harper and Row, 1976).

Study Guide: AS Questions

In the style of OCR

Study the five sources on the immediate causes of the Civil War in 1860–1, and then answer **both** sub-questions. It is recommended that you spend two-thirds of your time in answering part **(b)**.

(a) **Study Sources C and D.**

Compare these sources as evidence for differing views on the issues at stake when North and South went to war in 1861. (30 marks)

(b) **Study all of the sources.**

Use your own knowledge to assess how far the sources support the interpretation that the Civil War appeared inevitable by the early months of 1861. (70 marks)

Source A

From: The Vicksburg Mississippi Daily Whig, *January 1860. A Southern newspaper complaining about Northern economic domination.*

The people of the South have permitted Yankees [Northerners] to monopolise the carrying trade, with its immense profits. Until recently, we left manufacturing business to them without making any effort to become manufacturers ourselves. We have allowed the North to do all the importing and most of the exporting business, for the whole Union. Thus the North has grown more powerful to a most astonishing degree, at the expense of the South. It is no wonder that their villages have grown into magnificent towns and cities.

Source B

From: The Boston Transcript, *March 1861. A Northern newspaper questions the motives for secession, and fears the consequences.*

Alleged grievances in regard to slavery were originally the causes for the separation of the cotton states; but the mask has been thrown off, and it is apparent that the people of the principal seceding states are now in favour of commercial independence. They dream that the centres of traffic can be changed from Northern to Southern ports. The merchants of New Orleans, Charleston and Savannah are possessed with the idea that New York, Boston and Philadelphia may be deprived in the future of their mercantile greatness by a revenue system verging upon free trade. If the Southern Confederation is allowed to carry out a policy by which only a very low duty is charged on imports, no doubt the business of the chief Northern cities will be seriously injured.

Source C

From: Jefferson Davis, in a message to the Confederate Congress, April 1861. Davis blames the North for a situation in which war seemed inevitable.

As soon as the Northern states that prohibited African slavery within their limits had reached a number sufficient to give their representation a controlling voice in the Congress, a persistent and organised system of hostile measures against the rights of owners of slaves in the Southern states was introduced and gradually extended. A great party was organised for the purpose of obtaining the administration of the government, with the object of rendering property in slaves so insecure as to be comparatively worthless, and thereby annihilating in effect property worth thousands of millions of dollars.

Source D

From: The Philadelphia Public Ledger, June 1861. A Northern newspaper argues that democratic principles are the essential issue in the Civil War that had just broken out.

We are fighting for the fundamental principle of republican government – the right of the majority to rule. We are fighting to prove to the world that the free democratic spirit which first established the American government in 1776 is now equal to its protection and its maintenance. If this is not worth fighting for, then our revolt against England in 1776 was a crime, and our republican government is a fraud.

Source E

From: B.H. Reid, The Origins of the American Civil War, 1996. A modern historian analyses the attempts in 1861 at compromise.

All previous crises of the Union had ended with some final effort at compromise which succeeded. Although the state of affairs in the early months of 1861 was much graver than it had been in 1850 or in 1820, many hoped and others worked in 1861 for a last-minute compromise solution acceptable to both parties. Hopes were raised because the American system of government was now expert at resolving such conflict. That contemporaries expected reconciliation to succeed and save the Union in 1861 is not surprising. Whether such proposals were workable in 1861 is, however, quite another matter.

Exam tips

(a) The key here is to stick to the sources and the focus of the question. It is useful to point out the origin of the sources. What does Davis see as the main cause of Southern secession? Are his views likely to be held by most Southerners? *The Philadelphia Public Ledger* was just one of hundreds of Northern newspapers. Do its views represent the opinions of most Northerners?

(b) There is a need to balance your answer between what can be gleaned from the sources and your own knowledge. What are the sources saying about the issues dividing North from South in 1860–1? Given these issues, was there any hope of compromise? What attempts at compromise were made? Did foolish politicians fail to find an obvious solution to the crisis or had North and South become so divided that compromise was impossible?

In the style of OCR

How successful was Lincoln in his handling of events from November 1860 to April 1861?   (50 marks)

Exam tips

The cross-references are intended to take you straight to the material that will help you to answer the question.

You need to identify Lincoln's main actions and assess their impact.

*   Identify Republican policies – that is, policies to which Lincoln was committed – in November 1860.
*   Outline the process of secession – and the extent to which secession was caused by the Southern perception of what Lincoln might do. Could Lincoln have done something to reassure Southerners (page 99)?
*   What efforts at compromise were made in 1860–1? To what extent was Lincoln involved in the compromise process? Was compromise possible? If it was impossible, then it is somewhat unfair to blame Lincoln. However, if compromise was a real possibility, then Lincoln must be put in the 'dock', along with other blundering politicians (pages 98–100).
*   How did Lincoln manage events in March–April 1861, particularly the Fort Sumter crisis (pages 101–4)?

To score highly it is crucial that you offer clear judgements all the way through your answer. Use your concluding paragraph to pull the main judgements together.

Study Guide: A2 Question

In the style of Edexcel

Source 1

From: Charles W. Ramsdell, 'The natural limits of slavery expansion', 1929 (published in Mississippi Valley Historical Review, *XVI, pp. 151–71, reproduced from K. Stamp,* The Causes of the Civil War, *1991).*

By 1860 the institution of slavery had virtually reached its natural frontiers. There was, in brief, no further place for it to go. In the cold facts of the situation, there was no longer any basis for excited sectional controversy over slavery extension; but the public mind had so long been concerned with the debate that it could not see that the issue had ceased to have validity. In the existing state of the popular mind, therefore, there was still abundant opportunity for the politician to work to his own ends, to play upon prejudice and fear. Sowers of the wind, not seeing how near was the approaching harvest of the whirlwind!

Source 2

From: Michael F. Holt, 'The political crises of the 1850s', 1978 (reproduced from K. Stamp, The Causes of the Civil War, *1991).*

It was not events alone that caused Northerners and Southerners to view each other as enemies of the basic rights they both cherished. Politicians who pursued partisan strategies were largely responsible for the ultimate breakdown of the political process. Much of the story of the coming Civil War is the story of the successful efforts of Democratic politicians in the South and Republican politicians in the North to keep sectional conflict at the centre of political debate and to defeat political rivals who hope to exploit other issues to achieve election.

Source 3

From: Alan Farmer and Vivienne Sanders, American History 1860–1990, *2002.*

Slavery was the sole institution not shared by North and South. It defined the South, permeating almost every aspect of its life. The rise of militant abolitionism in the North exacerbated tension between the sections. But it was the issue of slavery expansion, rather than the mere existence of slavery, that polarised the nation. Most of the crises that threatened the bonds of the Union arose over this matter. Convinced that a slave power conspiracy was at work, Northerners came to support the Republican Party, which was pledged to stop slavery expansion. For many Southerners the election of a Republican president in 1860 was the last straw – an affront to their honour. So, the lower South seceded.

Use Sources 1, 2 and 3 and your own knowledge.

How far do you agree that the outbreak of the Civil War in the USA was primarily the result of political rivalries? Explain your answer, using the evidence of the sources and your own knowledge of the issues related to this controversy.   (40 marks)

Exam tips

The cross-references are intended to take you straight to the material that will help you to answer the question.

In answering questions of this type you are asked to use the sources and your own knowledge. It is important to treat these questions differently from the way that you would plan an essay answer. The sources raise issues for you and you should see them as a support. You can use them as the core of your plan since they will always contain points that relate to the claim stated in the question. Make sure you have identified all the issues raised by the sources, and then add in your own knowledge – both to make more of the issues in the sources (add depth to the coverage) and to add new points (extend the range covered). In the advice given below, links are made to the relevant pages where information can be found which relates to the points in the sources.

In this collection of material, you can find the following points:

- There need not have been any continuing controversy over slavery expansion (page 73).
- The issue of slavery expansion polarised the nation and was at the heart of the threat to the Union (pages 38–42 and 61–2).
- The North feared a 'slave power conspiracy' (page 93).
- There were fears and prejudices which politicians played upon (pages 88–9).
- The Republican Party was pledged to stop slavery expansion (page 87).
- Partisan party policies and strategies played a key part in the road to war (page 107).
- The election of a Republican president was the trigger for the secession of the lower South (pages 90–3).

Your task is to group and organise these points into an argument for and against the view stated in the question, adding in material from the sources and your own knowledge. Your own information will also help you challenge as well as expand on points in the sources. Try to use the sources together to support the points you wish to make. For example, Sources 1 and 2 both suggest that the irresponsible actions of politicians were largely responsible for triggering the war. How do they do this? Aim to select a few words from each of them to support that point, and then develop it further from information of your own.

You will also need to cover key areas which the sources do not include. In this case, you will also need to explore why attempts at compromise failed after the secession of 'the lower South' (see pages 98–101) and give additional coverage to the role of Lincoln.

5 War on the Home and Foreign Fronts

POINTS TO CONSIDER
With fewer people, far less industry and a less well-developed railway system, the odds were stacked heavily against the Confederacy. To fight – never mind to win – the war, Southerners would need to make far greater sacrifices than Northerners. The Union was always favourite to win. However, 'big battalions' do sometimes lose wars. If Northern morale had collapsed, the Union could have been defeated. Moreover, resources by themselves do not win wars; they need efficient management. How effective was the Union war effort? How well did the Confederacy manage the war? Did it lose the war at home rather than on the battlefield? Or did it lose it on the diplomatic front? This chapter will consider the following themes:

- The Confederate war effort
- The economic and social impact of the war on the Confederacy
- Confederate opposition to the war
- The Union war effort
- The economic and social impact of the war on the Union
- Union opposition to the war
- Britain and the Civil War

Key dates
1861 *Trent* affair
1862 Introduction of conscription by the Confederacy
        Homestead Act
        Legal Tender Act
1863 New York draft riots
        Laird rams crisis

1 | The Confederate War Effort

Jefferson Davis

Davis remains a controversial figure. His Vice-President, Stephens, thought him, 'weak, timid, petulant, peevish, obstinate' and blamed him for practically everything that went wrong in the war. Historian David Potter saw Davis's performance as the most important reason why the Confederacy lost the war, claiming that if Davis and Lincoln had reversed roles, the Confederacy might well have won.

Key question
How competent was Jefferson Davis's government?

The case against Davis

Certainly Davis had his failings. One of these was his inability to establish good working relationships with many of his colleagues. He quarrelled with military commanders and leading politicians and found it hard to work with men who enjoyed less than his full approval. Perhaps the high turnover in his cabinet is proof of his inability to cement firm relationships. In the course of the war he appointed no fewer than four secretaries of state and six secretaries of war.

Davis is also blamed for meddling in the affairs of subordinates. Finding it hard to prioritise and to delegate, he got bogged down in detail. Indecision is seen as another of his failings; lengthy cabinet meetings often came to no conclusion. While some contemporaries accused Davis of having despotic tendencies, historians have criticised him for exercising his powers too sparingly. He has also been blamed for failing to communicate effectively. At a time when the Confederacy needed revolutionary inspiration, he is seen as being too conservative.

The case for Davis

Davis did and does have his defenders. In 1861, unlike Lincoln, he came to the presidency with useful military and administrative experience. He had, from the outset, a more realistic view of the situation than most Southerners. He never under-estimated the Yankees and expected a long struggle. Robert E. Lee praised Davis and said he could think of no-one who could have done a better job.

The fact that Davis appointed Lee says much for his military good sense. Despite later accusations, he did not over-command his forces. To generals he trusted, like Lee, he gave considerable freedom.

Although he had long been a **state rights** advocate, Davis supported tough measures when necessary, even when these ran contrary to concerns about state rights and individual liberty. He promoted the 1862 Conscription Act, imposed **martial law** in areas threatened by Union invasion, supported the **impressment of supplies** needed by Southern troops, and urged high taxes on cotton and slaves.

As the war went on, he forced himself to become a more public figure, making several tours of the South to try to rekindle flagging faith. He probably did as much as anyone could to hold together the Confederacy. Few have questioned his dedication to the rebel cause or the intense work he put into a difficult job, the stress of which increasingly took its toll. Far from his performance contributing to Confederate defeat, it may be that his leadership ensured that the Confederacy held out for as long as it did.

Davis's cabinet

In all, Davis made 16 appointments to head the six cabinet departments. Judah Benjamin accounted for three of these as he was appointed, in succession, to Justice, War and State. A brilliant lawyer (the first Jew to hold high political office in the USA), he

Key date

Introduction of conscription by the Confederacy: 1862

Key terms

State rights
Many, particularly Southern, politicians believed that most issues should be decided at state, not federal, level.

Martial law
The suspension of ordinary administration and policing and, in its place, the exercise of military power.

Impressment of supplies
Confiscation of goods.

Profile: Jefferson Davis 1808–89

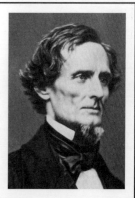

1808	– Born in Kentucky
1825	– Graduated from West Point
1835	– Resigned from the army after marrying Zachary Taylor's daughter Sarah against her father's wishes Sarah died three months after their marriage
1835–45	– Planter at Brierfield, Mississippi
1845	– Married Varina Howell and elected to Congress
1846	– Fought in the Mexican War: helped to win the battle of Buena Vista
1847	– Elected to the US Senate
1853–7	– Secretary of War
1861	– Became Confederate president
1865	– Captured by Union troops; imprisoned
1867	– Released from prison
1889	– Died

How good a president was Davis? Historians have very different views.

Historian Bell Wiley:

> Davis neither realised the importance of cultivating good will nor was he willing to pay the price of being a popular leader.

Historians David Donald, Jean Baker and Michael Holt in *The Civil War and Reconstruction* (2001):

> Much of the criticism of the Confederate president fails to take into account the insuperable difficulties of his position and to realize that no other Southern political leader even approached Davis in stature.

owed his survival to his ability and to his close relationship with Davis; no other adviser had his ear so often or so influentially. Benjamin, Stephen Mallory (Navy) and John Reagan (Postmaster General) served in the cabinet from start to finish.

The high turnover in the War and State departments resulted not from feuds between Davis and his Secretaries, but from Congressional criticisms that sometimes forced Davis to accept resignations. Benjamin was usually prepared to take the blame for events, if by so doing he sheltered Davis. Davis's cabinet met frequently and deliberated for hours. He usually heeded the advice he was given. For the most part he left his Secretaries to get on with running their departments, involving himself only in the detailed decision making of the War Department.

Most of the Secretaries were capable men and government operations functioned reasonably smoothly for much of the war. The War Department, with over 57,000 civilian employees at its height, was easily the largest office. The longest serving War Secretary was James Seddon (November 1862–February 1865). Energetic and clear-thinking, Seddon, aided by Assistant Secretary John Campbell, oversaw the myriad details of running the war.

Key question
Did the Confederate
Congress support
Davis?

The Confederate Congress

Congressmen in the Provisional Congress (which met in 1861–2) were selected by their state legislatures. After this, there were two popularly elected Congresses, the first from 1862 to 1864, the second from 1864 to 1865, each consisting of a House and Senate.

Of the 267 men who served as Confederate Congressmen, about a third had sat in the US Congress. There was no two-party system. Men who had once been political enemies tried to present a united front. It may be, however, that the absence of an 'official' opposition resulted in less channelling of political activity and more squabbling. Davis, moreover, had no party organisation to mobilise support or to help him formulate legislative policy and guide bills through Congress.

The Confederate Congress often found itself on the horns of a dilemma. While wanting to pass measures that would ensure victory, it was aware of its 'sacred heritage' to preserve state rights. These two principles often clashed.

In 1861–2 most Congressmen rallied round Davis; not to do so smacked of treason. Accordingly, the administration's measures, even those seen as draconian and anti-state rights, passed almost intact. However, as morale deteriorated under the impact of military setbacks, inflation and terrible casualty lists, opposition grew, both inside and outside Congress.

This was reflected in the 1863 Congressional elections. Almost 40 per cent of the members of the second Congress were new to that body and many were opposed to Davis. His opponents defy easy categorisation. Some held extreme state rights views; others simply disagreed with the way the war was being waged. A small minority wanted peace. Not surprisingly the 'opposition' never formed a cohesive voting block. Thus there was no major rift between Congress and Davis.

Key question
Did the Confederacy
'die of state rights'?

State rights

To wage a successful war, the Confederacy had to have the full co-operation of all its states. It also needed a central government strong enough to make the most of the South's resources. Some state leaders were not keen to concede too much power to Richmond. Appealing to the principle of state rights (for which they had seceded), they resisted many of the efforts of Davis's administration to centralise the running of the war effort. Governors Joseph Brown of Georgia and Zebulon Vance of North Carolina are often blamed for not working for the common cause. Brown, for example, opposed conscription and exempted thousands of Georgians from the draft by enrolling them in bogus state militia units.

In reality, however, most state governments co-operated effectively with Davis. All the 28 men who served as state governors, including Brown and Vance, were committed to the Confederacy. As commanders-in-chief of their states, they had more power in war than in peace and were not averse to using this power. They initiated most of the necessary legislation at state level – **impressing** slaves and even declaring martial law.

Key term
Impressing
Forcing into
government service.

As a result, they often found themselves vying more with their own state legislatures than with Richmond. Usually they got their legislatures to comply with their actions.

'Died of democracy'?

Key question
Did the Confederacy 'die of democracy'?

In 1862 Davis boasted that, in contrast to the Union, 'there has been no act on our part to impair personal liberty or the freedom of speech, of thought or of the press'. Protecting individual rights might seem an important aim (albeit an unusual one for a state whose cornerstone was slavery). However, historian David Donald has claimed that concern for individual liberties cost the South the war. Unwilling to take tough action against internal dissent, Donald thinks the Confederacy 'died of democracy'.

Donald's argument is not convincing. The notion that Davis could have created a government machine that could have suppressed **civil liberties** – and that if it had done so it might have triumphed – is nonsense. Davis, like most Southerners, was fighting for what he saw as traditional American values; he could not easily abandon those values. Such action would have alienated the public whose support was essential.

Donald's supposition that the Confederacy allowed total individual freedom is also mistaken. In 1862 Congress authorised Davis to declare martial law in areas threatened by the enemy and, given the widespread opposition to conscription, allowed him to suspend the right of habeas corpus in order that **draft evaders** might be apprehended. Nor was there total freedom of speech. Although there was no specific legislation, public pressures that had long stifled discussion about slavery generally succeeded in imposing loyalty to the Confederacy. Opposition newspapers could find their presses destroyed by **vigilantes**.

In short, it is unlikely that the preservation of basic freedoms, in so far as they were preserved, had more than a marginal impact on the Confederacy's demise.

Key terms

Civil liberties
The rights of individuals.

Draft evaders
Those who avoided conscription.

Vigilantes
Self-appointed and unofficial police.

Gold reserves
Most currencies are based on a country's gold holding.

Voluntary associations

Key question
How successfully did the Confederacy finance the war?

Much of what was achieved in the Confederacy was due more to local initiative than to government order.

- Men who led the local community were likely to lead either on the battlefield or on the home front. Planters often organised and outfitted regiments with their own money.
- In 1861 most states relied on local communities to supply the troops with basic necessities.
- Clergymen played an important role, preaching and writing in defence of the Confederacy.
- Women's groups made clothing, flags and other materials for the troops, and tried to feed the poor and help orphans.

Financing the war

The Confederacy was always likely to find it difficult to finance a long war. It had few **gold reserves** and the Union blockade made it difficult to sell cotton and to raise money from tariffs. Taxes on income, profits and property, levied in 1863, were unpopular, difficult to administer and failed to bring in sufficient revenue. State governments, which raised the taxes, were often reluctant to send money to Richmond. Rather than tax their citizens, states often borrowed money or printed it in the form of state notes to pay their dues, thus worsening **inflationary pressures**.

In 1863, in an effort to feed Southern troops, Congress passed the Impressment Act, allowing the seizure of goods to support the armies at the front line, and the Taxation-in-kind Act, authorising government agents to collect 10 per cent of produce from all farmers. Davis accepted the unfairness of these measures but thought it justified by 'absolute necessity'. He may have been right. Taxation-in-kind did help to supply rebel armies during the last two years of the war.

Only eight per cent of the Confederacy's income was derived from taxes. This meant it had to borrow. In February 1861 Congress allowed Treasury Secretary Christopher Memminger to raise $15 million in bonds and stock certificates. Guaranteed with cotton, there were initially many buyers, both within the Confederacy and abroad. But after 1863, when the tide of battle turned against the Confederacy, European financiers – and Southerners – were reluctant to risk loaning money to what seemed like a lost cause.

Given that the Confederacy was only able to raise one-third of its war costs through taxes, bonds and loans, Memminger had little option but to print vast amounts of Treasury paper money. Individual states, towns, banks and railway companies also issued paper notes. The result was serious inflation (see Figure 5.1). By

Key term

Inflationary pressure
An undue increase in the quantity of money in circulation. The result is that the value of money goes down.

Figure 5.1: Inflation in Richmond 1860–3

Extract from the *Richmond Dispatch* newspaper, July 1863

The Results of Extortion and Speculation. – The state of affairs brought about by the speculating and extortion practiced upon the public cannot be better illustrated than by the following grocery bill for one week for a small family, in which the prices before the war and those of the present are compared:

1860		1863	
Bacon, 10 lbs. at 12½c	$1.25	Bacon, 10 lbs. at $1	$10.00
Flour, 30 lbs. at 5c	1.50	Flour, 30 lbs. at 12½c	3.75
Sugar, 5 lbs. at 8c	.40	Sugar, 5 lbs. at $1.15	5.75
Coffee, 4 lbs. at 12½c	.50	Coffee, 4 lbs. at $5	20.00
Tea (green), ½ lb. at $1	.50	Tea (green), ½ lb. at $16	8.00
Lard, 4 lbs. at 12½c	.50	Lard, 4 lbs. at $1	4.00
Butter, 3 lbs. at 25c	.75	Butter, 3 lbs. at $1.75	5.25
Meal, 1 pk. at 25c	.25	Meal, 1 pk. at $1	1.00
Candles, 2 lbs. at 15c	.30	Candles, 2 lbs. at $1.25	2.50
Soap, 5 lbs. at 10c	.50	Soap, 5 lbs. at $1.10	5.50
Pepper and salt (about)	.10	Pepper and salt (about)	2.50
Total	$6.55	Total	$68.25

Key question
To what extent is the *Richmond Dispatch* likely to be a reliable source of evidence for food prices in the Confederacy?

1865 prices in the eastern Confederacy were over 5000 times the 1861 levels. This led to widespread suffering. Memminger's efforts to slow down inflation proved inadequate. Attempts to fix prices, for example, encouraged hoarding, thus exacerbating shortages of vital produce.

Massive inflation and a spiralling debt forced Memminger to resign in 1864. His successor, George Trenholm, tried to reduce the amount of money in circulation but by 1864–5 the Confederacy was on its last legs and the financial situation was desperate.

Given that inflation helped to erode Southern morale, it is not surprising that Memminger has often been singled out for blame. In fairness, it is hard to see what else he could have done. Shortages of basic commodities, resulting from the breakdown of the railway system and from the blockade, meant that inflation was inevitable.

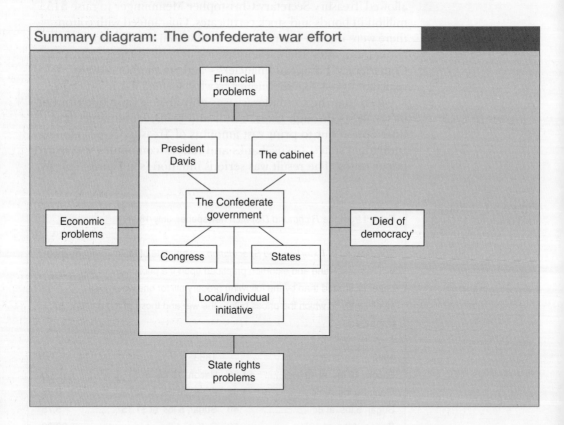

Summary diagram: The Confederate war effort

2 | The Economic and Social Impact of the War on the Confederacy

Efforts to manage the economy

In many respects Davis's government acted forcefully to place the South's economy on a war footing and to expand its industrial base. Before the war most Southerners took the view that economic development was beyond the proper scope of the central government's powers. But after 1861 officials intruded into almost

Key question
How successful was the Confederate economy?

every aspect of economic life as regulations abounded to manage conscription, manufacturing and transportation. The result was that the Richmond government played a much greater role in economic matters than Lincoln's government did in the North.

The **Ordnance Bureau**, ably led by Josiah Gorgas, a Northerner who stayed loyal to his Southern wife rather than to Pennsylvania, played a crucial role. By 1863 there were enough arsenals, factories and gunpowder works in the South to keep its armies supplied with the basic tools of war.

The War Department also assumed increasing control over the South's railway system. Companies were required to share spare parts and rolling stock. Railway schedules were regulated. **Draft exemptions** were issued to ensure that railway companies had skilled workers.

Steps were taken to regulate foreign trade. In 1863 a law required all blockade-runners to carry, as at least one-third of their cargo, cotton out and war supplies in. In 1864 the importation of luxury goods without a special permit was banned. Blockade running was remarkably successful. Hundreds of ships – some state owned, some Confederate government owned, but most owned by private individuals from the Confederacy and Britain (where most were built) – were involved. The most popular routes were from Nassau in the Bahamas to Charleston and from Bermuda to Wilmington. Given the advantage of surprise and speed, blockade-runners stood a 75 per cent chance of success – a success rate which continued until the last months of the war. Overall, the South imported 60 per cent of its small arms, 75 per cent of its **saltpetre** and nearly all its paper for making cartridges.

State governments played an important economic role. Most tried to regulate the distribution of scarce goods, such as salt. Successful efforts were also made to ensure that farmers shifted from cotton to food production. There was a reduction in the cotton crop, from over four million bales in 1861 to only 300,000 bales in 1864.

However, 'Confederate socialism' should not be exaggerated. Short of trained personnel, Richmond was not up to the task of carrying out many of its ambitious schemes. In the final analysis, most of what was achieved was the result of private initiative, not Confederate order. Davis's government mainly confined its activities to the military sphere. Even here, private enterprise was crucial. The Tredegar Ironworks at Richmond, the South's main ordnance producer, remained in private control.

Confederate government economic failure

There were steps that the Confederate government could have taken to limit the economic effects of the war.

- More could have been done to supervise the railway system which, handicapped by shortages of materials and labour, slowly collapsed. Thus raw materials destined for factories and foodstuffs bound for armies or towns were often left at depots for want of transport.

Key terms

Ordnance Bureau The government agency responsible for acquiring war materials.

Draft exemptions Workers in key industries, such as the railways, did not have to serve in the armed forces.

Saltpetre Potassium nitrate – a vital ingredient of gunpowder.

Confederate socialism The Richmond government's attempts to control the Confederate economy.

- Cotton might have been used to better effect, especially early in the war. The embargo on cotton exports, supported if not officially sanctioned by Davis, had two aims: to ensure that planters turned to food production, and to create a cotton scarcity that might lead to foreign recognition. More food was produced but the embargo failed to have much impact on Britain (see pages 138–43). Had cotton been exported in 1861 (when the Union blockade was weak), money from the proceeds could have been used to buy vital war supplies. Instead Southern agents in Europe were handicapped by lack of funds and often outbid by Union competitors.
- The Confederate government could have taken action sooner to control shipments on the blockade-runners. Before 1863, many blockade-runners were more concerned with making money than with helping the Confederacy, often bringing in luxury goods rather than essentials. By the time Davis's government got its blockade-running act together, many Southern ports had been captured.
- Given that many plantations turned to food production, which was less labour intensive than cotton growing, more slaves could have been impressed into government service and used for non-combat labour. Although slaves were impressed by state governments, planter political power ensured that Congress did not authorise Confederate impressment of slaves until 1863–4.

By 1865 the Confederate economy was near collapse. Machinery was wearing out and could not be replaced. Sources of raw materials were lost as Union forces took over large areas of the South. The breakdown of the railway system, much of which was destroyed by Union armies, proved decisive in the Confederacy's final demise.

The social impact
Confederate women
The Confederacy succeeded in mobilising about 900,000 men – over 40 per cent of its white males of fighting age. This had important implications for all aspects of Southern life, particularly the role of women.

> **Key question**
> What impact did the war have on Southern society?

- Wives of yeoman farmers had to work even longer hours to provide enough food for their families. They also had to practise strict domestic economy to conserve scarce resources.
- Wives of planters had to manage plantations and control restless slaves. In towns women took over jobs that had been done by men.

Without female support the Confederacy would soon have collapsed. By mid-1862 it is true that fewer women were willingly sending their men off to war. Some attempted to prevent them being drafted or even encouraged desertion. Nevertheless, until the winter of 1864–5 most women seemed to have remained committed to the rebel cause for which they were willing to accept huge sacrifice.

The impact of the war on slavery

The war affected the institution of slavery (see pages 207–8). Although there was no slave revolt, many slaves fled their plantations whenever it was safe to do so. Historian James Roark claims that, 'Slavery did not explode; it disintegrated ... eroded plantation by plantation, often slave by slave, like slabs of earth slipping into a Southern stream.' By 1864–5 slave owners sometimes had to negotiate with their slaves in order to get them to work.

Demoralisation

Shortages of basic commodities, inflation and impressment had a demoralising effect on all parts of the South. Some areas were also devastated by Union troops. Sherman's marches through Georgia and the Carolinas in 1864–5 (see pages 182–4) left a huge swathe of destruction.

Refugees flooded the South as whites fled contesting armies. In an effort to tackle the problem of refugees, and poverty in general, Confederate and state governments, local and town authorities, plus private charities and wealthy individuals became involved in huge relief efforts. Yet by the winter of 1864–5 the scale of the problem was so great that it overwhelmed the relief activities.

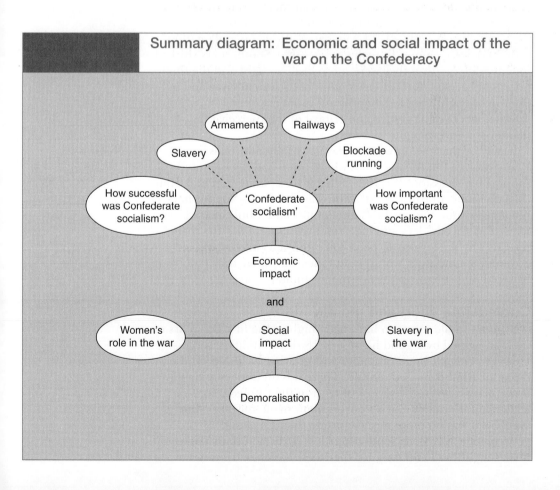

Summary diagram: Economic and social impact of the war on the Confederacy

3 | Confederate Opposition to the War

Key question
Did internal
opposition bring
about Confederate
defeat?

Many non-slaveholders in upland areas of the South opposed
secession from the start. There was so much support for the
Union in East Tennessee and West Virginia that both areas
effectively seceded from the Confederacy. This was a substantial
drain on Southern manpower; worse still was the fact that some
60,000 white men from these areas, and a further 30,000 from
other Southern states, joined the Union army. Nevertheless, most
white Southerners rallied to the Confederate cause in 1861; pro-
Union sympathisers were a small minority.

Opposition grew as the war progressed. The introduction of
conscription in 1862 was a major cause. Lukewarm Southerners
now faced a choice of military service or overt opposition. As the
war ground on, organised resistance to conscription intensified,
especially in the mountain regions of North Carolina and
Alabama. Armed men joined together to help one another in
eluding the enrolment officers and to fight them off when
necessary. Bands of draft evaders and deserters dominated some
areas of the South.

'A rich man's war and a poor man's fight'?

Conscription may have fuelled class conflict. Many ordinary
farmers resented the fact that rich Southerners could avoid
military service by either hiring substitutes or exempting
themselves because they held a managerial role on a plantation
with 20 slaves or more. In reality few wealthy Southerners shirked
military duty; indeed they were more likely to fight and die than
poor Southerners. But the perception of 'rich man's war and a
poor man's fight' rankled. Significant numbers of non-
slaveholders became restive and critical of the (perceived)
planter-led government.

It may be that the opposition was not essentially 'class' based.
It was strongest in upland areas where there had been limited
support for secession. It is thus difficult to separate regional from
class divisions. In truth, most – non-slaveholding – Southerners
remained committed to the Confederate cause until the end.
Hatred of slaveholders and class resentment were not the main
reasons why the loyalty of 'plain folks' to the Confederacy
wavered. Southerners' will to fight faded only after they had been
battered into submission by a stronger military force.

Confederate effort and morale

Southern morale seems to have been high in the first two years of
the war, helped by a good harvest in 1861 and military success.
However, defeats, huge casualties and growing hardship on the
domestic front damaged morale. There was an understandable,
if not necessarily justified, loss of faith in the Confederate
leadership. Certainly Davis's government made mistakes. But
arguably it was no more mistake-prone than Lincoln's
government. Nor were Southerners less dedicated than Yankees.
Most fought hard and long for their new nation, enduring far

more hardship than Northerners. Although ultimately not equal to the challenge, the Confederacy's efforts on the home front were, in most respects, better than might have been expected. The bitter truth was that most of its domestic problems were insurmountable.

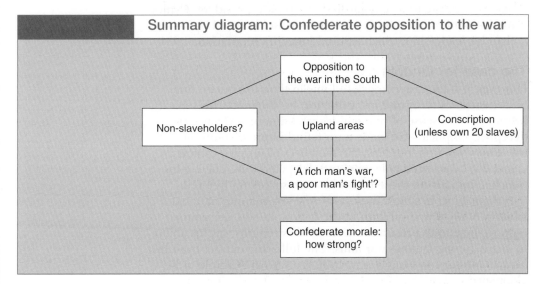

Summary diagram: Confederate opposition to the war

Key question
How effective was Lincoln's administration?

4 | The Union War Effort

Abraham Lincoln

Lincoln is usually regarded as the USA's greatest president. Contemporaries would have been staggered by this opinion. So unpopular was he in the summer of 1864 that it seemed he would not be re-elected president.

The case against Lincoln

- Pre-1861 Lincoln had had little administrative experience. He was to prove himself a poor bureaucrat and his small staff did not provide much assistance. Accordingly, the machinery of government often became clogged.
- He can be accused of meddling and incompetence, especially in military matters. His choice of commanders of the Army of the Potomac down to 1863 – McDowell, McClellan, Pope, McClellan (again), Burnside and Hooker – was uninspired.
- It is possible to depict Lincoln as essentially a devious politician – a man who spent hours each day dealing with political matters rather than devoting time to the war effort.
- Arguably he deserves little credit for foreign policy (handled by Seward), financial measures (handled by Chase) or economic matters (which were left to Congress).
- Democrats accused him of acting tyrannically. In 1862 he suspended the writ of habeas corpus: anyone could be imprisoned by military authority, for impeding conscription, or affording aid or comfort to the enemy. A horde of petty functionaries could decide who was loyal and who was not.

Some were over-zealous; others simply settled old scores. Over 40,000 people were subject to arbitrary arrest.

- It is debatable to what extent Lincoln deserves his reputation as the 'Great Emancipator' (see pages 197–202).
- Arguably Lincoln had an easier task than Davis. The Union was always favourite to win, regardless of who was president. Cynics might claim that it was his assassination (see page 211), rather than his leadership, which assured Lincoln's reputation.

The case for Lincoln

However, it is far easier to praise Lincoln than to criticise him. Most historians recognise his resilience, his diligence, his tenacity, his honesty, his sense of humour, his unassuming style and his deceptive simplicity. He made a profound impression on those who knew him well, not least the members of his own cabinet. Generally, he selected able men and delegated well, playing his hunches, and giving those men who were successful free rein.

Perhaps Lincoln's most important role was shaping national strategy. With a mystical faith in the Union, he was determined to fight to the end to preserve it. One of his strengths was his ability to articulate the Union's war aims. The following extract from his Annual Message to Congress in 1862 is a typical example of his eloquence:

> Fellow-citizens, we cannot escape history. We of this Congress and this administration, will be remembered in spite of ourselves ... The fiery trial through which we pass will light us down in honour or dishonour to the latest generation ... . We shall nobly save or meanly lose the last, best hope of earth.

He was certainly a consummate politician, keeping in touch with public opinion. The time devoted to matters of patronage and party organisation was time well spent. It ensured that there were many loyal men within both his party and the government, a fact that served him well in 1864.

Lincoln's man-management skills ensured that he did not really alienate any member of his cabinet. Historian James McPherson writes: 'The President's unique blend of firmness and deference, the iron fist of decision clothed in the velvet glove of humour and tact, enabled him to dominate his subordinates without the appearance of domination.'

Lincoln's main preoccupations throughout his presidency were military matters and race; he rarely focused hard on other issues. There was no need, for example, to involve himself in economic matters. The Republican-controlled Congress enacted the party's economic programme – a programme that he fully supported. He generally worked well with Congress. His views tended to represent the middle ground but he kept open lines of communication with both the radical and conservative wings of his party. Sensitive to the pulse of public opinion, he was concerned with what might – rather than what should – be achieved. His exquisite sense of political timing and his awareness of what was politically possible helped the Union to win the war and free the slaves.

As commander-in-chief, Lincoln did not shirk responsibility. Taking the view that waging war was essentially an executive function, he believed that he must use his powers to best effect. Where no precedent existed, he was prepared to improvise, stretching the authority of his office beyond any previous practice. In April 1861, for example, he called for troops, proclaimed a blockade of the South and ordered military spending of $2 million without Congressional approval.

Lincoln and civil liberty

Lincoln was totally committed to 'government of the people, by the people, for the people'. Nevertheless, he was willing to suspend civil liberties, including both freedom of speech and freedom of the press. Inevitably he came into conflict with both Congress and the Supreme Court over the legality of some of his actions. This does not seem to have unduly worried him. His main concern was to win the war.

Arguably Lincoln's vigorous policies in 1861 helped to keep the border states in the Union. Military rather than political goals were foremost in his mind when he allowed the restriction of civil liberties. Most of those imprisoned without trial came from states such as Missouri, which had many Southern sympathisers. Given the grim reality of guerrilla war, martial law was essential.

Elsewhere moderation was usually the norm. Many of those arrested – Confederate defectors, blockade runners, draft dodgers – would have been arrested whether the writ of habeas corpus had been suspended or not. Moreover, those who were arbitrarily arrested usually found themselves being arbitrarily released. Relatively few were brought to trial. Arrests rarely involved Democrat politicians or newspaper editors. Overall, Lincoln remained faithful to the spirit, if not always the letter, of the Constitution. Later generations have generally approved – even applauded – the way in which he tackled difficult issues of civil liberties.

Lincoln and military matters

Despite some initial insecurity about military matters, Lincoln was very much involved in the conduct of the war, cajoling, praising and urging his generals forward. Some historians think that he showed considerable military talent, with an ability to concentrate on the wider issues rather than getting bogged down in matters of detail. As early as January 1862 he said: 'I state my general idea of this war to be that we have the greater numbers and the enemy has the greater facility of concentrating forces upon points of collision; that we must fail, unless we can find some way of making our advantage an overmatch for his; and that this can only be done by menacing him with superior forces at different points, at the same time.' To Lincoln's chagrin, Union generals proved unable to carry out such a strategy until 1864–5.

Some of Lincoln's appointments, if not wise militarily, made sense politically. Appointing generals who represented important ethnic, regional and political constituencies ensured that the North remained united. Ultimately his military appointments gave the Union the winning team of Grant and Sherman.

Conclusion

For four years Lincoln stuck at his job. He worked hard – from 7 a.m. to 11 p.m. most days – granting favours, distributing jobs, corresponding with friends and enemies, giving or listening to advice, accepting or rejecting proposals. Although often severely depressed, he kept going even when the war was going badly. Nothing kept him from his work, not even his own personal tragedies. (His youngest son died in 1862 and his wife was mentally unstable thereafter.) He learned from his mistakes and revealed real qualities of leadership.

Lincoln's cabinet

Lincoln's cabinet was far more stable than that of Davis, with most of the Secretaries remaining at their posts for most of the war. Lincoln bothered little with the cabinet as such. He used the rare meetings as a sounding board to discuss the timing or language

Key question
How effective was Lincoln's cabinet?

The last photograph of Lincoln (April 1865). The war had clearly taken its toll on him.

An illustration after Francis Carpenter's famous painting of Lincoln and his cabinet. Treasury Secretary Chase stands to the left of Lincoln (who is reading the Emancipation Proclamation). Secretary of State Seward sits with legs crossed.

of statements he was about to issue or to get approval for actions he was about to take. The secretaries usually saw Lincoln individually rather than en masse. Within their departments, cabinet members performed well, working hard themselves and keeping their subordinates hard at work.

Secretary of State Seward was regarded as Lincoln's right-hand man. Salmon Chase, Secretary of the Treasury, was the main radical spokesman in the cabinet. Lincoln's first Secretary of War, Simon Cameron, had a reputation for corruption before the war and this reputation quickly grew. In 1862 he was replaced by Edwin Stanton, an ex-Democrat, who proved himself efficient and incorruptible. Once a severe critic of Lincoln, Stanton became one of his closest advisors. Gideon Welles, Secretary of the Navy, served the Union well throughout the war. Postmaster Montgomery Blair came from one of the best-known political families in the Union. On the conservative wing of the party, his father continued to own slaves until 1865. Caleb Smith, Secretary of the Interior, and Bates, the Attorney General, played minor roles.

Congress

Key question
How well did Congress co-operate with Lincoln?

Depleted by the loss of its Southern members, Congress was controlled by the Republicans throughout the war. In 1861 the House of Representatives had 105 Republicans, 43 Democrats and 28 'Unionists'. Of the 48 Senators, 31 were Republican. The

Republicans retained control after the 1862 mid-term elections. Given the Republican dominance, Congress generally co-operated with Lincoln. While there was some conflict over the boundaries of executive and legislative power, Congress loyally provided the means for Lincoln to conduct the war.

Radical Republicans, the most energetic wing of the party, often blamed Lincoln for failing to prosecute the war more vigorously or to move against slavery more rapidly. However, the radicals were not a disciplined group. Nor did they always oppose Lincoln. When he wanted their support, he usually got it.

State government

State governments provided invaluable assistance to Lincoln, especially in raising troops. Most states were Republican controlled. Those that did fall under Democrat control did little to hinder the Union war effort.

Voluntary associations

Neither the federal nor state governments had the apparatus or traditions to manage all aspects of the war. Voluntary organisations helped to fill the gaps. The United States Sanitary Commission, for example, did much to help the Army Medical Bureau. Sanitary Commissioners prowled Union camps and hospitals, insisting on better food and conditions. Thousands of women were the mainstay of the Commission, knitting, wrapping bandages and raising funds.

Financing the war

In 1861 the Union (unlike the Confederacy) had an established Treasury, gold reserves and an assured source of revenue from tariffs. Nevertheless, Northern financial structures were not ready for war, and over the winter of 1861–2 the whole Northern banking system seemed near to collapse. Secretary Chase kept the Treasury afloat by raising loans and issuing bonds, in which ordinary citizens, as well as bankers, were encouraged to invest. One million Northerners ended up owning shares in the national debt.

Two-thirds of the Union's revenue was raised by loans and bonds. One-fifth was raised by taxes. An income tax, the first in US history, was enacted in 1861 and imposed a three per cent tax on annual incomes over $800. Far more important (it brought in 10 times as much as the income tax) was the Internal Revenue Act (1862). This basically taxed everything.

Congress also approved an inflationary monetary policy. In 1862 the Legal Tender Act authorised the issuing of $150 million in paper currency, not redeemable in gold or silver. Ultimately 'greenback' notes to the value of $431 million were issued. The Legal Tender Act provided the Treasury with resources to pay its bills and restored investors' confidence sufficiently to make possible the sale of $500 million of new bonds.

Linked to these measures were attempts to reform the banking system. Chase's ideas finally bore fruit in the 1863 and 1864

> **Key question**
> How successfully did the Union finance the war?

> **Legal Tender Act:** 1862
>
> Key date

National Banking Acts. While the new national banks pumped paper money into the economy, a tax of 10 per cent on state bank notes ensured that the Union was not awash with paper money. Inflation, over the course of the war, was only 80 per cent.

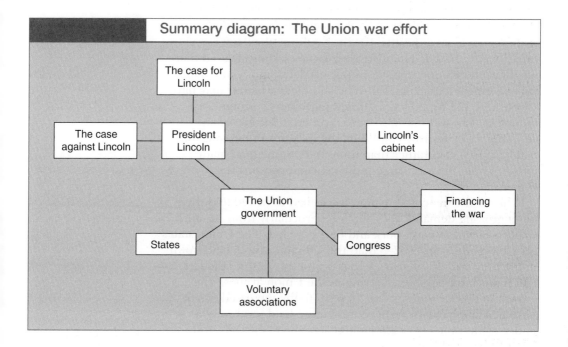

Summary diagram: The Union war effort

5 | The Economic and Social Impact of the War on the Union

Economic legislation

Key question
What impact did the war have on the Union's economy?

Key date

Homestead Act: 1862

After 1861 the Republicans were able to pass economic legislation, previously held up by Democratic opposition. The 1862 Homestead Act, for example, offered 160-acre farms out west, free of charge, to settlers who worked on them for five years. Higher tariffs not only provided the government with extra revenue but also protected US industry from foreign competition. Generous railway subsidies were meted out. The most important railway development was the decision to build a trans-continental line from Omaha to San Francisco.

By twentieth century standards there was little assertion of federal power in the management of the wartime economy. There was no rationing, no attempt to control prices, wages and profits, and no central control of the railways. Although the US government was now a huge customer, businessmen made their own decisions and controlled their own production.

Union economic success

The Northern economy, with its abundant raw materials, ready capital and technological expertise, was able to ensure that Union armies were well equipped and that civilians did not go short of basic commodities. It was not certain in 1861 that Northern industry would meet the challenge. The loss of Southern markets threatened disaster. However, the overall effect of the war, especially the need to feed, equip and arm the Union forces, is often seen as stimulating economic growth.

Production gains were especially notable in war-related industries such as canned food, shipbuilding and munitions. Railways made great profits. For the first time their full carrying capacity was utilised. The increased money supply ensured that manufacturers found it easier to pay off debts and secure loans for investment and expansion. The shortage of labour may have encouraged the introduction of new machinery in some industries. The war may also have resulted in businessmen adopting wider horizons and thinking in terms of millions (of bullets, boots, etc.) rather than thousands. Some men made fortunes from the war. Huge profits encouraged further expansion.

Farmers also benefited. Union forces had to be fed and there was a growing demand from abroad, particularly from Britain. Exports of wheat, corn, pork and beef doubled. The Union states grew more wheat in 1862–3 than the USA as a whole had grown in the previous record year of 1859 – and this despite the fact that many farm boys were serving in the Union armies. The growth in production was due, in part, to the increased use of farm machinery, but mainly because more land was brought under cultivation – over 2.5 million acres between 1862 and 1864.

Union economic problems
The war's effects were not all positive.

- Some industries, not least the New England cotton mills, suffered hard times.
- The fact that so much of the labour force was drawn into the army may have slowed down industrial and agricultural growth.
- The war probably reduced immigration by some 1.3 million people – nearly twice the number lost by both sides in the war.
- According to some estimates, the combined effect of loss in immigration and military deaths reduced the population by 5.6 per cent from what it would have been without the war.
- Economic growth in the 1860s was slower (some claim) than in any other decade in the nineteenth century.
- If there was a shift to **mass production**, this was arguably a trend that was well under way before the war and one that was not particularly affected by it.

Mass production Key term
Making large quantities of goods by a standardised process.

Conclusion
The North's economy grew, in spite, if not because, of the war. In March 1865 a New York paper reported: 'There never was a time in the history of New York when business prosperity was more general, when the demand for goods was greater … than

within the last two or three years.' According to historian Peter Parish, 'The abiding impression [of the Northern economy] is one of energy and enterprise, resilience and resource ... The war was not the soil in which industrial growth took root, nor a blight which stunted it, but a very effective fertiliser.'

The social impact

Key question
What impact did the war have on Northern society?

In many ways life for most Northerners during the war went on as usual. However, the fact that regiments were often made up of men from a single town or county could mean sudden calamity for a neighbourhood if that regiment suffered heavy casualties. The fact that so many men of military age left their homes to fight meant there were more job opportunities for women, who worked as teachers, in industry and in government service. However, the war did not bring women much closer to political or economic equality. They were not given the vote and after 1865 returned to their old roles.

There is some evidence that during the war the rich became richer while the poor became poorer. Some working men saw their real earnings drop as prices rose faster than wages. The result was labour unrest and some violent, albeit small-scale, strikes. However, some workers enjoyed rising wages resulting from a shortage of labour. Many working-class families also benefited from bounties and wages paid to soldiers who sent millions of dollars home. Overall, therefore, it is unlikely that there was a major rise in class tension.

In some areas, the war led to an increase in racial tensions. Some Northerners resented fighting a war to free the slaves. Anti-black feeling was also fanned by job competition and the employment of black **strike breakers**. In 1863 there were race riots in a number of northern cities – Chicago, Buffalo and Boston. The most serious was in New York (see below).

Key term

Strike breakers
Workers employed during a strike to do the work of those on strike.

The war initially led to a reduction in immigrant numbers – 92,000 in 1861–2 compared with 154,000 in 1860. But by 1863 there were over 176,000 immigrants and by 1865 nearly 250,000 – proof of the North's booming economy and also of the government's success in publicising opportunities and encouraging immigrants. Some immigrants, attracted by the high bounties, volunteered for the Union army. Others, by filling key jobs, helped the economy. The war may have helped the process of assimilation and possibly tamed anti-immigrant feeling. However, the assimilation process should not be exaggerated. Ethnic rivalry remained strong after 1865.

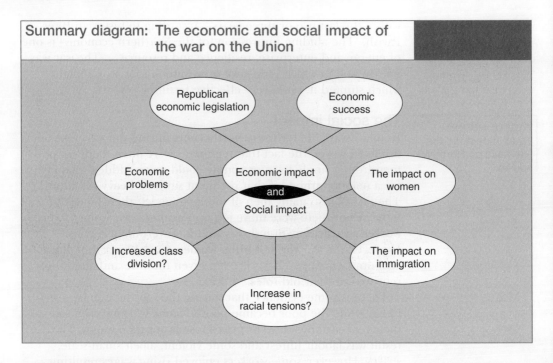

Summary diagram: The economic and social impact of the war on the Union

6 | Union Opposition to the War

In 1861 leading Northern Democrats like Senator Douglas called on all Northerners to rally round Lincoln. Lincoln, aware of the need to maintain unity, promoted Democrats to his cabinet and to high military command. Some **War Democrats** threw in their lot totally with Lincoln. But as the war went on, Democratic opposition increased. Democrats disliked:

- the way the war was being handled
- Republican economic policies
- Lincoln's arbitrary measures
- efforts to end slavery.

Reflecting and exploiting Northern racist views for all they were worth and capitalising on war weariness, the Democrats had some success in the 1862 mid-term elections.

The Copperheads

Although many Democrats saw the conflict as a Republican war, most still wanted to restore the Union: pro-Confederate Northerners were a small minority. This was not the way that many Republicans saw it. In the west, Republicans labelled their Democratic opponents 'Copperheads' (after a poisonous snake) and claimed that they belonged to subversive, pro-Southern secret societies which planned to set up a Northwest Confederacy that would make peace with the South. Republican leaders realised that charges of treason could be used to discredit the Democrat party as a whole and could serve as an excuse to organise Union Leagues – Republican-led societies pledged to defend the Union.

Key question
How serious was internal opposition to the Union war effort?

War Democrats
Those Democrats who were determined to see the war fought to a successful conclusion.

Key term

An 1863 cartoon from *Harper's Weekly*. It shows (Democratic) copperhead snakes threatening to attack an armed female (who represents the Union).

Clement Vallandigham

Democrat dissent reached its height in early 1863 when Union military failures fostered a sense of defeatism. Some Democrats thought that the time had come to make peace. Clement Vallandigham, campaigning to become governor of Ohio, denounced the war and called upon soldiers to desert. He was seeking to be made a martyr and a martyrdom of sorts duly followed. On the orders of General Burnside (whose political finesse was no more subtle that his military judgement), Vallandigham was arrested in the middle of the night. Tried by a military tribunal, he was found guilty of treason and sentenced to imprisonment for the rest of the war. This led to a chorus of protest from outraged Democrats. Even some Republicans were appalled that a civilian had been tried and sentenced by a military court merely for making a speech.

Lincoln, while not liking what Burnside had done, saw no alternative but to support him. By discouraging enlistment and encouraging desertion, Vallandigham had broken the law. 'Must I shoot a simple-minded soldier-boy who deserts, while I must not touch a hair of a wiley agitator who induces him to desert?', mused Lincoln. 'I think that in such a case, to silence the agitator, and save the boy is not only constitutional, but withal a great mercy.'

However, Lincoln was anxious to avoid making Vallandigham a martyr. Accordingly, he decided to banish him to the Confederacy for the duration of the war. Soon tiring of the South, Vallandigham moved to Canada where he continued to conduct his campaign for governor of Ohio. But the upturn in Union military fortunes after July 1863 undermined his peace platform. Along with other pro-peace Democrats, he lost his election contest in 1863.

The New York draft riots

The most serious internal violence came in New York in July 1863. The New York riots followed the enforcement of the 1863 Conscription Act. New York's Democrat Governor, Horatio Seymour, whipped up opposition to the draft. When the names of the first draftees were drawn, a mob of mostly Irish workers attacked the recruiting station. The mob then went on the rampage, venting its fury on blacks who were blamed for the war. For several days New York was in chaos. Economic, ethnic, racial and religious factors all played a part in causing the riots. Lincoln moved quickly, sending in 20,000 troops to restore order. At least 120 people – mainly rioters – died in the process.

New York draft riots: 1863

Key date

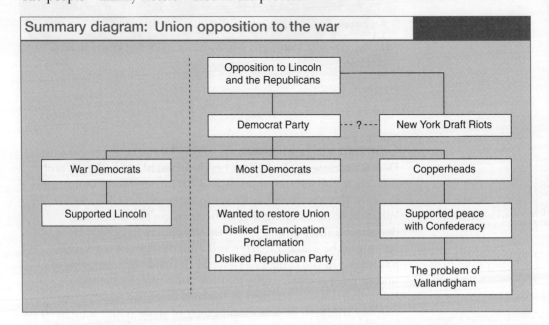

Summary diagram: Union opposition to the war

7 | Britain and the Civil War

Realising from the outset that the Confederacy's best hope of success was if Britain joined the war on its side, Jefferson Davis tried to secure British support. In May 1861 Confederate commissioners were sent to London and gained an informal interview with British Foreign Secretary Lord Russell. The Russian minister in Washington was convinced that, 'England will take advantage of the first opportunity to recognise the seceded states.' In the event, neither Britain nor any other foreign power recognised the Confederacy, never mind intervened on its behalf.

Key question
Why did Britain not intervene in the war?

Britain's attitude to the war

Prime Minister Lord Palmerston and Foreign Secretary Russell knew that there were good reasons for supporting the Confederacy:

Key question
Why was British opinion divided?

- Britain's immediate and long-term self-interest might well be served by the break-up of the USA.

- An independent Confederacy would have strong economic links with Britain, providing raw cotton in return for manufactured goods.
- Cotton was an issue of immediate concern. In order to prevent economic hardship at home, it might be necessary for Britain to break the Union blockade to acquire Southern cotton.
- Many Britons sympathised with the Confederacy and thought the North had no right to force people back into an unpopular Union.
- Given that four slave states remained in the Union, slavery did not seem to be a crucial issue. Indeed, Lincoln's administration insisted for most of 1861–2 that the war was not a crusade to abolish slavery. This made it easier for influential newspapers, such as *The Times*, to support the Confederacy.

However, there were many good reasons for not getting involved in the war:

- Conflict with the Union might result in the loss of Canada.
- War would certainly result in the loss of valuable markets and investments in the North.
- British opinion was far from united. Aware that slavery lay at the heart of the conflict, many Britons supported the Union.
- The **Crimean War** (1854–6) had indicated the difficulties of fighting a war thousands of miles from home.

Not surprisingly, Palmerston believed that Britain's best policy was neutrality.

British neutrality

One immediate problem was whether Britain should recognise the Confederacy as a sovereign state. Lincoln's administration made it clear that the conflict was a rebellion. Thus, recognition of the Confederacy was tantamount to a declaration of war against the USA. However, in legal terms the situation was confused because Lincoln had proclaimed a blockade against the Confederacy. A blockade was an instrument of war. If a state of war existed, Britain could make a reasonable case for recognising the Confederacy.

In May 1861 the British government adopted a compromise position. While declaring its neutrality and not recognising the Confederacy as a sovereign state, Britain recognised its **belligerent status**. Under international law belligerents had the right to contract loans and purchase arms in neutral nations. However, Britain's neutrality proclamation prevented the Confederacy fitting out its warships in British ports. It also recognised the Union blockade. Having declared itself neutral, Britain made every effort to remain so.

Confederate actions

In 1861 Southerners believed that Britain would be forced to recognise the Confederacy and break the blockade because of its need for cotton. In order to tighten the screw, an unofficial cotton

Key terms

Crimean War
In 1854 Britain and France went to war against Russia to protect Turkey. Most of the war was fought in the area of Russia known as the Crimea.

Belligerent status
Recognised legally as waging war.

Key question
How did the Confederacy try to win British support?

embargo was introduced. While the Confederate Congress did not establish a formal embargo, local 'committees of public safety' halted the export of cotton. The *Charleston Mercury* summed up the argument in June 1861: 'the cards are in our hands and we intend to play them out to the bankruptcy of every cotton factory in Great Britain and France or the acknowledgement of our independence'.

Unfortunately for the Confederacy, the embargo ploy failed. European warehouses were full of cotton purchased in 1859–60, and so there was no immediate shortage. The cotton embargo thus backfired. Southerners failed to sell their most valuable commodity at a time when the blockade was at its least effective. Moreover, the embargo angered Europeans: 'To intervene on behalf of the South because they have kept cotton from us would be ignominious beyond measure', declared Russell.

Nevertheless, the British government did consider breaking the Union blockade. 'We cannot allow some millions of our people to perish to please the Northern states', said Palmerston. British and French diplomats discussed the possibility of joint action to lift the blockade. In the event, the talks were not followed by action.

The Confederacy did its best. Agents were sent across the Atlantic to establish contacts with sympathetic British MPs. In an attempt to influence British opinion, the Confederacy also set up a newspaper, the *Index*, devoted to presenting the rebel case. Confederate purchasing agents had spectacular successes purchasing British armaments. It is difficult to see what more the Confederacy could have done.

Union diplomacy

Northern politicians and diplomats, from Lincoln downwards, deserve some praise for their dealings with Britain:

- Charles Francis Adams, the US minister in London, employed every means at his disposal to ensure the strict maintenance of British neutrality.
- Secretary of State Seward displayed skilful statesmanship.
- Lincoln usually left policy to Seward. Only when there was a serious crisis (for example, the *Trent* affair) did he interfere.

The *Trent* affair

In November 1861 James Mason and John Slidell, **Confederate commissioners** to Britain and France, respectively, left Cuba for Europe in the *Trent*, a British steamer. Soon after leaving Havana, the *Trent* was stopped by Captain Wilkes, commanding the USS *San Jacinto*. Wilkes forcibly removed Mason and Slidell from the British ship.

This action created a wave of anger in Britain: 'You may stand for this but damned if I will', Palmerston told his cabinet. Russell demanded that Mason and Slidell should be released and the US must make a public apology. To back up the threat, the British fleet prepared for action and soldiers were sent to Canada. Britain also stopped the export of essential war materials to the Union.

Trent affair: November 1861 | Key date

Confederate commissioners
Men representing the Confederate government. | Key term

In this cartoon, published in New York at the height of the *Trent* affair, US Secretary of State Seward (*beside the American eagle*) returns the Confederate commissioners Slidell and Mason (*in boat*) to Europe. His act appeases Lord Russell (*foot on the British lion*) and frustrates Jefferson Davis (*far right*), who had hoped that Britain would enter the war as a Confederate ally.

The *Trent* affair posed a serious dilemma for Lincoln. While there was a danger of war if his government did not satisfy Britain, Union opinion would be outraged if he cravenly surrendered. Wilkes had become something of a national hero, so much so that the House of Representatives had passed a resolution praising his action. A compromise was eventually found. The US government, while not apologising for Wilkes's action, admitted he had committed an illegal act and freed Mason and Slidell.

British mediation?

The closest the Confederacy came to getting British recognition was in the autumn of 1862 after its triumph at Second Manassas (see page 167). French Emperor Napoleon III's proposal that Britain and France should attempt to mediate in the conflict was seriously considered by Palmerston and Russell. Given that mediation meant recognition of the Confederacy, Britain and France might easily have found themselves at war with the Union. However, the failure of Lee's Maryland invasion (see pages 167–8) convinced Palmerston that it would be unwise to intervene.

Even after Lincoln's Emancipation Proclamation, some members of Palmerston's cabinet still wanted to take action. In October 1862 Chancellor of the Exchequer William Gladstone claimed that 'Jefferson Davis and other leaders have made an army, and are making, it appears, a navy, and they have made what is more than either, they have made a nation.' Supported by Gladstone, Russell prepared a memorandum arguing for mediation. Palmerston rejected the idea.

The cotton famine

The full impact of the cotton shortage hit Britain over the winter of 1862–3 and caused high unemployment in Lancashire. However, given that the British economy was generally prospering, there was limited pressure on the government to take action. During 1863 the situation in Lancashire improved as a result of increased imports of cotton from India, China and Egypt.

Commerce raiders

Although denied British recognition, the Confederacy received valuable aid from Britain. Confederate agents worked effectively to secure British military supplies. In particular, British shipbuilders built vessels for a variety of Confederate purposes. The majority were employed in running cargoes through the blockade. The Confederacy also purchased **commerce raiders**. In theory, British law forbad the construction of warships for a belligerent power. However, Confederate agents got round this by purchasing unarmed ships and then adding the guns elsewhere.

Confederate commerce raiders caused considerable damage to Union merchant shipping. The *Alabama*, for example, took 64 Union ships before finally being sunk off Brest. Altogether the North lost some 200 ships. While scarcely crippling trade, the raiders were a nuisance, driving Union shipping insurance rates to astonishing heights. Consequently, more and more Atlantic trade was transferred to neutral ships, which were not attacked by Confederate raiders. The main beneficiary was Britain.

The Laird rams

The last serious crisis between the Union and Britain came during the summer of 1863. Lincoln's government was aware that the Laird Brothers shipbuilders were building two ironclad ships for the Confederacy. These boats – the **Laird rams** – would be the strongest ships afloat. Charles Adams threatened war against Britain if the boats were sold to the Confederacy. The British government eventually bought the 'rams' itself and the crisis quickly fizzled out.

Conclusion

One of Palmerston's favourite sayings was: 'They who in quarrels interpose, will often get a bloody nose.' Given his cautious policy, it was always likely that Britain would remain neutral. While Seward, Lincoln and Adams deserve some credit, their diplomatic skill should not be over-rated. Confederate diplomacy should not be castigated. Only if the Confederacy looked like winning would Britain recognise the Confederacy. Yet only if Britain recognised the Confederacy and went to war on its side, was it likely that the Confederacy would win.

Key terms

Commerce raiders
Confederate warships that attacked Union merchant ships.

Laird rams
The distinguishing feature of these vessels was an iron ram that projected from the bow, enabling them to sink an enemy by smashing its hull.

Key date

Laird rams crisis: 1863

Summary diagram: Britain and the Civil War

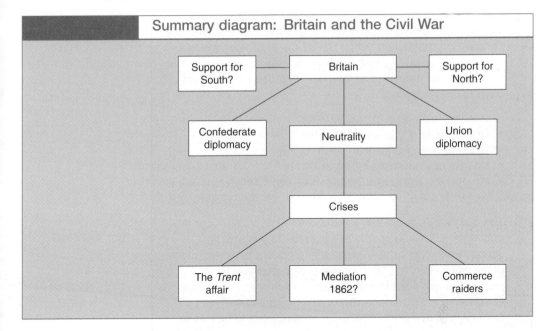

Study Guide: AS Questions

In the style of OCR

(a) 'If the Union and Confederacy had exchanged presidents with one another, the Confederacy might have won its independence.' How far do you agree with this view? (30 marks)

(b) Assess the strength of the internal opposition to both Lincoln and Davis in the Civil War. (70 marks)

Exam tips
The cross-references are intended to take you straight to the material that will help you to answer the questions.

(a) It is deceptively easy to write an all-I-know-about answer, starting with Lincoln and finishing with Davis. Such answers usually score low marks. You are asked to make a relative assessment of reasons. The key is to reach a balanced judgement, revealed in the introduction and then supported by the rest of your answer. The best answers will consider the criteria by which Lincoln and Davis are to be judged. They will then go on to examine the extent to which the two men met these criteria. Compile a list of half a dozen or so criteria by which you might wish to judge Lincoln and Davis's performance. (They might include military leadership, political skill, handling of the economy, diplomacy and maintaining morale.) This list should provide a good framework for an essay plan. But remember you are also specifically asked to decide whether the war would have had a different outcome if Lincoln had led the Confederacy and Davis the Union. You might well reach the conclusion that Lincoln was the better leader: he did ultimately lead the winning side. But the best answers will consider Union advantages and Southern weaknesses. Was Lincoln's job easier than that of Davis? Could (almost) anyone have led the Union to victory? Did Davis's leadership ensure that the Confederacy survived as long as it did? The main content areas to look at are:

- Lincoln's leadership (pages 127–30)
- Davis's leadership (pages 116–18)
- Union advantages (pages 146–7)
- Confederate advantages (pages 147–9)
- Why did the war end in Union victory and Confederate defeat (pages 185–92)?

(b) This question does not ask you to write all you know about the opposition to Lincoln and Davis but rather to evaluate the strength of the opposition. Marks are given for the development of the arguments, so plan your response before you try to answer. You will need to consider opposition within the respective Congresses and also opposition in the Union and the Confederacy as a whole. The main content areas to look at are:

- opposition to the war in the Union (pages 136–8)
- opposition to the war in the Confederacy (pages 126–7).

Who faced stronger internal opposition – Lincoln or Davis – and why?

6 The War 1861–5

POINTS TO CONSIDER

The situation in the USA in the spring of 1861 was similar to that in Europe in 1914. Thousands of men, egged on by family, friends and neighbours, rushed to volunteer, their main fear being that the war would be over before they could get a shot at the enemy. The war was to be different from their expectations. It was to drag on for four terrible years. Why did this happen? Why did the Union eventually win? This chapter will address these questions by examining the following themes:

- Union and Confederate strengths
- The nature of the war
- The soldiers' experience
- The main military events in 1861–2
- The main military events in 1863
- Union victory 1864–5

Key dates

1861	July	First Manassas
1862	April	Battle of Shiloh
	June–July	Seven Day battles
	August	Second Manassas
	September	Battle of Antietam
	December	Battle of Fredericksburg
1863	May	Battle of Chancellorsville
	July	Battle of Gettysburg
	July	Capture of Vicksburg
	September	Battle of Chickamauga
1864	March	Grant became General-in-Chief
	May–June	Wilderness–Petersburg campaign
	September	Fall of Atlanta
	November	Lincoln re-elected president
1865	April	Fall of Petersburg and Richmond
	April	Lee surrendered at Appomattox

1 | Union and Confederate Strengths

Union advantages

Key question
What were the main
Union strengths?

Napoleon Bonaparte thought most wars were won by the side with the 'big battalions' – that is, the side with most men and materials. The Union had the 'big battalions':

- There were 22 million people in the North compared with only nine million in the South (of whom only 5.5 million were whites).
- Four slave states, containing some two million people, remained loyal to the Union. These states would have added 80 per cent to the Confederacy's industrial capacity.
- The Union had a stronger pool of military experience. Most men in the US regular army remained loyal to the Union. Between 1820 and 1860, two-thirds of all the graduates at West Point, the USA's chief military academy, had been Northerners.
- The Union enjoyed a huge naval supremacy (see pages 153–5).
- In 1860 the North had six times as many factories as the South, 10 times its industrial productive capacity, and twice as many miles of railway track (see Figure 6.1 on page 147).
- The North had more horses, cows and sheep and produced over 80 per cent of the country's wheat and oats.
- Not all the people within the Confederacy were committed to its cause. Pockets of Unionism existed, especially in the Appalachian Mountains. The Confederacy suffered a major setback when West Virginia seceded from Virginia. Eastern Tennessee was also strongly Unionist.

Union slave states
Delaware and Maryland

Key question
Why did four slave
states remain loyal to
the Union?

There was never any likelihood that Delaware would secede. Less than two per cent of its population were slaves and its economic ties were with the North.

Maryland was another matter. In April 1861 Union soldiers passing through Baltimore on their way to Washington were attacked by pro-Confederate townspeople. Four soldiers and 12 civilians were killed – the first fatalities of the war. Helped by the pro-Union Maryland governor, Lincoln took strong action. Stretching the constitution to its limits (and probably beyond), he sent in troops, suspended the **writ of habeas corpus** and allowed the arrest of suspected trouble-makers. Lincoln's tough measures helped to save Maryland for the Union. In June elections in Maryland were won by Unionist candidates and the state legislature voted against secession.

Writ of habeas
corpus
The right to know
why one has been
arrested.

Key term

Kentucky

Kentucky was deeply divided. Its governor leaned to the South but its legislature was opposed to secession. Attempting to remain neutral, Kentucky rejected calls for recruits from both sides and warned Lincoln and Davis to keep out of the state. Lincoln, aware that a false move on his part could drive Kentucky into the Confederacy, relied on patience, tact and backstage manoeuvring rather than direct action. While paying (apparent) respect for the integrity of Kentucky, his government supplied arms to Unionists within the state. Kentucky's neutrality was short-lived. In September 1861 Confederate forces occupied Columbus. Union forces were quickly ordered into Kentucky and soon controlled most of the state.

Missouri

In the spring of 1861 it seemed likely that Missouri would join the Confederacy. In June its pro-Confederate governor called for 50,000 volunteers to defend the state against Union invasion. However, there was also considerable Unionist support, especially from the state's German population. Congressman Francis Blair and Captain Nathaniel Lyon helped to ensure that the state did not fall into Confederate hands. Although Lyon was defeated and killed at the battle of Wilson's Creek in August, Unionists kept control of most of Missouri.

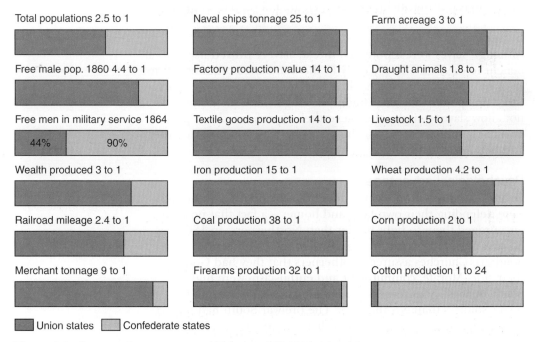

Total populations 2.5 to 1

Free male pop. 1860 4.4 to 1

Free men in military service 1864
44%   90%

Wealth produced 3 to 1

Railroad mileage 2.4 to 1

Merchant tonnage 9 to 1

Naval ships tonnage 25 to 1

Factory production value 14 to 1

Textile goods production 14 to 1

Iron production 15 to 1

Coal production 38 to 1

Firearms production 32 to 1

Farm acreage 3 to 1

Draught animals 1.8 to 1

Livestock 1.5 to 1

Wheat production 4.2 to 1

Corn production 2 to 1

Cotton production 1 to 24

Union states   Confederate states

Figure 6.1: Comparative resources of Union and Confederate states

Key question
What were the main Confederate strengths?

Confederate advantages

Although the odds were stacked heavily against the South, most Southerners, and many European observers, were confident that the Confederacy would triumph. Even after the war, many Southerners were convinced that the Confederacy should have won. 'No people ever warred for independence', said General Beauregard, 'with more relative advantages than the Confederacy.'

The size of the Confederacy

The sheer size of the Confederacy – 750,000 square miles – was its greatest asset. It would be difficult to blockade and conquer. Even if Union armies succeeded in occupying Confederate territory, they would have difficulty holding down a resentful population and maintaining their **supply lines**.

The advantage of defending

Confederate forces did not have to invade the North, hold down occupied territory or capture Washington and New York to win. All they had to do was defend. Defence is usually an easier option in war than attack. The Union had little option but to attack. Southerners hoped that Northern opinion might come to question high losses. If Union will collapsed, the Confederacy would win by default.

Geographical advantages

The crucial theatre of the war was the land between Washington and Richmond in North Virginia. Here a series of west to east running rivers were to provide a useful barrier to Union armies intent on capturing Richmond (see Figure 6.3 on page 164).

Slavery

Although slaves were a potential threat, slavery proved itself a real benefit to the Confederacy early in the war. Slaves could be left to work on the home front, enabling the South to raise more of its white manpower than the Union. Although the Confederacy did not allow slaves to fight, they nevertheless performed many invaluable military tasks – such as transporting goods to the front and building fortifications.

Psychological advantages

Given that most of the war was fought in the South, Southerners were defending their own land and homes – a fact that perhaps encouraged them to fight harder than Northerners. In 1861 few Southerners questioned the rightness of the Confederate cause. Southern Churches assured Southerners that they had God on their side. Morale, commitment and enthusiasm were high in the South in 1861. Southerners were confident that they were far better soldiers than Northerners. The pre-war South had placed more emphasis on martial virtues than the North. In 1860 most of the military colleges in the USA were in slave states. Southerners had usually dominated the senior posts in the US army. The élite of the nation's generals had all been Southerners. Most military experts assumed that farmers, who knew how to ride and shoot, were better soldiers than industrial workers.

Interior lines of communication

By using its road and rail systems, the Confederacy could move its forces quickly from one area to another. This meant that it should be able to concentrate its forces against dispersed Union forces.

Maryland, Missouri and Kentucky

Although Maryland, Missouri and Kentucky did not secede, thousands of pro-Confederates in the three states fought for the South.

'King Cotton'

Cotton was the Confederacy's great economic weapon. Cotton sales should enable it to buy military supplies from Europe. There was also the hope that Britain might break the Union naval blockade (see pages 138–42) to ensure that cotton supplies got through to its textile mills. This would lead to war between Britain and the Union.

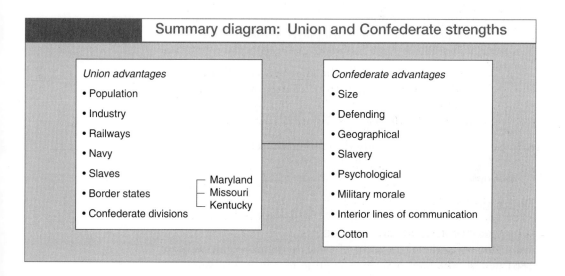

Summary diagram: Union and Confederate strengths

Union advantages
• Population
• Industry
• Railways
• Navy
• Slaves
• Border states ⎡ Maryland
⎢ Missouri
⎣ Kentucky
• Confederate divisions

Confederate advantages
• Size
• Defending
• Geographical
• Slavery
• Psychological
• Military morale
• Interior lines of communication
• Cotton

Key question
How prepared for war were both combatants in 1861?

2 | The Nature of the War

Neither side was prepared for war in 1861. The Union had only a 16,000-strong regular army, most of which was scattered out West. The War Department totalled only 90 men. Lincoln had no military experience. Seventy-four-year-old General Winfield Scott, the leading Union general, suffered from dropsy and vertigo. He had no general staff, no carefully prepared strategic plans and no programme for **mobilisation**. In April 1861 Lincoln appealed for 75,000 volunteers to serve for three months. It was soon obvious that this was insufficient. In July Congress agreed to raise 500,000 men who would serve for three years.

The Confederacy had to start its military organisation from scratch. Davis at least had some military experience. The 300 or so officers who resigned from the regular army to fight for the Confederacy provided a useful pool of talent. Southern **state militias**, were, on balance, better prepared for war than those in the North. In February 1861 the Confederate Congress agreed to raise 100,000 volunteers for up to a year's service. In May it authorised an additional 400,000 troops for three years' service. Given its limited manufacturing capacity, the South's main problem was equipping the volunteers. In April it was estimated that there were only 160,000 muskets in the whole of the South.

Key terms

Mobilisation
Preparing for war, especially by raising troops.

State militias
Traditionally every able-bodied male, aged 18–45, had been required to muster in state militia units once or twice a year. By the 1850s, most militias were shambolic; many men did not bother turning up for drill practice.

'Armed mobs'?

Moltke, the Prussian Chief of Staff in the 1860s and 1870s, characterised the military operations of the Civil War as merely, 'Two armed mobs chasing each other around the country, from which nothing could be learned.' There was some justification for this view in 1861. Compared with European armies, both the Union and Confederate armies were amateurish – from the top down.

- Neither side had a recognisable high command structure.
- Taking whatever advice seemed appropriate, both Lincoln and Davis had the job of appointing the chief officers. Political criteria, not just military concerns, played a role in these appointments. While some 'political' generals became first-rate soldiers, many were incompetent.
- Only a few junior officers had any military qualifications. Many were elected by the men under their command or were appointed by state governors, usually because of their social standing or political influence.
- Most ordinary soldiers, unused to military discipline, had little time for army spit and polish. There was thus widespread insubordination.

Mass armies

Why was conscription introduced?

From Lincoln and Davis's point of view, the main requirement in 1861 was to raise men quickly. Accepting locally and privately raised volunteer units met those needs much more rapidly and at less expense than recruiting regular troops. In 1861 the problem was not for authorities to obtain men but to hold volunteers to manageable numbers.

By early 1862 the flood of recruits had become a trickle. In March 1862 Davis decided he had no option but to introduce conscription. Every white male, aged 18 to 35 (soon raised to 45), was liable for military service. The length of service of those already in the army was extended to the duration of the war.

In the North most states adopted a carrot and stick approach. The carrot was bounties – large sums of money offered to men who enlisted. The stick, initially, was the Militia Law (July 1862). This empowered Lincoln to call state militias into Union service. Most states managed to enrol enough men but some had to introduce a **militia draft** to fill their quotas. In March 1863 the Union introduced conscription for all able-bodied men aged 20 to 45. As in the South, this was criticised, not least because it was possible to avoid the draft by hiring a substitute.

> **Militia draft**
> Conscription of men in the state militias.
>
> *Key term*

Under one-tenth of the men who fought in the Civil War were conscripted. But this statistic does not reflect the full effect of the Conscription Laws. The fact that conscripts were treated with contempt by veteran soldiers and had no choice in which regiment they would serve encouraged men to volunteer.

Both sides managed to raise massive armies. By 1865 some 900,000 men had fought for the Confederacy; the Union enlisted about 2.1 million men.

Key question
What was the impact
of the rifle-musket?

The impact of the rifle-musket

Improvements in military technology were to change the nature of warfare. In previous wars the smoothbore musket, which had an effective range of less than 100 yards, had been the main infantry weapon. Given the range of the smoothbore musket, infantry charges could often overwhelm an enemy position, as US troops had shown in the Mexican War (pages 35–6). However, by 1861 the smoothbore had been supplanted by the rifle-musket.

Rifling itself was not new, but loading rifled weapons prior to 1855 was a slow process. With the adoption of the **minié ball**, the rifle-musket could be fired as quickly as the smoothbore. Rifle-muskets were still **muzzle-loading** and single-shot (skilled men could fire three shots a minute) but the vital fact was that they were accurate at up to 600 yards. This was to have a huge impact on the battlefield. However, the production of the weapon had been so limited that not until 1863 did nearly all the infantry on both sides have rifle-muskets.

In 1861–2 Union Ordnance Chief Ripley opposed the introduction of repeating rifles on the grounds that soldiers might waste ammunition, which was in short supply. In 1864–5 repeating rifles, used mainly by cavalry units, gave Union armies an important advantage. If Ripley had contracted for repeating rifles in 1861–2, the war might have ended sooner.

Battle: attack and defence

In 1861–2, with smoothbore muskets still the norm, troops tended to attack in mass formations. The defender stood in line ready to return volleys. Once the rifle-musket became commonplace the defending force had a great advantage, especially if it had some protection. By 1864 virtually every position was entrenched. Given that frontal assaults tended to result in appalling casualties, commanders usually tried to turn the enemy's flank. The defenders' response was to keep the flanks well guarded. Thus, frontal charges were often inevitable if there was to be any battle at all.

In large-scale battles attacking infantry usually approached the enemy in lines of two ranks each, perhaps 1000 men long. A second line followed about 250 yards behind the first. A third line was often held in reserve for rapid movement to a point of opportunity. The attack usually broke down into an 'advance by rushes', men of the first line working forward, from one bit of cover to the next, with pauses to build up enough fire to cover the next rush. If the first line stalled, the second line would be fed in to restore the attack's momentum, followed, if necessary, by the third line. The assaulting force, at the moment of collision with the enemy, would thus usually consist of one disordered mass with units intermixed. It was difficult for officers to retain control and follow up any success that might be achieved.

Battles usually disintegrated into a series of engagements during which infantry traded volleys, charged and counter-charged. Most battles were hammering matches, not because of the stupidity of the commanders, but simply because of the

Key terms

Minié ball
An inch-long lead ball that expanded into the groove of the rifle-musket's barrel.

Muzzle-loading
Loaded down the barrel.

nature of the combat. In May 1864 some 19 million bullets were fired in a single week in North Virginia. Both sides, and especially the attacker, invariably sustained heavy losses. This made it difficult for the successful army to follow up its victory. Usually the beaten army retreated a few miles to lick its wounds; the winners stayed in place to lick theirs.

Politicians on both sides often denounced their generals for not pursuing a beaten foe, not understanding how difficult it was for a victorious army to gather supply trains and exhausted soldiers for a new attack.

The use of cavalry

The accuracy of rifle-fire meant that cavalry were no longer a major force on the battlefield. Cavalry charges against unbroken infantry were suicidal. The main role of cavalry was now to scout, make raids against supply lines, guard an army's flanks, screen its movements, obtain supplies and cover retreats. In battle cavalrymen usually dismounted and fought as infantry rather than charging with sabres. About 20 per cent of Confederate troops and 15 per cent of Union troops were cavalry.

At the start of the war the Confederate cavalry was superior to that of the Union. This was partly the result of good morale and excellent leaders like Jeb Stuart and Nathan Bedford Forrest. Confederate superiority was also helped by the fact that cavalry units were organised into one autonomous unit, rather than being attached piecemeal to infantry regiments as was the case in the Union army until 1863. By 1863 Union cavalry were certainly as good as Confederate cavalry and thereafter probably better, as Northerners were better armed and had better horses.

The use of artillery

Artillery had proved itself a crucial weapon in the Mexican War. However, the rifled-musket forced artillerymen to retire to safer, but less effective, ranges. The terrain over which much of the war was fought did not help the artillery. Rugged country and extensive forests ensured that few battlefields offered large areas of open ground where guns could be used to maximum effect. Union armies almost always had greater artillery strength than **rebel armies**. The North had the manufacturing potential to produce more – and better – guns. Rebel artillery units possessed a patchwork of widely different guns. Some were purchased abroad. Others were captured from Union armies. The Confederacy did manufacture some of its own guns but these were usually inferior to Union cannon.

Rebel armies
Confederates were called rebels or 'rebs' by Union forces.

Key term

The importance of communications

Civil War strategy and tactics were considerably affected by improvements in communication.

- Both sides made use of railways to move masses of men and to keep them supplied. The Confederacy found it hard to maintain its railway system and thus maximise its lines of interior communication.

- On the Mississippi and its tributaries, steamboats played a vital supply role.
- The telegraph enabled commanders to communicate directly with units on widely separated fronts, thus ensuring co-ordinated movement.

The war's main theatres

The Civil War was fought mainly in the Confederacy, with the most decisive battles in North Virginia and the West.

North Virginia was seen as crucial to the war's outcome. In this area a flat coastal strip gave way initially to rolling hills and then to the Appalachian Mountains. The Confederate capital Richmond, the principal target of Union forces, was only a hundred miles or so from Washington. The area north of Richmond was to be the scene of bitter fighting. Geographical factors – dense forests, swampy areas and a half-dozen major rivers running west to east – favoured the defender. So did the fertile Shenandoah Valley. This ran from north-east (near Washington) to south-west (away from Richmond).

Between the Appalachians and the Mississippi lay a vast region of plains and hills, extending from Kentucky and Tennessee in the north to the Gulf Coast in the south. The sheer size of the West, its lack of natural lines of defence, and the fact that the main rivers flowed into the heart of the Confederacy meant that the West was the rebels' 'soft underbelly'.

West of the Mississippi was a huge but thinly populated area. The fighting here was small scale; none of the campaigns had a major effect on the war's outcome.

Guerrilla war

There was a guerrilla dimension to the war, especially in Missouri, Kentucky, Arkansas and Tennessee. Confederate guerrilla units gathered when the call went out, engaged in an operation (for example, attacking Union outposts, patrols and civilian sympathisers) and then returned to homes and hideouts until needed again.

The naval war

Key question
How important was naval warfare?

In April 1861, the Union, on paper, had a fleet of 90 ships but few were ready for action. There were only 8800 men in the navy. However, the Union did have a large **merchant marine**, from which it could draw vessels and men. The Confederacy had no navy at all in 1861. Although some 300 naval officers joined the Confederacy, the likelihood of their finding ships to command seemed minimal. Nearly all US shipbuilding capacity was in the North.

Key term
Merchant marine
Ships involved in trade, not war.

As soon as the war began the North bought scores of merchant ships, armed them and sent them to do blockade duty. By December 1861 the Union had over 260 warships on duty and 100 more were under construction. Much of this expansion was due to the dynamism of Navy Secretary Gideon Welles and Assistant Secretary Gustavus Fox. They were helped by several factors:

- most naval officers remained loyal to the Union
- the North had a proud naval tradition
- the Union had the industrial capacity to build a colossal fleet.

Blockading the South was crucial. If the Confederacy could sell its cotton in Europe and purchase weapons and manufactured goods in return, the war might continue indefinitely. Given the 3500 miles of Southern coastline, the blockade was easier to declare than to enforce. But as the months went by the blockade grew tighter, hindering the Confederacy's war effort.

The Union was also able to use its naval supremacy to transport its troops and to strike at Confederate coastal targets. In April 1862 New Orleans, the Confederacy's largest town, was captured by Admiral Farragut. Loss of many of its coastal towns weakened the Confederacy and depressed Southern morale.

Secretary of the Confederate Navy Stephen Mallory had the unenviable job of creating a navy from scratch. Appreciating that the Confederacy could never outbuild the Union, he realised that its only hope was the bold adoption of new weapons. Aware of British and French experiments with **ironclad warships**, Mallory believed that the best chance to break the Union blockade was for the Confederacy to build several of these revolutionary vessels. In

Ironclad warship
Ship made of iron or protected by iron plates.

Key term

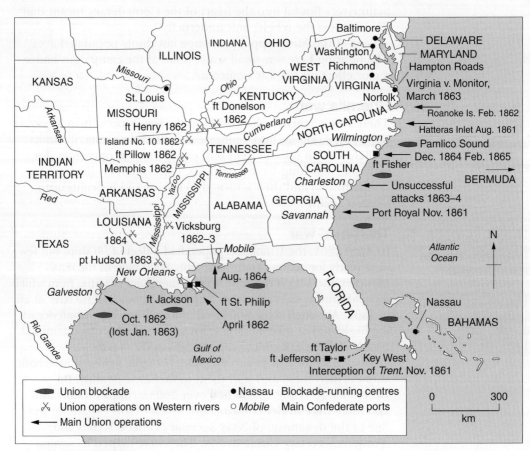

Figure 6.2: The naval war

the summer of 1861 he ordered the conversion of the *Merrimack* (a scuttled Union frigate which the Confederacy had managed to raise) into an ironclad.

The Confederacy's greatest moment in the naval war came on 8 March 1862 when the *Merrimack* (now renamed the *Virginia* and with its sides sheathed with iron plate) succeeded in sinking two blockading ships. For one day the Confederate navy ruled the waves. Unfortunately for Mallory, by March 1862 the Union had its own ironclad, the *Monitor*. On 9 March the first ironclad encounter in history occurred. Neither the *Virginia* nor the *Monitor* was able to sink the other, but the *Virginia* was so damaged that it was forced to return to port and was later abandoned.

The Confederacy could scarcely retain a monopoly of new naval weapons. It had to stretch its resources to build one ironclad, whereas the Union was able to mass-produce them.

The 'inland sea'

Confederate craft were no match for the heavily armed and armoured Union squadrons operating on the Western rivers. Gunboats played a crucial role in helping Union troops capture a number of key Confederate fortresses. By August 1862 Union forces controlled all the Mississippi except a 150-mile stretch from Vicksburg to Port Hudson.

Commerce raiders

The Confederacy purchased a number of fast raiders such as the *Alabama* and the *Florida* from Britain. These raiders sank or captured some 200 Union merchant ships. Although never seriously threatening Union commerce, the raiders' exploits helped Southern morale. Unable to find safe ports for refitting, most were eventually hunted down and sunk.

Was the Civil War a 'total' war?

Historian Mark Neely has claimed that the war was not total. He stresses that the Union government never tried to control the North's economy or to mobilise all its resources. Moreover, there was little of the ruthlessness and cruelty that characterised twentieth century wars. On the whole civilians were safe. Women were rarely raped. The 'hard war' policies adopted by Union generals Sherman and Sheridan in 1864 (see pages 182–3) were designed to damage property, not kill.

However, as James McPherson has pointed out, 'The Civil War mobilised human resources on a scale unmatched by any other event in American history except, perhaps, World War II.' In fact, far more American men (proportionately) were mustered than in the Second World War. The war was more total in the South than in the North. A quarter of white men of military age in the Confederacy lost their lives. Moreover, the Union eventually did all it could to destroy the South's economic resources as well as the morale of its civilians.

Was the Civil War the first modern war?

Given railways, the telegraph, the rifle-musket and iron, steam-driven ships, many historians see the Civil War as more akin to World War I than the Napoleonic Wars.

However, there was no battle in the entire war when there were more than 100,000 men on each side. The strategy and tactics of the armies would have been familiar to Napoleon (just as Nelson would have felt at home in most of the ships). Horse-drawn transport remained the norm. Experiments with machine guns, submarines and underwater mines were rudimentary and made little impact on the war's outcome. Given the state of communications, Civil War generals could barely command, still less control, their men on battlefields.

The war came half way between the Napoleonic Wars and World War I. Not surprisingly it showed features of both.

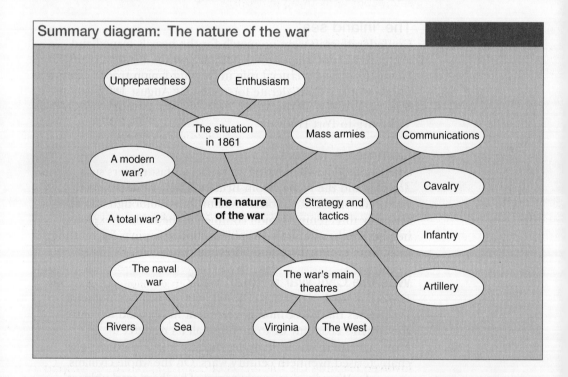

Summary diagram: The nature of the war

- Unpreparedness
- Enthusiasm
- The situation in 1861
- A modern war?
- A total war?
- The nature of the war
- Mass armies
- Communications
- Strategy and tactics
- Cavalry
- Infantry
- Artillery
- The naval war
  - Rivers
  - Sea
- The war's main theatres
  - Virginia
  - The West

3 | The Soldiers' Experience

Historian Bell Wiley believed that the similarities between '**Johnny Reb**' and '**Billy Yank**' far outweighed the differences. Nevertheless, he accepted that there were some differences. Some 20 per cent of Union troops had been born overseas, mainly in Ireland and Germany. By 1865 10 per cent of Union troops were African Americans. In contrast, 95 per cent of rebel soldiers were white native-born Southerners. According to Wiley, Union soldiers were better educated and held a less romantic view of the war. Southern troops were reputed to be more independent and less likely to take military discipline seriously.

Key question
What was the war like for Billy Yank and Johnny Reb?

Johnny Reb
Confederate soldiers' nickname.

Billy Yank
Union soldiers' nickname.

Key terms

Why did men fight?

Bell Wiley believed that most soldiers had little idea of what they were fighting for. Historian Reid Mitchell reached a similar conclusion: the soldiers 'may well have fought during the Civil War for reasons having less to do with ideology than with masculine identity'. Certainly many men fought bravely not for a cause but because they did not want to let their comrades – and themselves – down.

Historian James McPherson, after examining a cross-section of letters, claims that the majority of men on both sides were fully aware of the issues at stake and passionately concerned about them. Southerners believed that they were defending hearth and home against an invading army and saw the conflict as the second War for Independence. Northerners knew they were fighting to save the Union. Thus men on both sides were motivated by simple but very strong patriotism.

Military organisation

Military units usually consisted of men who came from the same neighbourhoods. This was important. The closeness of the soldiers to their home community was a powerful impetus for military service. Soldiers were aware that any cowardice or misdoing was reported home. So too was bravery, which earned a soldier respect both at home and among his comrades.

Age, health and fitness

The average age of soldiers was 25. Eighty per cent of the men were between 18 and 30 years old, but drummer boys as young as nine signed on (the youngest boy killed in battle was 12) and there were also soldiers over 60. Those responsible for recruitment rarely bothered about potential soldiers' fitness. Physical examinations of recruits were often a sham. This accounts for the fact that scores of women managed to enlist by passing as men.

Army life

Following enlistment, recruits underwent basic training. This involved learning the rudiments of camp life, marching, weapon training and (hours of) drilling. The goal of drill was to move disciplined manpower quickly into position on the battlefield to deliver the maximum firepower. Men had to be trained to follow orders so automatically that even amid the frenzy of battle they would respond to them.

Union soldiers were better equipped than the 'rebels'. By 1862 most Union infantry wore a blue uniform. Confederate soldiers wore more assorted colours. Some wore grey. Others wore clothes they had stripped from the enemy dead and dyed butternut – a yellowish-brown colour. The common soldier carried on his back nearly everything he would need to fight the enemy and survive the elements. At the very least a soldier had to carry a rifle with bayonet, a cartridge box, a haversack, a cape, a blanket and a canteen. Many also carried a razor, towel, soap, comb, knife, writing implement, Bible, family portraits, an oil-cloth groundsheet, socks, money, sewing kit, tobacco pouch, matches, a pipe, eating utensils and a cup.

Union soldiers were better fed than Confederates. The only criticism that British observers could make of the Union army ration (which mainly comprised salted meat and hard bread) was that there was too much of it! Supply problems meant that Southern troops often had to scavenge for whatever they could get.

For most men the novelty of army life was short-lived. In its place came homesickness, loneliness and sheer tedium. In the summer, soldiers suffered from heat and from the fact that they were constantly on the move. During the winter, tents, log huts or makeshift shanties were poor protection from the weather. Inattention to latrine procedures and garbage pits meant that there was usually an overbearing stench.

In camp, and on the march, there was a constant search for diversions to overcome the boredom of army routine. Music helped to sustain morale. Regimental bands welcomed recruits, provided entertainment in camp and inspired troops both on the march and in battle. Each side had its own favourite songs: Union troops liked 'Battle Cry of Freedom' and 'John Brown's Body'; Confederates liked 'Dixie' and the 'Bonnie Blue Flag'. Sports – boxing, wresting and baseball – were popular. So was gambling. Soldiers often frequented brothels when they were on leave. Leave, however, was something of a rarity in both armies.

While actual fighting took up only a small part of a soldier's time, battle – the ultimate test – was often at the forefront of men's minds. Most soldiers, initially shocked by the smoke, crash of musketry and cannon-fire, fought well. Amazingly, men in the early part of the war often begged for the privilege of carrying their regiment's colours, knowing full well that in battle colour bearers were among the first to die.

Medical care

Of about 360,000 deaths, about 67,000 Union soldiers were killed in action, 43,000 died of wounds and 224,000 died of disease (24,000 died from unknown – or other – causes). Confederate statistics (which are less accurate) indicate a comparable situation. Disease was thus the main killer of Civil War soldiers. Epidemics of mumps and measles could put whole regiments out of action. Dysentery, typhoid, pneumonia and malaria, caused by bad sanitation, bad water, bad food, exposure and mosquitoes, were the main killers.

By today's standards, disease mortality was terribly high. But far fewer soldiers died from disease than in the Napoleonic or Crimean Wars. Indeed the US Surgeon General wrote that the Union army's death rate from disease was 'lower than has been observed in any army since the world began'. This was largely because, by the standards of the time, medical care was good.

Although neither side had adequate facilities in 1861, this was generally put right as the war progressed. Ambulance corps were

Key question
How effective was medical care?

Confederate soldiers, killed during the Battle of Antietam, lie along a dirt road near Hagerstown Pike.

Confederate soldiers pose outside their tent.

established to give first aid on the battlefield and remove the wounded to dressing stations and field hospitals. Both sides quickly constructed a network of hospitals of astonishing size (the Confederate Chimborazo Hospital could cope with 8000 patients) and commendable efficiency. Soon over 3200 women were working as nurses. (Previously army nursing had been an all-male concern.) Female nurses such as Clara Barton won reputations

Confederate prisoners after Gettysburg.

akin to Florence Nightingale's in the Crimean War. The main problem was the state of knowledge of medicine and public health, rather than lack of competence on the part of army doctors and nurses. The revolutionary developments that were to transform medicine came a decade or so later.

Desertion

One in seven Confederate and one in 10 Union troops deserted. They did so for a variety of reasons: boredom, fear, concern for families at home and lack of commitment. The fact that the odds were in favour of the escape attempt succeeding also encouraged desertion. Union and Confederate authorities did their best to lure deserters back into the ranks with periodic amnesties. There was little consistency in the punishment meted out to deserters who were caught. Some were branded with the letter D for deserter; some were sentenced to hard labour; a few were shot.

Prisoners of war

Prisoner exchange was the norm in the first two years of the war. In 1863 the Union suspended exchange of prisoners, technically on the grounds of Confederate violations of agreements (not least with regard to black prisoners), but actually because the smaller populated South had more to gain from exchanges than the North. Thus, in 1863–4 both sides had to deal with thousands of captives. Warehouses, schools, even open fields, were used as prison camps. Most were over-crowded and prisoners had inadequate food, shelter, clothing and medical services, resulting in high mortality rates. Union prisoners particularly suffered. This was more by accident than intent. By 1864 the Confederacy was having difficulty feeding its own people, never mind captured Yankees. The most notorious Confederate prison camp was Andersonville – the fourth biggest 'settlement' within the Confederacy by 1864. Over a quarter of the camp's 50,000 inmates died from malnutrition and disease. During the war, 194,743 Union soldiers were imprisoned. Some 30,128 died. 214,865 Confederate prisoners were taken; 25,976 died.

Conclusion

The romantic assumptions of 1861 were soon shattered by the terrible reality of war. One in five of the soldiers who fought in the Civil War died in it. Yet most soldiers came to look back on the war with pride and nostalgia. Perhaps there was more reason for pride than nostalgia. The hard school of experience turned the enthusiastic mobs of 1861 into resilient soldiers whose powers of endurance astounded European observers.

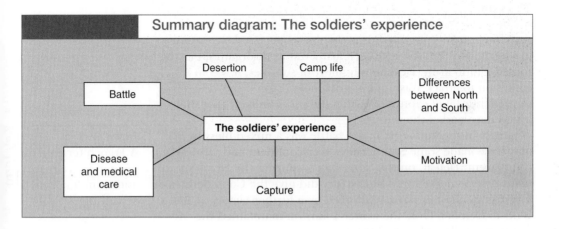

Summary diagram: The soldiers' experience

Desertion — Camp life — Differences between North and South — Battle — The soldiers' experience — Disease and medical care — Capture — Motivation

Key question
Why did the war not end in 1861 or 1862?

4 | The War 1861–2

Union and Confederate plans in 1861

Winfield Scott, Union General-in-Chief, thought it would take many months to train and equip the armies needed to crush the insurrection. He supported the Anaconda Plan, the aim of which was slowly to squeeze life out of the Confederacy by naval blockade and by winning control of the Mississippi river. But Lincoln, like most Northerners, looked for a quick decisive blow. He accepted that Union troops were untrained but as he wrote to General McDowell, who commanded Union forces around Washington: 'You are green, it is true, but they are green; you are all green alike.' Lincoln thus urged McDowell to march on Richmond.

Meanwhile Jefferson Davis pledged himself to defend every part of the Confederacy. He realised that lost territory would result in a depletion of resources and a decline in morale.

Key date

The first battle of Manassas: July 1861

First Manassas

In 1861 both sides saw Virginia as the crucial theatre of war. The main Confederate army of 22,000 men, led by Beauregard, was positioned south of the Bull Run river at Manassas. General Joe Johnston commanded another army of 11,000 men in the

Shenandoah Valley. On 16 July Union General McDowell marched south with some 30,000 men. His attack on 21 July was well conceived and he came near to winning a decisive victory.

Confederate forces fought bravely, especially Thomas Jackson's brigade which stood 'like a stonewall' (hereafter Jackson became known as 'Stonewall') and were saved by the arrival of Johnston's troops, many of whom travelled by train from the Shenandoah. Union troops panicked and fled. The Confederacy had won the first major battle. The South suffered 2000 casualties (including 440 dead); the Union suffered 3000 casualties (with over 600 dead). Southerners, who usually named battles after the nearest settlement, called the battle Manassas. Northerners, who usually named battles after the nearest geographical feature, called it Bull Run.

The Confederacy made no attempt to follow up its victory by marching on Washington. Some see this as a missed opportunity to win the war. But the Southern army was as disorganised as the routed Union army. Desperately short of supplies, it was in no condition to attack Washington's defences. Even if the Confederates had captured Washington, it is unlikely that this would have ended the war.

Victory in the war's first major battle was a mixed blessing. It may have made some Southerners over-confident and complacent. Defeat, on the other hand, spurred the North on to more determined efforts. But victory did give the Confederates in Virginia an *esprit de corps*, reinforced by a further victory at Ball's Bluff in October. Over the winter Johnston maintained the Confederate line along the Potomac river.

> **Esprit de corps**
> A French term meaning loyalty to, and confidence in, something.

(margin: Key term)

General McClellan

After Manassas, McDowell was replaced by 34-year-old General George McClellan. Credited with some minor victories in West Virginia, he exuded an air of optimism and soon replaced Scott as General-in-Chief. McClellan is one of the most controversial figures of the war. An able administrator, he restored the morale of the main Union army, now called the Army of the Potomac. He was popular with the soldiers, who referred to him affectionately as 'Little Mac'. McClellan's supporters claim he was a man of strategic vision who was betrayed by Republican political intrigue (McClellan was a Democrat who had no wish to free the slaves) and by poor intelligence. Anxious not to create scars that might take a generation to heal, his hope of winning the war by manoeuvre and bringing it to an end without too much gore, made – humane – sense.

Even McClellan's supporters concede, however, that he was an arrogant egotist. He failed to work collaboratively with his political masters, whom he constantly derided. (Lincoln was 'nothing more than a well-meaning baboon ... the original gorilla'.) The main charge levied against McClellan is that, having built a fine army, he was too reluctant to use it. Over-cautious and indecisive, he had a chronic disposition to exaggerate the odds against him. This was apparent over the winter of 1861–2.

> **Key question**
> How good a general was McClellan?

Although his army was twice the size of the rebel force facing him, he believed he was outnumbered. Lincoln and the Northern public grew increasingly impatient as McClellan refused to move.

The Peninsula campaign

In late January 1862 a frustrated Lincoln ordered McClellan to attack. But McClellan now went down with typhoid fever and was confined to bed for three weeks. On his recovery, rather than lead a direct march on Richmond, he devised an ambitious flanking attack, intending to ferry the bulk of his army to Urbana so that it was between Richmond and the rebel army at Manassas. Just as he was ready to move, Johnston withdrew to new lines south of the Rappahannock river. Still anxious to avoid a frontal attack, McClellan now planned to attack Richmond up the peninsula between the York and James rivers.

In April 1862 the Army of Potomac, 121,000 strong, was transported to Fortress Monroe – 70 miles from Richmond. 'I have not come here to wage war upon the defenceless, upon non-combatants, upon private property, nor upon the domestic institutions of the land', announced McClellan. It soon seemed as though he had not come to wage war at all. The only rebel army

'Stonewall' Jackson was a Confederate war hero.

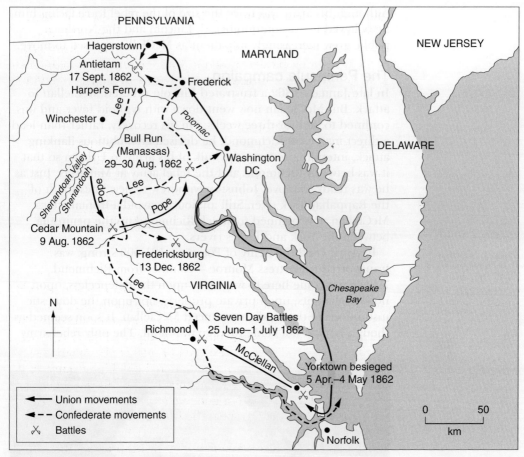

Figure 6.3: The war in the East: 1861–2

ready to impede McClellan's advance was a force of 11,000 men commanded by General Magruder. Magruder convinced McClellan that he had thousands more men, simply by marching his small force up and down. Instead of attacking, McClellan settled down to besiege Yorktown, giving Davis time to send more men to the peninsula. Just as he was ready to attack Yorktown, the Confederates withdrew. McClellan, delighted to have won another bloodless 'victory', advanced cautiously, not reaching the outskirts of Richmond until late May. His forces greatly outnumbered the Confederates opposing him, but McClellan, convinced he was outnumbered, awaited reinforcements.

The Shenandoah valley

McClellan never got his reinforcements, largely because of Stonewall Jackson's Shenandoah valley campaign. Jackson, with 18,000 men, was sent into the valley to ensure that (far larger) Union forces did not move south to Richmond. Jackson, a religious fanatic who saw himself as God's instrument, demanded a great deal of his men, who at first regarded him with suspicion. However, from March to June 1862 he proved himself a brilliant soldier and won their grudging respect. During that period he fought six battles, marched his 'foot cavalry' hundreds of miles, inflicted 7000 casualties on the enemy, diverted 60,000 Union troops from other tasks, and inspired the South. Lincoln, worried at the threat that Jackson posed to Washington, did not send men to help McClellan. Instead, it was Jackson who marched south to fight McClellan.

Confederate problems

Despite Jackson's success, the Confederacy seemed to be on the verge of defeat in May. Confederate forces had suffered severe setbacks, not least the loss of New Orleans in April. Most of the Mississippi valley was now in Union hands and McClellan seemed certain to capture Richmond. In April Stanton, Lincoln's Secretary for War, anticipating victory, called a halt to federal recruiting.

Robert E. Lee

On 31 May General Johnston attacked McClellan's forces outside Richmond. The result was a costly draw: the South lost 6000 casualties and the North 5000. The most important outcome was the fact that Johnston was wounded and replaced by 55-year-old Virginian Robert E. Lee. Considered by many to be America's finest soldier in 1861, Lincoln had offered him high command in the Union army but Lee had remained loyal to his state. The early part of the war had not gone well for him: after setbacks in West Virginia and the Carolinas, he became Davis's military adviser.

Lee now had the opportunity to display his prowess. Renaming his army the Army of Northern Virginia, he determined to seize the initiative. He planned to join up with Jackson and carry out an audacious flanking movement on the Union army. Although some historians have been critical of Lee's so-called 'offensive–defensive' strategy (which he was to use time and again in 1862–3), it is hard to imagine a better one. A war fought purely on the defensive was unlikely to be successful. The Union would be able to pick off the South almost at will. By going on the offensive, Lee hoped to win a major victory which would seriously damage Northern morale.

The Seven Days

Lee attacked at the end of June. The week of battles that followed is known as 'The Seven Days'. Lee struck first at Mechanicsville. Jackson's late arrival meant that little was achieved. On 27 June Lee attacked at Gaines Mill. Again Jackson failed to perform well but rebel forces finally broke the enemy line. Pursuit of the beaten foe proceeded sluggishly from 28 to 30 June. In the last battle of the campaign, at Malvern Hill on 1 July, Lee lost 5000 men to the Union's 3000.

The Seven Days cost the Confederacy 20,614 men; Union losses were only 15,849. Over-complicated battle-plans and defects in command structure led to Lee making a number of disjointed attacks. He was also let down by his subordinates, not

---

Key question
How good a general was Robert E. Lee?

Key date
The Seven Days: Lee's campaign to drive McClellan from Richmond: June–July 1862

Profile: Robert E(dward) Lee 1807–70

1807		– Born in Virginia: son of Revolutionary War General 'Light Horse' Lee
1829		– Graduated from West Point
1831		– Married Mary Custis, the daughter of George Washington's adopted son: he inherited her father's mansion at Arlington, along with 63 slaves
1846–8		– Won renown in the Mexican War
1848–61		– Remained in the army, serving as an engineer out West and superintendent at West Point
1861		– Resigned from the Union army and became commander of Virginia's forces
1862	March	– Became Davis's chief military adviser
	June	– Appointed commander of the Army of Northern Virginia
	June–July	– Seven Day battles
	August	– Second Manassas
	September	– Battle of Antietam
	December	– Battle of Fredericksburg
1863	May	– Battle of Chancellorsville
	July	– Battle of Gettysburg
1864	May	– Battle of the Wilderness
1865	February	– Became General-in-Chief of all the Confederate armies
	April	– Surrendered to Grant at Appomattox Court House
1870		– Died

Historians disagree about Robert E. Lee. Some think he was the Confederacy's greatest hero. Others think that he was the reason the Confederacy lost.

Edward Hagerman, *The American Civil War and the Origins of Modern Warfare* (1988): 'Lee took longer to learn from his experience that the frontal assault contributed only to attrition without victory than any other field commander in the Civil War.'

James McPherson, *Drawn with the Sword* (1996):

… the Confederacy had a chance to win the war – not by conquering the North or destroying its armies, but by sapping the Northern will and capacity to conquer the South and destroy Confederate armies. On three occasions the Confederacy came close to winning on these terms. Each time it was Lee who almost pulled it off. His victories at the Seven Days and second Manassas battles and the invasion of Maryland in the summer of 1862; his triumph at Chancellorsville and the invasion of Pennsylvania in 1863; and the casualties his army inflicted on Grant's forces in the Wilderness–Petersburg campaign in the spring and summer of 1864 … these three campaigns each came close to sapping the Northern will to continue the war … . Of all Confederate commanders, Lee was the only one whose victories had some potential for winning the war. The notion that a more gradual strategy would have done better is speculative at best.

least Jackson who was strangely lethargic. Lee, who had failed
to destroy the Union army, was disappointed with the results
of his offensive. Nevertheless, he had saved Richmond and
forced a demoralised McClellan to retreat back down the
peninsula.

Second Manassas

Key dates

The second Battle of
Manassas (or Bull
Run): August 1862

The Battle of Antietam
(or Sharpsburg):
September 1862

Lincoln now appointed General Pope, who had won some small
victories in the West, to command the Union forces around
Washington. McClellan was ordered to evacuate the peninsula
and join Pope. With a united army, Pope would then advance on
Richmond.

Lee, determined to strike first, headed north in mid-August
with some 55,000 men. Dividing his army, Lee sent Jackson on a
long sweep west and north of Pope, who was still awaiting
McClellan's – slow – arrival. On 26–27 August, Jackson's 25,000
troops captured Pope's main supply depot at Manassas.

Pope, strengthened at last by advanced units of McClellan's
army, attacked Jackson's outnumbered force. Second Manassas,
fought on 29–30 August, was a Union disaster. Failing to
appreciate that the rest of Lee's army was marching to Jackson's
aid, Pope was defeated when General Longstreet attacked his left
flank. Lee came close to winning the decisive victory that he was
seeking. However, most Union troops escaped and retreated
towards Washington. Pope's poor generalship had cost the Union
16,000 men (Lee lost 9000). Reluctantly Lincoln re-appointed
McClellan as commander-in-chief.

Antietam

Key question
Why was Antietam a
crucial battle?

In September, Lee sent Jackson to capture Harper's Ferry while
he himself invaded Maryland with 40,000 men. He aimed:

- to protect Virginia's harvest
- to gain Maryland volunteers
- to win a decisive victory
- to demoralise the North
- to persuade Britain to recognise the Confederacy.

After Second Manassas, thought Longstreet, 'we had the most
brilliant prospects the Confederates ever had'.

However, Lee's invasion did not go to plan. He lost more soldiers
by straggling and desertion than he gained from pro-Confederate
Marylanders. He also lost a copy of his operational orders which
mysteriously fell into McClellan's hands. Aware that Lee's army was
divided, McClellan was in a tremendous position to defeat him.
Although he frittered away much of his dazzling advantage, he did
force Lee back toward the Potomac river. Instead of retreating into
Virginia, Lee took up a position behind Antietam Creek.

Given that he was hopelessly outnumbered, that both his flanks
were vulnerable, and that he had the Potomac behind him, Lee's
decision to offer battle seems incredible. If McClellan had
attacked on 15 or 16 September Lee must surely have been
defeated. Fortunately for Lee's reputation, McClellan did not

attack. On 16 September Jackson's corps rejoined Lee's army, which reduced the odds. Even so McClellan still had a two-to-one advantage when he finally attacked on 17 September.

Antietam, partly because it was so badly handled by McClellan, was really three separate battles. All three Union attacks were partially successful but none was followed through to complete success and Lee managed to hang on. Antietam was the bloodiest single-day battle of the war. Lee lost 10,000 men, McClellan 14,000.

Although Lee's army had staged one of its most impressive performances, McClellan was able to claim victory because on 18 September Lee retreated into Virginia. Indeed, Antietam can be seen as the turning point of the war. Within days of the battle Lincoln issued his famous Emancipation Proclamation (page 200). Lee's failure to win a decisive victory meant there was now little likelihood of British intervention. But McClellan failed to follow up his 'victory'. Exasperated with his excuses for inactivity, Lincoln relieved him of command in November, replacing him with General Burnside.

Fredericksburg

Burnside's plan was simple: his 100,000 men would advance to Fredericksburg and then strike south. Lee's 75,000 strong army took up a strong position behind Fredericksburg. On 13 December

The Battle of Fredericksburg: December 1862

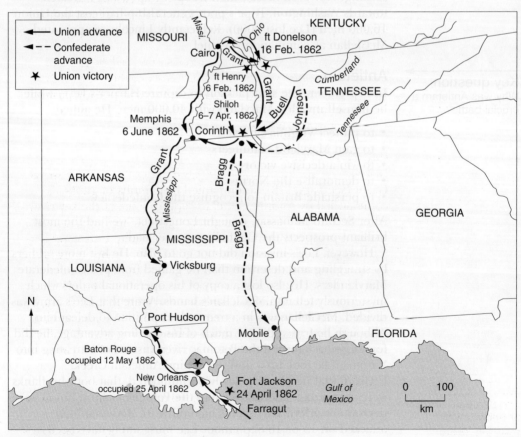

Figure 6.4: The war in the West: 1861–2

Burnside launched a series of suicidal attacks. Union forces lost 11,000 men. Lee lost less than 5000. Burnside, dissuaded from launching more attacks by his senior generals, pulled back across the Rappahannock. Union morale was not helped when Burnside's attempt to turn Lee's flank in January 1863 got bogged down in mud.

The West 1861–2

The Confederates won the first major battle in the West – at Wilson's Creek in Missouri in August 1861. They were unable to follow up their victory. In Missouri, and across the West as a whole, Confederate forces were greatly outnumbered by Union troops.

In 1861 Lincoln divided the Union's western forces: General Halleck was to concentrate on winning control of the Mississippi while General Buell was to drive Confederate forces from Kentucky and Tennessee. Lincoln hoped for a joint offensive. However, the divided command led to some confusion. Moreover, neither Halleck nor Buell was prepared to risk failure by attacking too soon. Both men had good excuses for delay. Their forces were short of arms, equipment and transport for most of 1861.

General Albert Sidney Johnston commanded the Confederate forces between the Appalachian and Ozark Mountains. Aware that Davis wished to defend every foot of Southern territory, Johnston scattered his 40,000 troops along the southern borders of Kentucky and Missouri, hoping that a number of forts built at strategic points on the important rivers would hold up any Union advance.

In January 1862 troops from Buell's army, led by General Thomas, won the North's first real victory of the war at Mill Springs, Kentucky. Another branch of the Union army pushed the rebels out of Missouri and defeated the rebels in March at Elkhorn Tavern, Arkansas.

Grant's success

In February Halleck sent 15,000 men under General Ulysses S. Grant (see page 178), accompanied by a flotilla of gunboats commanded by Andrew Foote, to capture some of the key river forts. In February Foote's ships forced Fort Henry to surrender. Union gunboats were not sufficient to capture the stronger and more important Fort Donelson. Accordingly, Grant besieged the Fort and demanded 'unconditional and immediate surrender'. The 16,000 Confederate garrison duly surrendered and Union forces now controlled the Tennessee and Cumberland rivers, vital arteries into the South. Johnston retreated to Corinth, leaving Kentucky and most of Tennessee under Union control. Halleck now ordered Grant and Buell to push into south-west Tennessee.

Shiloh

In early April Grant, with over 40,000 men, encamped on the west bank of the Tennessee river at Shiloh, waiting for Buell's army. On 6 April Johnston launched a surprise attack. Many Union troops panicked and fled but enough regiments held out to ensure that

Key date

The Battle of Shiloh (a Hebrew word meaning 'place of peace'): April 1862 the rebels did not win a total victory. The Confederate cause was not helped by the death of Johnston in the midst of battle. Beauregard took over. As the first day of battle ended, he telegraphed to Davis that he had won a 'complete victory'.

Grant remained calm – with good reason. That night, 25,000 men from Buell's army arrived. The next day the outnumbered Confederate army was forced to retreat. At Shiloh the rebels suffered 10,600 and the Union 13,000 casualties.

While Shiloh was certainly not Grant's best-fought battle, its outcome was of great importance. The Union had turned back the rebel bid to regain the initiative. Halleck now assumed full command and advanced – or rather crawled – towards Corinth. (It took him nearly a month to cover 22 miles.) Davis, displeased by Beauregard's evacuation of Corinth, replaced him with General Bragg.

On the Union side, Halleck was appointed General-in-Chief. Lincoln hoped he would become a vigorous commander, co-ordinating Union strategy. Instead, he became something of a pen-pusher who neither laid down nor enforced a comprehensive strategy for the war as a whole.

Kentucky and Tennessee 1862

In the late summer Bragg advanced into Kentucky. Few Kentuckians joined the Confederates and Bragg failed to make the most of his opportunities. Blundering into a Union army at Perryville in October, Bragg won a tactical victory but, facing serious supply problems, had to retreat into Tennessee. If Bragg's raid had raised then dashed Southern hopes, at least he had transferred the

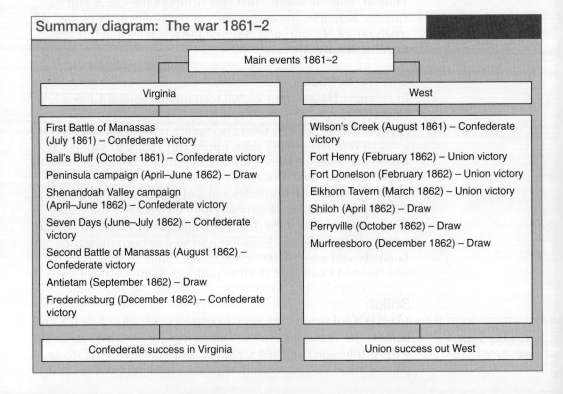

Summary diagram: The war 1861–2

Main events 1861–2

Virginia	West
First Battle of Manassas (July 1861) – Confederate victory	Wilson's Creek (August 1861) – Confederate victory
Ball's Bluff (October 1861) – Confederate victory	Fort Henry (February 1862) – Union victory
Peninsula campaign (April–June 1862) – Draw	Fort Donelson (February 1862) – Union victory
Shenandoah Valley campaign (April–June 1862) – Confederate victory	Elkhorn Tavern (March 1862) – Union victory
Seven Days (June–July 1862) – Confederate victory	Shiloh (April 1862) – Draw
Second Battle of Manassas (August 1862) – Confederate victory	Perryville (October 1862) – Draw
Antietam (September 1862) – Draw	Murfreesboro (December 1862) – Draw
Fredericksburg (December 1862) – Confederate victory	
Confederate success in Virginia	Union success out West

Confederates' main western operations from Mississippi to Tennessee. By the end of 1862, the Confederacy's position in the West was far from hopeless. Union forces had failed to take Vicksburg and thus did not control the entire Mississippi river.

In December 1862 General Rosecrans tried to drive the Confederate Army of Tennessee out of Tennessee. On 31 December the two armies severely mauled each other at Murfreesboro (or Stones River). Bragg renewed the battle two days later but his attack was beaten back and he had to withdraw. Tennessee remained quiet for six months. The main 'fighting' was in-fighting in the Confederate army between the quarrelsome Bragg and most of his generals.

5 | The War in 1863

Chancellorsville

Key date

The Battle of Chancellorsville: May 1863

In January 1863 Lincoln replaced Burnside with 'Fighting' Joe Hooker. Hooker had a hot temper and was known to be an intriguer. There were even rumours that he intended to set himself up as military dictator. Lincoln was prepared to risk the dictatorship. What he wanted more than anything else was military success. By April Hooker, with 130,000 men – twice as many as Lee – was ready to move. While General Sedgewick threatened Lee at Fredericksburg, the bulk of Hooker's army crossed the Rappahannock upstream, threatening Lee's left flank. By 30 April the main Union army had reached Chancellorsville in the heart of the area known as the Wilderness. Unfortunately for Hooker, the Wilderness's scrubby undergrowth made movement and fighting difficult and helped to negate the Union's numerical advantage.

Lee now showed himself at his most brilliant. Leaving General Early with 10,000 men to hold Sedgewick, Lee led 50,000 Confederates to meet Hooker. On 2 May, he further divided his army by sending Jackson with 28,000 men to attack Hooker's right flank. Jackson attacked just before dusk, driving Union troops back in confusion. Nightfall brought an end to the fighting – and to Jackson, mistakenly shot in the arm by his own men while inspecting the battlefield. Jackson's arm was amputated but he contracted pneumonia and died on 10 May.

Jackson's efforts at least ensured a Confederate victory. Injured (by falling masonry) and bemused by events, Hooker retreated. This enabled Lee to send half his army to head off Sedgewick, who had driven Early from Fredericksburg. Sedgewick was forced to retreat with the rest of Hooker's army. Lee had achieved what many see as his most impressive victory. With far fewer men, Lee had inflicted greater casualties on the enemy: Union losses were 17,000 men; Lee's losses were 13,000. Although Jackson's death cast a long shadow, Confederate morale was sky high.

Gettysburg

Key question

How important was Gettysburg?

Davis's advisers were split on how best to use the Army of Northern Virginia. Some favoured sending forces to relieve Vicksburg. Others thought a better tactic was to reinforce Bragg's

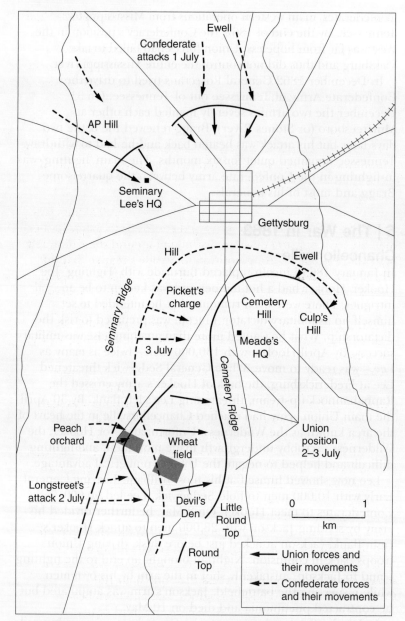

Figure 6.5: The Battle of Gettysburg, 1–3 July 1863

army and launch a major advance through Tennessee and
Kentucky. Convinced that only victories on Northern soil would
force Lincoln to accept Southern independence, Lee insisted on
an invasion of Pennsylvania. Such a move would ease pressure in
Virginia while the capture of a major Northern town would be a
severe blow to Union morale. Lee got his way and in mid-June
began his advance northwards.

Hooker tried to follow Lee but with little real idea of where he
was heading. On 28 June Lincoln replaced Hooker with General
Meade. Meade, an unpretentious, competent soldier, had little

time to get to grips with his new command. Lee, meanwhile, had no real idea of the Union army's situation.

On 1 July rebel soldiers, looking for shoes, stumbled across Union troops at Gettysburg. Lee and Meade ordered their forces to converge on the small town. Thus began the greatest battle ever fought on the American continent.

Key date The Battle of Gettysburg: 1–3 July 1863

The battle

The first day of the battle – 1 July – belonged to the Confederacy. Union troops retreated on to Culp's Hill and Cemetery Hill. If the rebels had pushed home their attack they might have triumphed.

Lee considered his options. Meade's army of 85,000 men was strongly positioned on hills south and east of Gettysburg. Rather than attack, Longstreet favoured swinging around the Union left flank and finding a strong position in Meade's rear so that the rebels were between the Army of the Potomac and Washington. Longstreet believed that Meade would then be forced to attack, and it was better to fight a defensive rather than an offensive action. Lee, aware of his army's supply problems, would have none of this. 'I am going to whip them here' he declared, 'or they are going to whip me.'

On 2 July serious fighting did not start until well into the afternoon when Longstreet attacked the Union left. The Confederates had some success against Union troops who had unwisely advanced into the Peach Orchard. They also nearly captured the strategically important Little Round Top on the extreme left of the Union position. The fighting on Little Round Top was symbolic of rebel fortunes on 2 July. Lee's men came close, but not close enough, to victory. They failed to break through in the centre and had no more success on the Union right. The day ended in stalemate.

On 3 July Lee launched his main attack on the Union centre. A total of 15,000 men, led by General Pickett, advanced up Cemetery Ridge. The charge was a disaster. Rebel troops were mown down by Union fire. In less than one hour the Confederates suffered 6500 casualties. Lee had been beaten. In three days he had lost 28,000 men – one-third of his command. (The Union army lost 23,000 men.) Lee retreated back to Virginia. He accepted full responsibility for Gettysburg: 'The army did all it could. I fear I required of it impossibilities.' He offered his resignation. Davis refused to accept it.

The results of Gettysburg

Gettysburg was a serious defeat for the Confederacy. The myth of Lee's invincibility had been broken and this in itself was a huge morale booster for the Union. After Gettysburg Lee was never again strong enough to launch a major invasion of the North. But Gettysburg was probably not the main turning point of the war.

- If Lee had won (and afterwards he maintained that he would have triumphed if he had had Stonewall Jackson), he could not have held a single Northern city for any length of time and would ultimately have had to retreat. Given the situation in the West, it seems unlikely that Union morale would have collapsed.

- Defeat at Gettysburg did not make Confederate defeat inevitable. The battle was not decisive because Meade, despite Lincoln's urgings, was unable to follow up his victory. For the rest of 1863 there were few major engagements in Virginia.

Vicksburg

From August 1862 Union forces under Grant had tried to take the fortified town of Vicksburg, as it prevented Union control of the Mississippi. In Davis's view Vicksburg was vital to the Confederate cause: it was 'the nail-head that held the South's two halves together'. The town was probably not as important as Davis thought. By this stage there was actually little Confederate traffic across the Mississippi. Nevertheless Vicksburg did have a symbolic importance. Its capture would demoralise the South and bolster the North.

As the Union threat to Vicksburg grew, Davis appointed Joseph Johnston to oversee Confederate operations in the West. However, Johnston's exact power was ill-defined and Bragg (in Tennessee) and Pemberton (at Vicksburg) continued to exercise independent command. Davis's hope that Johnston would bring a unified vision to the West was not realised.

Vicksburg's natural defences made it difficult to capture. Rebel cavalry constantly threatened the Union supply line. Over the winter Grant probed unsuccessfully for a crossing that would enable him to get his forces east of the Mississippi. Finally he determined to gamble. Marching his army down the west side of the Mississippi, he relied upon Admiral Porter's ironclad fleet sailing past Vicksburg. This was achieved on the night of 16–17 April. Two weeks later Grant's army was ferried across the Mississippi.

> **Key question**
> How important was the loss of Vicksburg?

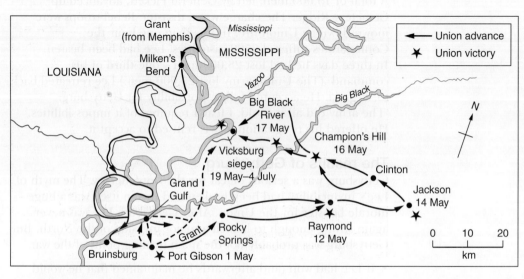

Figure 6.6: The Vicksburg Campaign 1863

The ensuing campaign was brilliant. Aware that he would be outnumbered if the Confederate forces in the vicinity (Pemberton with 30,000 men at Vicksburg and Johnston with 25,000 men near Jackson) united, Grant's aim was to defeat the two rebel armies separately. Largely ignoring his line of communications, he cut inland. In three weeks he won several battles, defeating Johnston and forcing Pemberton to retreat into Vicksburg. After failing to storm the defences, Grant besieged the town. On 4 July 30,000 Confederate troops in Vicksburg surrendered. The capture of Port Hudson five days later meant that the Confederacy was cut in two.

Chattanooga

Lincoln, anxious to press the Confederacy on all fronts, demanded more decisive action from General Rosecrans in Tennessee. Threatened with dismissal, Rosecrans advanced in June, forcing Bragg to retreat to Chattanooga. Unable to hold the town, Bragg withdrew to Chickamauga, where he was reinforced by 12,000 men from the Army of Northern Virginia, led by Longstreet. In September Rosecrans advanced in three columns. On 19–20 September Bragg gave battle at Chickamauga – the only major battle in the entire war in which the rebels outnumbered Union forces. Bragg came close to winning a decisive victory. Only a brave rearguard action by Thomas prevented a rout and enabled the Union army to retreat to Chattanooga. The battle of Chickamauga cost the Confederates 18,500 casualties compared to the Union's 16,500.

Bragg besieged Chattanooga but failed to cut the frail Union supply line. Despite Bragg's failings, the Union position was

Key dates

The fall of Vicksburg: 4 July 1863

The Battle of Chickamauga: September 1863

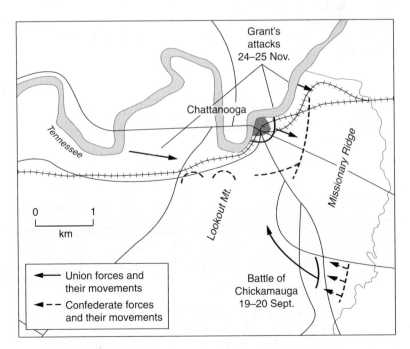

Figure 6.7: Chickamauga and Chattanooga, September–November 1863

critical. The Union army was so short of food it seemed it might be forced to surrender. Lincoln now gave Grant command of all the Union's western forces. Grant acted swiftly, establishing the '**cracker line**' to Chattanooga. Then, on 24 November Union troops stormed Lookout Mountain. The next day Grant's men seized Missionary Ridge. Rebel forces retreated in disarray. Weeks too late, Bragg was relieved of his command. The Union victory confirmed that Grant was the Union's greatest general.

Cracker line
The term given to Grant's success in establishing a supply route to Chattanooga. Army rations very much depended on hard bread – or crackers.

Key term

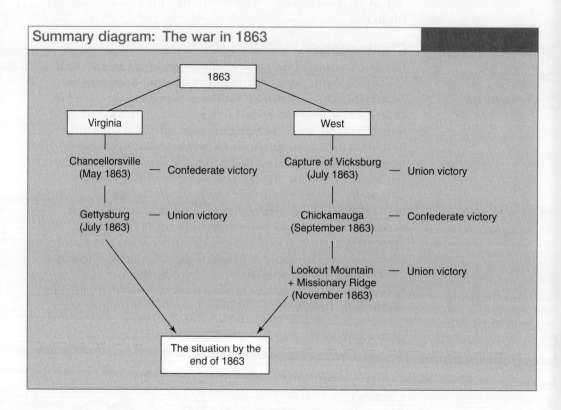

Summary diagram: The war in 1863

critical. The Union army was so short of food it seemed it might

6 | Union Victory 1864–5

The defeats at Gettysburg, Vicksburg and Chattanooga were severe blows to Southern morale. By December 1863, Union forces were preparing to invade Georgia. Large areas of Arkansas, Tennessee and Louisiana were under Union control. Nevertheless, the South was far from beaten. Out west the Union faced the problem of long supply lines. In the east the Confederacy still had Lee and the Army of Northern Virginia. If Lee could continue to inflict heavy casualties on the Union, there was every chance that the Northern electorate might oust Lincoln in the 1864 election and vote in a peace candidate.

In March 1864 Lincoln appointed U.S. Grant General-in-Chief of all the Union armies. He immediately came east to supervise the effort to destroy Lee. Sherman took over command in the

Key question
How successful were Union armies in 1864?

Grant became General-in-Chief: March 1864

Key date

West. Determined to make use of the Union's greater manpower, Grant planned for a 'simultaneous movement all along the line'.

- The 115,000-strong Army of the Potomac would attack Lee.
- Sherman's Western army would capture Atlanta and then 'get into the interior of the enemy's country ... inflicting all the damage you can'.
- 30,000 men in Louisiana, led by General Banks, were to capture Mobile.
- Butler's 30,000-strong army at Yorktown was to threaten Richmond.
- Sigel, with 26,000 men, was to occupy the Shenandoah Valley.

Lincoln approved of this strategy; it was the one he had advocated from the start.

The Confederacy by 1864 had to scrape the bottom of its manpower barrel. Men between the ages of 17 and 50 were now liable for conscription. Even so, rebel forces were less than half those of the Union. Nevertheless, the morale of the Army of North Virginia remained high and General Joe Johnston, re-appointed to command the Army of Tennessee, had done a good job in improving Confederate morale in the West.

Although they would be outnumbered in the coming campaigns, at least most rebel soldiers were veterans. Many experienced Union troops, on the other hand, were due to go home in 1864 when the three-year enlistment period ended. This would seriously weaken the Union army. Rather than force the veterans to re-enlist, the Union offered them $400 and 30 days' leave. Some 136,000 men, scenting victory, re-enlisted; 100,000 decided not to do so.

Key date

The Wilderness campaign: May–June 1864

Grant's plan unfolds

Grant's strategy did not go to plan:

- Banks was defeated in the Red river area.
- Butler failed to exert pressure on Richmond.
- Union forces in the Shenandoah were defeated. In July a 10,000-strong rebel force pushed up the valley and reached the suburbs of Washington, forcing Grant to send reinforcements to defend the capital.

The Army of the Potomac had mixed success. With a two-to-one superiority in manpower, Grant hoped to manoeuvre Lee into an open-field combat. Lee's strategy was straightforward: keep Grant from Richmond, force him to attack fortified positions, and make the cost of trying to defeat the Confederacy so high that Northerners would refuse to pay the price and vote out Lincoln in November.

In May Grant crossed the Rapidan river, threatening to slip round Lee's flank. The bloodiest six weeks of the war now began. On 5–6 May Union and rebel forces met again in the same Wilderness area that had foiled Hooker one year earlier (see page 171). The Union army suffered 18,000 casualties in

Profile: Ulysses S. Grant 1822–85

1822		– Born Hiram Ulysses Grant
1839		– Entered West Point: as a result of an error, he was called Ulysses S. Grant
1846–8		– Served in the Mexican War
1854		– Unhappy with his posting out West, he resigned from the army
1854–61		– Failed in a number of civilian trades; finally became clerk in his father's shop in Galena, Illinois
1861		– Promoted to General thanks to political influence
1862	February–April	– Captured Fort Donelson (page 169)
		– Battle of Shiloh (pages 169–70)
1863	April–July	– Masterminded the capture of Vicksburg (pages 174–5)
	November	– Saved Chattanooga (pages 175–6)
1864	March	– Appointed General-in-Chief
	May–June	– Wilderness–Petersburg campaign
1865		– Received Lee's surrender at Appomatox
1868		– Won presidential election
1872		– Re-elected president
1885		– Died

Contemporaries at the time and historians since have debated what made Grant such a good general.

President Lincoln:

The great thing about Grant ... is his perfect coolness and persistency of purpose. I judge he is not easily excited – which is a great element in an officer.

General Sherman:

I am a damn sight smarter than Grant. I know a great deal more about war, military history, strategy, and administration, and about everything else than he does. But I tell you where he beats me, and where he beats the world. He don't care a damn for what the enemy does out of his sight, but he scares me like hell.

Grant had his own views:

The art of war is simple enough. Find out where your enemy is. Get at him as soon as you can. Strike at him as hard as you can and as often as you can, and keep moving on.

confused, ferocious fighting; twice the losses sustained by Lee. But Grant (unlike Hooker in 1863) had no intention of retreating. Instead he edged southwards, trying to get between Lee and Richmond.

For the next month the opposing armies were never out of contact. Grant's probings were foiled by Lee's skilful defence. On 3 June at Cold Harbour Grant lost 7000 men in just over one hour; Lee lost 1500. In the first 30 days of his offensive, Grant lost 50,000 men; twice as many as Lee. Northern Democrats denounced him as 'Butcher' Grant. But the slogging match had just as great an impact on the Army of Northern Virginia. By June Lee was desperately short of men and many of his best officers were dead or wounded.

Grant threatens Petersburg

Grant's perseverance paid off. On 12 June Union forces crossed the James river, threatening Richmond from the south and almost capturing Petersburg, a crucial railway junction. Luck and inspired resistance from a small force led by General Beauregard saved the day for the Confederacy. Lee, aware that the loss of Petersburg would result in the loss of Richmond, was forced to defend the town. Both sides dug trenches and the siege of Petersburg began. On 30 July the Union army tried to blast a way through the Southern defences, exploding tons of gunpowder below the rebel lines. In the fighting which followed, Union forces got bogged down in the crater created by the explosion and suffered 4500 casualties. The Confederates hung on.

Although Grant had not yet defeated Lee, he had at least forced him onto the defensive and ensured he was no longer able to fight the type of war at which he excelled – a war of manoeuvre. Both Grant and Lee knew that a **war of attrition** favoured the Union.

Key term

War of attrition
A conflict in which each side tries to wear down the other.

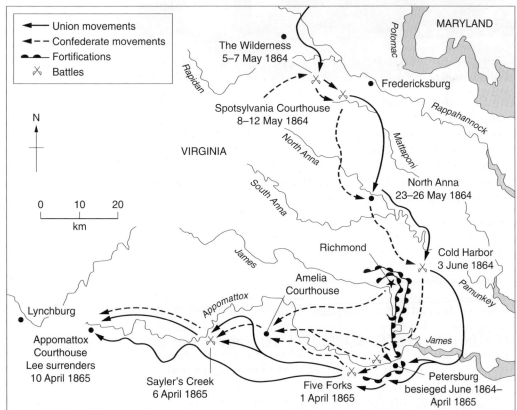

Figure 6.8: The Virginian Campaign 1864–5

General William T. Sherman. Sherman commanded the Union's Western forces in 1864–5.

The Shenandoah Valley

In the autumn of 1864 the Confederacy suffered serious set-backs in the Shenandoah. Sheridan, the new Union commander, chased the Confederates up the valley, winning battles at Winchester and at Cedar Creek.

The Atlanta Campaign

In May 1864 Sherman, with 100,000 men, left Chattanooga and headed towards Atlanta, state capital of Georgia and an important industrial and rail centre. His Confederate opponent, General Johnston, commanded some 70,000 men. Rather than go on the offensive (as Davis wanted), Johnston retreated, taking up strong positions and hoping that Sherman would launch costly frontal offensives. Instead Sherman repeatedly turned Johnston's flank, forcing him back. Sherman did try one frontal attack at Kennesaw Mountain in June but this was a disaster. Thereafter he returned to his flanking manoeuvres.

Johnston seemed impervious to the rising discontent over his continuous retreat. By July Union forces had reached the outskirts of Atlanta. Davis now replaced Johnston with 33-year-old John Bell Hood. Hood, who had lost an arm at Gettysburg

Union Poster 1864. The Republicans called themselves the National Union Party in 1864, hoping to encourage Democrats to vote for Lincoln. What does this source tell you about Republican propaganda?

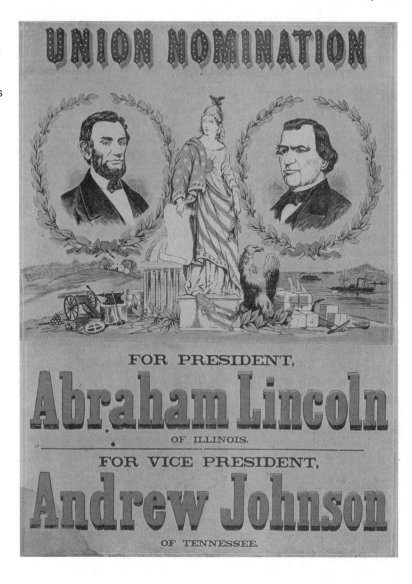

and a leg at Chickamauga, was a brave fighter but had little skill as a commander. 'All lion, none of the fox', was Lee's view, a view that Hood was now to confirm. A series of attacks on Union lines resulted in the loss of 20,000 Confederates. At the end of August, Hood was forced to abandon Atlanta. Its capture was an important boost to Northern morale.

Key date
Sherman captured Atlanta: September 1864

Key question
Why was the slavery issue so difficult for Lincoln in 1861?

The 1864 election
The Confederacy's last (and best) hope was that Lincoln would be defeated in the 1864 election. This hope was a realistic one. In August, with the war going badly, Lincoln said, 'I am going to be beaten and unless some great change takes place, badly beaten.' The Democrat convention, hoping to capitalise on Northern war weariness, called for a negotiated peace, condemned Lincoln's arbitrary measures and pledged to preserve states' rights. However, General McClellan, the Democrat presidential

candidate, would not agree to the peace platform. This meant that his party was in something of a muddle. Its strongest card was accusing Lincoln of plotting '**miscegenation**'.

Lincoln was not popular with all Republicans. Many wanted to nominate General Grant as presidential candidate but he made it clear that he would not stand. Treasury Secretary Chase had presidential ambitions but failed to mount a challenge. John C. Frémont, the 1856 Republican candidate, created his own political party (the Radical Democrats) and threatened to split the Republican vote.

Lincoln was easily renominated at the Republican convention in June. Andrew Johnson of Tennessee was chosen as his running mate. The fact that Johnson was both a Southerner and a War Democrat seemed to strengthen the Republican ticket. The Republican platform endorsed a policy of unconditional surrender and called for the 'utter and complete extirpation of slavery' by means of a constitutional amendment.

Lincoln's problems were not quite over. In August wide cracks appeared between the President and his party over reconstruction policy (see pages 209–11). But with the election only a few weeks away, Republicans rallied round Lincoln.

In September the war turned in Lincoln's favour. Admiral Farragut won an important naval victory at Mobile, Atlanta fell and Sheridan was successful in the Shenandoah. Frémont now withdrew from the race and the election became a straight contest between Lincoln and McClellan. Republicans ridiculed McClellan's military record and did their best to depict the Democrats as at best unpatriotic defeatists and at worst traitors.

> **Miscegenation**
> The blending of the white and black races.
>
> *Key term*

The election results

In November Lincoln won 2,213,645 popular votes (55 per cent of the total) and 212 electoral college votes to McClellan's 1,802,237 votes (45 per cent) and 21 electoral votes. The Republicans increased their majorities in both houses of Congress. Native-born, Protestant Americans remained loyal to Lincoln. Particularly remarkable was the backing Lincoln received from Union troops. Most states enacted provision for soldiers to vote in the field. Those states which blocked this measure failed to stop the soldiers from voting. The War Department allowed whole regiments to return home to vote. Lincoln received 78 per cent of the soldier vote. The election was really a referendum on whether the North should continue fighting. Lincoln's success was the death knell of the Confederacy.

> Lincoln re-elected president: November 1864
>
> *Key date*

Marching through Georgia

In the autumn of 1864 Sherman divided his army. Leaving Thomas to watch Hood, Sherman set off from Atlanta in mid-November with 62,000 men on a march through Georgia to Savannah on the coast. Cutting adrift from supply lines, Sherman's aim was to demoralise the South, destroying both its capacity and its will to fight. Convinced his men could live off the land, he was aware that the Confederacy was not in a position to

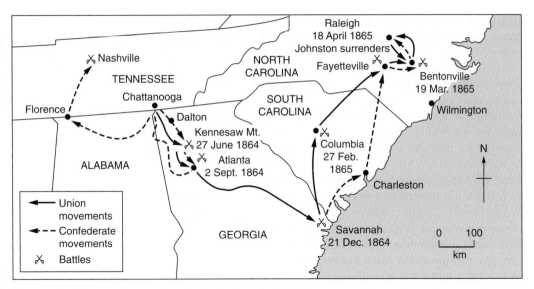

Figure 6.9: Sherman's march through the South 1864–5

mount effective opposition. His march – intended to make
Georgia 'howl' – went much to plan. Leaving a swathe of
destruction some 60 miles wide, Union forces reached and
captured Savannah in mid-December. The 285-mile march
inflicted some $100 million damage on Georgia, crippled much
of the state's railway network, and gave a lie to the Confederate
government's promise of protection for its people.

Nashville

Instead of trying to stop Sherman, Hood invaded Tennessee. His
scheme – to defeat Thomas, reconquer Kentucky and then march
to help Lee – came to nothing. On 30 November Hood ordered a
suicidal assault on Union forces at Franklin. His losses were three
times those of the North. The Union army now pulled back to
Nashville, which Hood 'besieged' for two weeks. Given that Hood
had 23,000 men and Thomas 50,000, it was hard to know who
was besieging whom. Despite pressure from Lincoln, Thomas
(one of the Union's unsung heroes) delayed his counter-attack
until he was fully prepared. When he struck on 15–16 December
he won the most complete victory of the war. The battle of
Nashville effectively destroyed Hood's Army of Tennessee. In
January 1865 Hood resigned what little was left of his command.

Key date

Battle of Nashville:
December 1864

The end of the Confederacy

In his December 1864 address to Congress Lincoln spoke
confidently of victory. Union resources, he said, were unexhausted
and inexhaustible; its military and naval forces were larger than
ever, and its economy was prospering. The Confederacy's
situation, by contrast, was desperate. Its Western armies were in
tatters and Lee's Army of Northern Virginia suffered from mass
desertions as troops received despairing letters from home.

In early February Confederate Vice-President Stephens (with Davis's approval) met Lincoln to see if it was possible to arrange peace. The talks were unproductive. Lincoln was not prepared to compromise on either slavery or disunion and Davis was not prepared to surrender.

Lee, now given overall command of all that was left of the Confederate armies, asked for regiments of slaves to be raised to fight for the Southern cause. In March, the Confederate Congress approved a measure it had previously opposed. It came too late to have any effect. The Confederacy was falling apart. In January 1865 Wilmington, the last major Confederate port, was closed with the Union capture of Fort Fisher. In February Sherman headed north. South Carolina suffered worse deprivation than Georgia. Lee gave Johnston the thankless task of trying to resist Sherman's remorseless march towards Richmond.

Grant did not really need Sherman's army. By March rebel trench lines extended 35 miles around Petersburg and Lee had fewer than 50,000 half-starved troops to man them. Grant had 125,000 men, not counting Sheridan approaching from the north and Sherman approaching from the south. On 1 April Sheridan won a decisive victory at Five Forks. The following day Grant ordered a full-scale assault and the Union army broke through Lee's lines. Lee had no option but to abandon both Petersburg and Richmond. Davis fled. On 3 April Lincoln visited Richmond. He was mobbed by ex-slaves who greeted him as a messiah.

key dates

Fall of Petersburg and Richmond: April 1865

Lee surrendered at Appomattox: April 1865

Confederate surrender

Lee headed westwards, hoping to join up with Johnston's forces. Instead he found himself surrounded by Union forces. On 6 April, he fought his last battle at Sayler's Creek. He achieved nothing, except the loss of 8000 men. On 9 April, he realised, 'There is nothing left for me to do but to go and see General Grant and I would rather die a thousand deaths.'

Lee and Grant met at Appomattox Court House on 10 April. Lee surrendered and Grant was magnanimous in victory: Confederate troops could keep their side arms and horses, and Grant gave the hungry rebels Union army rations. Lee, meeting his troops for the last time, said, 'Boys I have done the best I could for you. Go home now, and if you make as good citizens as you have soldiers, you will do well, and I shall always be proud of you.'

Lee's surrender was the effective end of the war. Davis, fleeing southwards, exhorted the Confederacy to fight on and spoke of a new phase of the struggle. But most Southerners heeded Lee's advice and showed no interest in a guerrilla war. On 16 April Johnston surrendered to Sherman. Davis was captured on 10 May. The last skirmish, fought in Texas on 13 May, was ironically a rebel victory.

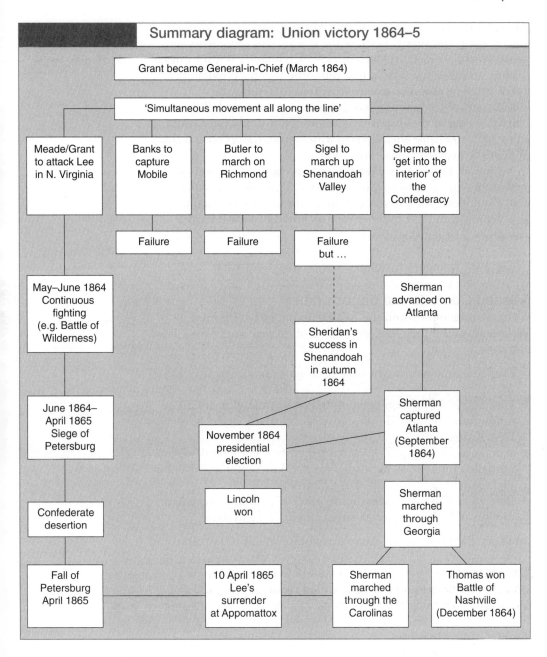

Summary diagram: Union victory 1864–5

Grant became General-in-Chief (March 1864)

'Simultaneous movement all along the line'

| Meade/Grant to attack Lee in N. Virginia | Banks to capture Mobile | Butler to march on Richmond | Sigel to march up Shenandoah Valley | Sherman to 'get into the interior' of the Confederacy |

Failure — Failure — Failure but …

May–June 1864 Continuous fighting (e.g. Battle of Wilderness)

Sherman advanced on Atlanta

Sheridan's success in Shenandoah in autumn 1864

June 1864– April 1865 Siege of Petersburg

November 1864 presidential election

Sherman captured Atlanta (September 1864)

Lincoln won

Sherman marched through Georgia

Confederate desertion

| Fall of Petersburg April 1865 | 10 April 1865 Lee's surrender at Appomattox | Sherman marched through the Carolinas | Thomas won Battle of Nashville (December 1864) |

Key question
Did the Confederacy defeat itself or was it defeated?

7 | Key Debate

On 10 April 1865 Robert E. Lee, having just surrendered to Grant at Appomattox, wrote a farewell address to his soldiers.

> After four years' arduous service, marked by unsurpassed courage and fortitude, the Army of Northern Virginia has been compelled to yield to overwhelming numbers and resources.

According to Lee, the Confederacy lost the war not because it fought badly but simply because the enemy had more men and guns. Historian Richard Current (1960), reviewing the statistics of Union strength – two and a half times the South's population, three times its railway capacity, nine times its industrial production, overwhelming naval supremacy – concluded that 'surely in view of the disparity of resources, it would have taken a miracle ... to enable the South to win. As usual, God was on the side of the heaviest battalions.'

Yet not all historians would accept that the Union's superior resources were the prime cause of Confederate defeat. Many insist that Confederate defeat was due to Confederate mistakes and/or problems within the Confederacy which had little to do with resources. The key question is:

> Did the Confederacy defeat itself or was it defeated?

Missed Confederate opportunities

At many stages events on the battlefield might have gone differently and if they had, the course of the war might have been different.

- Confederate forces might have been more proactive after First Manassas.
- Had Stonewall Jackson been up to par in June–July 1862 Lee might have triumphed even more spectacularly in the Seven Days battles.
- Who knows what would have happened had Lee's battle orders not fallen into Union hands in Maryland in September 1862 or Jackson had not been killed at Chancellorsville.
- Better Confederate leadership in 1863 might have prevented the loss of Vicksburg and brought victory at Gettysburg.

In short, the Confederate cause was not inevitably a 'lost cause'.

Leadership

Superior leadership is often seen as the main reason for Union victory.

Political leadership

Historian David Potter claimed that 'If the Union and Confederacy had exchanged presidents with one another, the Confederacy might have won its independence.' Lincoln is generally seen as more eloquent in expressing war aims, more successful in communicating with the people, more skilful in keeping political factions working together, and better able to endure criticism and work with his critics. He is lauded for appointing the winning military team, for picking able administrative subordinates, and for knowing how to delegate.

Lincoln's superiority to Davis might seem self-evident. Nevertheless, Lee could think of no-one in the South who could have done a better job than Davis. Davis certainly worked hard and did his best to inspire Southerners.

Davis's government is often charged with failing to manage the country's economy and finances efficiently. The main criticism is that it printed too much money. This fuelled inflation, which ravaged the economy and damaged Southern morale. However, given the Union blockade, inflation was inevitable. Despite its economic problems, the Confederacy maintained over three per cent of its population under arms – a higher figure than the North. In terms of the management of military supply, the Confederacy could boast some organisational successes. Ordnance Chief Josiah Gorgas, for example, built an arms industry virtually from scratch. The main problem was the shortage, not the management, of supplies.

Military leadership

The key aspect of leadership in the Civil War, as in any war, was military leadership.

Was the Confederacy too attack-minded?

Many historians claim that Davis and Lee pursued a flawed military strategy. They chose to pursue what has been labelled an 'offensive–defensive' strategy. This consisted of placing conventional armies in an essentially defensive posture to protect as much territory as possible and launching offensive movements when circumstances seemed promising. Lee emphasised the 'offensive' in 'offensive–defensive', seeking to gain and hold the initiative.

Lee's penchant for attack has been criticised. Arguably a more defensive strategy would have conserved manpower, thereby enabling the Confederacy to prolong the war and perhaps exhaust Union will. Historians Grade McWhiney and Perry Jamieson argue that the Confederacy literally bled itself to death in the first three years of the war by making costly attacks and losing its bravest men. Lee is seen as a main culprit. His battles in 1862–3 were certainly costly: from Seven Days to Chancellorsville his army suffered 65,000 casualties.

But would a purely defensive strategy have been more successful? General Joe Johnston was the Confederate exponent of defensive warfare. Rather than stand and fight, he surrendered huge chunks of land virtually without a struggle in North Virginia in 1862 and in Georgia in 1864. This did not enhance Southern morale. Moreover Confederate retreats often led to disastrous sieges and huge surrenders, for example Fort Donelson (1862), Vicksburg (1863) and Atlanta (1864).

In Lee's view, an 'offensive–defensive' strategy was the best hope of winning a decisive, overwhelming military victory. On several occasions he came tantalisingly close to success. When finally forced on the defensive in 1864–5 and deprived of the opportunity to manoeuvre, his defeat was inevitable.

Although Lee has become a target for revisionist historians, most scholars still think he should be held in high regard. Despite being outnumbered in every major campaign, he won victories which depressed Union and bolstered Confederate morale. Without Lee's generalship the Confederacy would have crumbled earlier. If other Confederate generals had fought as well, the war might have had a different outcome.

Should the Confederacy have relied more on guerrilla warfare?

The Confederate leadership has been taken to task for attempting to fight a conventional rather than a guerrilla war. However, a purely guerrilla-style war strategy in 1861 was inconceivable.

- It would have meant the loss of territory (and thus of slaves). This would have alienated most Southerners and seriously damaged Confederate morale.
- Davis hoped to win British and French recognition. Neither country would have recognised a fledgling Confederacy that relied on guerrilla units rather than on a formal army.
- Those who have waged successful guerrilla wars in the past have almost always been dependent on outside support. No such support was available to the Confederacy.

During the war there was considerable Confederate guerrilla activity in Florida, Tennessee, Virginia and Missouri (where it was particularly nasty). However, when Davis called for an all-out guerrilla war in April 1865 there were few takers. Most Southerners recognised that a guerrilla war would simply prolong the misery with little prospect of winning independence.

Did the Confederacy focus too much on Virginia?

Some historians think that Lee's strategic vision was limited to Virginia, where his influence concentrated Confederate resources at the expense of the West. The result was that the Confederacy lost the West, and thus lost the war.

Such criticism is unfounded. Lee was commander of the Army of Northern Virginia; Virginia was thus his rightful priority. If anyone was to blame for a Virginia-focused strategy it was Davis. In fairness to Davis, it seems highly unlikely that the Confederacy could have won the war by concentrating most of its forces in the West, where military conditions, especially control of the major rivers, favoured the Union. Virginia, the South's most important industrial state, had to be defended. In Virginia geographical conditions favoured the defender. It thus made sense to give most resources to the best army (the Army of Northern Virginia) and the best general (Lee).

Indeed Davis might be criticised not so much for his pre-occupation with Virginia, but instead for dividing scarce resources more or less equally between East and West. However, Davis knew that the Confederacy could not survive long without both Virginia and the West. He had to try and hold both, with limited manpower and limited talent.

How inept were the Confederacy's Western commanders?

Many of the Confederacy's problems in the West stemmed from its poor commanders. The first overall Western commander, Albert Johnston, let Union forces break through the Tennessee and Cumberland river defence line in early 1862. Beauregard made plans not based on realities. Bragg quarrelled with everyone and had a poor record. Joe Johnston always had one eye fixed on retreat. Hood was a disaster. However, in fairness to the rebel generals, their armies were under-resourced and they had major problems of supply.

How skilful were Union generals?

The Union did finally find the winning team of Grant and Sherman. Grant, often regarded as the war's greatest soldier, displayed his talent when capturing Fort Donelson (1862) and Vicksburg (1863). He became overall Union commander in March 1864. According to his supporters, he had a concept of the total-war strategy necessary to win the conflict, the skill to carry out that strategy, and the determination to keep pressing it despite the high cost in casualties.

Historians have also sung the praises of Sherman. His capture of Atlanta and his marches through Georgia and the Carolinas, reaching parts of the Confederacy that the Confederate government thought could not be reached, weakened the South logistically and psychologically.

However, the Union army had more than its fair share of blunderers. Inept Union leadership, on several occasions, gave the Confederacy a chance of victory.

Moreover, Grant and Sherman were far from supermen. Their 1864–5 campaigns were won mainly because their forces were larger and better equipped than those of the enemy.

Confederate will

Today, many scholars insist that the Confederacy could have won if its people had possessed the will to make the necessary sacrifices.

Lack of nationalism?

Some scholars (for example, Beringer, Hattaway and Still) claim that the Confederacy did not generate a strong sense of nationalism. Thus, when the going got tough, Southerners found it tough to keep going. If the nationalist spirit had been strong enough, the argument goes, Southerners would have waged a savage guerrilla war after April 1865.

The lack of nationalism argument, however, is not convincing. The strength of patriotic feeling in 1861 produced 500,000 volunteers for military service. Confederate politicians, clergymen and newspaper editors, invoking memories of 1776, did their utmost to create a sense of nationalism. The war, by creating both a unifying hatred of the enemy and a new set of heroes, strengthened Confederate nationalism. So did military service.

James McPherson found evidence of very strong patriotism in the letters of Southern soldiers. Most soldiers faithfully discharged their duty.

Historian Gary Gallagher suggests that the most nationalistic Southerners were young officers. They had few, if any, doubts about slavery, attributed base motives to Northerners in general and Republicans in particular, and supported secession. Their personal example in combat inspired their men and their achievements helped to nourish patriotism and resolve among civilians.

Far from explaining Confederate defeat, nationalism helps to explain why Southerners fought as long as they did. Northerners almost threw in the towel in the summer of 1864 when they suffered casualty rates that Southerners had endured for more than two years. The Confederacy's death toll was far greater than France's in the Franco-Prussian War (1870–1). Nobody suggests that Frenchmen in 1870 did not have a strong sense of national identity. Yet France lost, defeated by the stronger and more military adept Prussians. Nationalism is not a magic shield ensuring invulnerability to those who possess it.

Religious doubts?

Given so much death and destruction, some Southerners began to wonder if God was really on their side. Did these doubts help to corrode morale? It seems unlikely. Southern Church leaders supported the Confederate cause until the bitter end. During the war a great religious revival movement swept through the Confederate armies. Many men were convinced that God was testing the new nation and that out of suffering would come victory. Rather than explaining defeat, religion played a vital role in sustaining Southern will.

Slavery qualms?

The notion that many Southerners felt moral qualms about slavery, which undermined their will to fight to preserve it, is unconvincing. All the evidence suggests that most Southerners went to war to preserve slavery and remained committed to it to the end.

Divisions within the Confederacy?

Recent scholarship has stressed that many groups within the South became disenchanted as the war progressed. Two-thirds of the Confederacy's white population were non-slaveholders who may have come to resent risking their lives and property to defend slavery. Some of them had opposed secession in 1861. Others became alienated as a result of hardship during the war. However, McPherson found little if any evidence of class division in the letters of Southern soldiers. Many non-slaveholders were ready to fight and die for the Confederacy from start to finish.

Confederate women?

'Historians have wondered in recent years why the Confederacy did not endure longer', wrote historian Drew Gilpin Faust: 'In considerable measure … it was because so many women did not want it to. It may well have been because of its women that the South lost the Civil War.' Severe hardship on the home front, Faust claims, led to a growth of defeatism which was conveyed by uncensored letters to Southern soldiers. Women told their men to put family before national loyalty.

In reality, however, many Southern women remained loyal to the end, exhorting their men to stay at the front and fight. Increased privation, the experience of living under Federal occupation, and the loss of loved ones often reinforced rather than eroded loyalty to the Confederacy.

The strength of Confederate will

Even in 1864–5, letters, diaries and newspapers reveal a tenacious popular will rooted in a sense of national community. 'The devils seem to have a determination that cannot but be admired', wrote Sherman in March 1864. 'No amount of poverty or adversity seems to shake their faith – niggers gone, wealth and luxury gone, money worthless, starvation in view within a period of two or three years, are causes enough to make the bravest tremble, yet I see no sign of let up – some few deserters – plenty tired of war, but the masses determined to fight it out.'

What is remarkable about the Confederacy is not its internal weaknesses but its staying power and the huge sacrifices that so many of its people made. The most sobering statistic is that half of the Confederacy's soldiers were killed or seriously wounded.

The strength of Union will

Historians have tended to examine why Southern will collapsed rather than ask the equally important question: why did Northern will hold? It is often said that the Confederacy had no chance in a war of attrition. In fact a war of attrition was the best chance it had. To win, the Confederacy had to wear down Northern will: a long, bloody war was the best way to do this. The war was long and bloody but Northern will endured. Civilian morale was helped by the fact that for many Northerners life during the war went on much the same as usual. Northern losses were (relatively) less than those sustained by Southerners. The North was never seriously invaded and many Northerners experienced increased prosperity during the war. But ultimately Northern, like Southern, will, was crucially affected by the outcome of campaigns and battles. The morale of Northern troops was particularly crucial. In 1864 80 per cent of Union soldiers voted for Lincoln, proof that soldier morale still held strong. Union victories from mid-1863 onwards undoubtedly helped to sustain that morale.

Robert E. Lee and Confederate morale

As the war progressed, Lee and his Army of Northern Virginia embodied the Confederacy in the minds of most Southerners. His success sustained Southern hopes. Contemporaries understood the importance of military events to national morale and, by extension, to the outcome of the war. In March 1865 Lincoln spoke of the 'progress of our arms, upon which all else chiefly depends'. But for victories at Atlanta and in the Shenandoah Valley, Lincoln might well have lost the 1864 election. The symbolic importance of the Army of Northern Virginia was such that few Southerners contemplated serious resistance after Lee's surrender at Appomattox, despite the fact that he surrendered only a fraction of Southerners under arms in April 1865.

Conclusion

When asked some years afterwards why the Confederates lost at Gettysburg, General Pickett replied, 'I think the Yankees had something to do with it.' The Yankees also explain why the Confederacy lost the war. The Union defeated the Confederacy; the Confederacy did not defeat itself.

The Confederacy surrendered in 1865 because Union armies had demonstrated their ability to crush Southern military resistance. Defeat caused defeatism, not vice versa. A people whose armies are beaten, railways wrecked, cities burned, countryside occupied and crops laid waste, lose their will – and ability – to continue fighting. In war 'big battalions' do normally triumph. The Civil War was to be no exception. Unable to fight a perfect war, the stubborn Confederacy finally fell before the enemy's superior resources. The final epitaph of the Confederacy should be 'Expired after a brave (but foolish) fight.'

Some key books in the debate

Richard E. Beringer, Herman Hattaway and William N. Still, *Why the South Lost the Civil War* (University of Georgia Press, 1986).
David Donald (ed.), *Why the North Won the Civil War* (Collier, 1960).
Gary W. Gallagher, *The Confederate War* (Harvard UP, 1997).
James. M. MacPherson, *Battle Cry of Freedom* (Penguin, 1988).

Study Guide: AS Questions

In the style of OCR

(a) Assess the reasons why the Union failed to win the Civil War by 1863. (30 marks)

(b) How successful were Confederate military forces from 1861 to 1863? (70 marks)

Exam tips

The cross-references are intended to take you straight to the material that will help you to answer the questions.

(a) The golden rule for writing essays is simple: answer the set question. Do not simply write a narrative account of all that happened in the war between 1861 and 1863. Instead, and as a general rule, go for development of a few key themes rather than breadth of coverage. You will need to evaluate some of the following factors:

- Union strengths – and expectations (pages 146–7).
- Confederate strengths, which helped to counter Union expectations (pages 147–9).
- Confederate success at Manassas (pages 161–2).
- Union success in the first part of 1862 (pages 162–5).
- The leadership of Robert E. Lee in 1862–3 (pages 165–74).
- The situation in late 1863 (page 176).

Remember you need to reach a balanced conclusion, which should draw together the threads of your argument. You should not spring a new idea (that you have just thought of) on the reader. Do not be afraid to give your view, but try not to use phrases such as 'I think'. This does not sound very authoritative. It is better style to write 'the evidence suggests' or 'it seems likely that'.

(b) This is a standard evaluative question requiring a clear and balanced judgement. Remember that your first paragraph – or introduction – is crucial. It is the first opportunity for you to impress or depress an examiner. There is no perfect way of writing an introduction, but you should certainly be identifying key issues which you will go on to develop. Ideally you should establish criteria against which the Confederate military forces will be judged (for example, against aims or against results). Did Confederate forces fight better or worse than might have been expected? Thanks to Robert E. Lee, they certainly achieved some success in Virginia. However, Lee was not a superman: Gettysburg was proof of that. And Lee's victories were often costly.

Confederate forces did less well elsewhere. Indeed by late 1863, the Confederacy had lost a string of important towns, forts and battles in the West – and also lost control of the Mississippi. Could Confederate forces have done better out West? Who – or what – was responsible for their failure?

Study Guide: A2 Question

In the style of Edexcel

Source 1

From: Stanley Lebergott, Why the South Lost: Commercial Purpose in the Confederacy, 1861–5, *1983.*

Given Southern unwillingness to be taxed or to pay taxes due, and given planter unwillingness to support Confederate war bonds, the Confederacy was left with only one policy – impressments*. This led to the hiding of the very items necessary for continuing the war: cotton, wheat, horses and mules.

From that came shortages for the armies and the cities. However, impressments did more than restrict the supply of material for battle and block food to both the army and civilians. It increased desertion from the army, further increasing the likelihood of military defeat. By late 1864, about half the Confederate soldiers were absent from the ranks as they returned to their farms to support their destitute families.

[*impressments: the requisitioning and confiscation of essential materials]

Source 2

From: Alan Farmer, The American Civil War 1861–65, *2002.*

The strength of patriotic feeling in 1861 produced 500,000 volunteers for the Confederate army. After 1861, Confederate politicians, clergymen and newspaper editors all did their best to create a sense of nationalism and the war further strengthened this. It created an intense and unifying hatred of the Yankee.

Hatred and a desire for revenge seems to have been a consuming passion for many southern soldiers. But hostility to the North was not the only reason why Southerners fought. Many soldiers believed they were fighting for liberty and constitutional rights, principles for which they were ready to die.

However, a people whose armies are beaten, railways wrecked, factories and cities burnt, countryside occupied and crops laid waste, quite naturally lose their will to continue fighting because they have lost the means to do so. By 1865 the Confederacy had lost its will for sacrifice; some 97,000 Confederate soldiers were killed and thousands wounded. But primarily it was military defeat which caused defeatism and the victory for the North.

Source: Edexcel GCE in History © Edexcel Limited 2007 Sample Assessment Materials

Use Sources 1 and 2 and your own knowledge.
How far do you agree that resistance to taxation in the South was the main factor in explaining its defeat in the Civil War? Explain your answer, using the evidence of Sources 1 and 2 and your own knowledge of the issues related to this controversy.   (40 marks)

Exam tips

The cross-references are intended to take you straight to the material that will help you to answer the question.

Source 1 shows the Southern unwillingness to pay taxes or to support Confederate war bonds. Use your own knowledge together with the source to explore the implications of this for the South's defeat. You should expand on the problems brought about by impressments. These are well developed in the source itself: the hiding of the very items necessary for the war, shortages for the armies and cities. Note, too, that Lebergott links the increase in desertion directly to it as well.

You have material in Source 2 from which to develop a counter-argument. Note here the emphasis on military defeat and loss of will to continue the fight because they 'had lost the means to do so'. Note, however, the areas of agreement within the sources: both provide evidence of demoralisation within Southern forces (how do they do this?).

Your own knowledge of the military roles of Robert E. Lee, Grant and Sherman, the significance of the naval blockade and the North's industrial strength can be added as you explore how significant the resistance to taxation was in explaining the South's defeat. You should consider the advantages possessed by the South initially (pages 147–9) and show the factors which nevertheless enabled the Union forces to succeed (pages 146–7 and 186–92).

You should also look back to Chapter 5 for additional information on Confederate problems in financing the war and its economic problems (pages 120–4) and demoralisation (pages 126–7).

7 Reconstruction

POINTS TO CONSIDER

In 1861 Frederick Douglass predicted, 'The American people and the government of Washington may refuse to recognise it for a time but the inexorable logic of events will force it upon them in the end; that the war now being waged in this land is a war for and against slavery.' Douglass's prediction proved correct. By 1865 American slaves had been freed. The impact of emancipation was one of the problems of Reconstruction – the process of restoring the 11 Confederate states to the Union. How successful was Reconstruction? What impact did Reconstruction – and indeed the Civil War – have on the USA as a whole? In examining these issues, this chapter will focus on:

- The emancipation of the slaves
- The African American war effort
- The problem of Reconstruction
- Reconstruction in the South 1867–77
- The impact of the Civil War

Key dates

1861	July	Crittenden Resolution
	August	First Confiscation Act
1862	July	Second Confiscation Act
	September	Emancipation Proclamation
1863	January	Emancipation Proclamation came into effect
	December	Lincoln's 10 per cent plan
1864		Wade–Davis bill
1865	April	Lincoln assassinated. Andrew Johnson became president
	December	13th Amendment added to the Constitution
1866		Civil Rights Act
1867		Military Reconstruction Act
1868	July	14th Amendment added to the Constitution
	November	Ulysses S. Grant elected president
1870		15th Amendment added to the Constitution
1876		Disputed presidential election
1877		Rutherford B. Hayes inaugurated president

1 | The Emancipation of the Slaves

Key question
Why was the slavery issue so difficult for Lincoln in 1861?

Key terms

Emancipation
The act of setting free from bondage.

Contraband of war
Goods which can be confiscated from the enemy.

In 1861 Lincoln was determined to maintain Northern unity. An avowed policy of **emancipation** of the slaves would alienate not only Northern Democrats, but also the four Union slave states (Kentucky, Maryland, Missouri and Delaware), which together had about 400,000 slaves. It would also spur Southerners to an even greater effort and leave no possibility of a compromise peace.

In April 1861, Lincoln declared, 'I have no purpose, directly or indirectly, to interfere with the institution of slavery in the states where it exists. I believe I have no lawful right to do so, and I have no inclination to do so.' Congress supported this stance. In July the Crittenden Resolution, which disclaimed any intention of meddling with 'the rights or established institutions' of the South, won overwhelming approval in Congress.

'Contraband'

A set of forces placed pressure on the federal government to take some action with regard to emancipation. One problem was what to do with refugee slaves who came to the camps of Union armies occupying parts of the South. By the letter of the Fugitive Slave Act (see page 47), they should have been returned to their owners. Some Union soldiers did just that. Others, on both humane and pragmatic grounds – the slaves would be punished and could also help the rebel war effort – opposed such action.

Key dates

Crittenden Resolution: July 1861

First Confiscation Act: August 1861

In May 1861 General Benjamin Butler declared that slaves who came to his camp were to be confiscated as '**contraband of war**', thus ensuring they were not returned to their Confederate owners. This neatly avoided the question of whether or not the fugitives were free and turned the Southerners' argument that

A family of former slaves outside their ramshackle house in Virginia in 1862.

slaves were property against them. Butler's action was supported by the terms of the Confiscation Act (August 1861) which threatened any property used 'for insurrectionary purposes' with confiscation. It left unsettled the issue of whether or not 'confiscated' slaves became free.

Radical Republicans

As the months went by and it became clear that there was little likelihood of the Confederate states being enticed back into the Union, radical Republicans began to make their influence felt. To most radicals it seemed that to fight slaveholders without fighting slavery, was (in Frederick Douglass's words) 'a half-hearted business'. Radicals wanted to abolish slavery and create a new order in the South. They had a variety of motives:

- Some, but not all, were genuinely concerned for black Americans.
- Most, if not all, had a loathing of slaveholders who they blamed for causing the war.
- All were concerned that if the Union was restored without slavery being abolished, nothing would have been solved.
- If emancipation became a Union war aim there was little chance that Britain would support the Confederacy (see page 138–42). 'It is often said that war will make an end of slavery', said Charles Sumner in October 1861. 'This is probable. But it is surer still that the overthrow of slavery will make an end of the war.'

By December 1861 most Republicans supported a tougher stand against slavery. The House of Representatives now refused to reaffirm Crittenden's resolution. To one Congressman it seemed a powerful faction was already forming whose watchword was 'Emancipation – the utter extinction of slavery.'

Lincoln's views in 1861

In August 1861 General Frémont, the 1856 Republican presidential candidate and now Union commander in Missouri, issued a proclamation freeing the slaves of all Confederate supporters in Missouri. In Lincoln's view this was a step too far and he ordered that Frémont rescind his order. When Frémont refused, Lincoln removed him from his Missouri command.

Radicals implored Lincoln to declare his support for emancipation. He remained hesitant. He referred to men like Sumner as the conscience of his party and shared the radical conviction that slavery was a moral evil. However, he still had no wish to alienate Northern Democrats or the Union slave states, and feared that if emancipation became a Union war aim, the conflict would degenerate into a 'violent and remorseless struggle'. 'We didn't go to war to put down slavery – but to put the flag back', declared Lincoln in December 1861: '... the thunderbolt will keep.'

Key date

Second Confiscation Act: July 1862

Key term

Colonisation
The movement of people to a different country or area, which they then take over.

Congressional measures in 1862

In the spring of 1862 Congress began to take action against slavery. In April slavery in Washington was abolished: provision was made to compensate slave owners and to support the **colonisation** of ex-slaves to Liberia or Haiti. In June, Congress, voting on straight party lines, abolished slavery in all federal territories. In July a second and much more sweeping Confiscation Act was enacted. This allowed the seizure of all enemy 'property': slaves in such cases were to be set 'forever free'. Lincoln also received authority to employ 'persons of African descent' in any capacity deemed necessary for the suppression of the rebellion. As a sweetener to Lincoln, Congress again set aside $500,000 for colonisation expenses.

The Confiscation Act met with considerable resistance in Congress. Some thought it went too far. Others thought it didn't go far enough and were disappointed that the measure proposed to do nothing about slavery in the Union slave states. Lincoln had doubts about the bill, but in the end signed it. In fact, the second Confiscation Act was not as radical as it seemed. The only way that a slave could actually gain freedom was on a case-by-case basis before a federal court: this court had to find that the slave owner was, in fact, a rebel.

Key question
Why did Lincoln's views change in 1862?

Lincoln's views: spring/summer 1862

In July 1862 abolitionist William Lloyd Garrison described Lincoln's handling of the slavery issue as, 'stumbling, halting, prevaricating, irresolute, weak, besotted'. At best Lincoln had followed Northern opinion: others – Congressmen and army officers – had led it. However, by mid-1862, Lincoln, certain that it was his responsibility to make the final decision on the emancipation issue, was convinced that a bold step was necessary.

Even before the summer of 1862 Lincoln had begun to take action. In March 1862 he sent Congress a request that compensation be given to any state which adopted the principle of gradual abolition of slavery. Owners would be given $400 for every slave freed. He hoped that the Union slave states would adopt their own emancipation laws and that some of the rebel states might then follow suit. Abolitionists denounced Lincoln's measure, arguing that justice would be better served by compensating the slaves for their long years in bondage rather than by indemnifying slaveholders. Nevertheless, Congress approved the scheme for gradual compensated emancipation. However, to Lincoln's chagrin, the Union slave states refused to implement emancipation on any terms.

Thwarted in the North, Lincoln determined to act in the South. The situation had changed since 1861. The allegiance of Kentucky, Maryland and Missouri was now secure. He was aware of the pressure from radical Republicans and reluctant to alienate them. Lincoln was also concerned that if the Union won, and the Southern states re-entered the Union with slavery untouched, it would remain a source of future strife. His main belief, however, was that a bold statement on emancipation would weaken the Confederacy.

In July 1862 Lincoln presented his Emancipation Proclamation to his cabinet. Many of its members greeted the news with astonishment. 'The measure goes beyond anything I have recommended', said Stanton. All except Blair – who feared that the Proclamation would harm Republican chances in the autumn mid-term elections – approved. However, Seward recommended that it should only be issued after a military success; otherwise it would seem like an act of desperation born of weakness. Lincoln accepted the logic of this and waited patiently.

When Horace Greeley wrote a bitter editorial criticising him for not doing more on the slavery front, Lincoln still did not reveal his intentions. He responded to Greeley by saying, 'If I could save the Union without freeing any slave I would do so and if I could save it by freeing all the slaves I would do it; and if I could save it by freeing some and leaving others alone I would also do that.'

The Emancipation Proclamation

The Proclamation was issued on 22 September 1862 after the battle of Antietam (see page 167). Justified by Lincoln as 'a fit and necessary war measure', it seemed, on the surface, to be cautious.

- Slavery was to be left untouched in states that returned to the Union before 1 January 1863.
- Thereafter all slaves in enemy territory conquered by Union armies would be 'forever free'.

Thus, the Proclamation had no effect whatsoever in the Union slave states. It did not even affect slavery in those areas that had already been brought back under Union control. British Prime Minister Palmerston was unimpressed: 'It is not easy to estimate how utterly powerless and contemptible a government must have become which could sanction such trash.' The London *Spectator* said that the principle behind the proclamation seemed to be, 'not that a human being cannot justly own another, but that he cannot own him unless he is loyal to the United States'.

Nevertheless, most abolitionists were delighted. 'God bless Abraham Lincoln', wrote Greeley. 'Thank God, the skies are brighter and the air is purer, now that slavery has been handed over to judgement', said Sumner. Radical Republicans appreciated that Lincoln had gone as far as his powers allowed in making the war a war to end slavery. (Many British commentators misunderstood Lincoln's constitutional powers and the fact that he had no power to act against slavery in areas loyal to the USA unless this could be seen as essential to the Union war effort.) As Union forces advanced, slavery in the Confederacy would end – and once it ended there it could not survive in the border states. According to historian Richard Ransom, 'with the stroke of a pen, the president had turned the war into a revolution'.

Key question
How significant was the Emancipation Proclamation?

Emancipation Proclamation: September 1862

Emancipation Proclamation came into effect: January 1863

Key dates

Opposition to the Proclamation

Northern Democrats, convinced that the Proclamation would
make it impossible to bring the Confederate states back into the
Union, denounced the measure. Aware of the fear of a migration
of ex-slaves northwards, Democrats made emancipation a central
issue in the mid-term elections in autumn 1862.

Historians once claimed that these elections were a triumph for
the Democrats, and thus proof that most Northerners were
opposed to emancipation. The Republicans lost control of several
states, and also lost 35 Congressional seats. Lincoln
acknowledged that his Proclamation contributed to the setbacks.
However, on closer analysis, the election results suggest that
emancipation had less impact than Lincoln believed. Overall the
Republicans retained control of most states and easily kept control
of Congress. Democrat majorities in Pennsylvania, Ohio, New
York and Indiana were very small and could be explained by the
inability of Republican-supporting soldiers to vote. The
Republicans actually suffered the smallest net loss of a party in
power for 20 years.

The impact of the Emancipation Proclamation

On 1 January 1863 Lincoln proclaimed that the freedom of all
slaves in rebellious regions was now a Union war aim – 'an act of
justice' as well as 'military necessity'. Not wishing to be held
responsible for a bloody slave revolt, he urged slaves 'to abstain
from all violence, unless in necessary self-defence'. At the same
time, he called on Union forces to protect the rights of those they
made free.

Davis condemned the Proclamation as 'the most execrable
measure recorded in the history of guilty man'. In the short term
it may well have helped to stiffen Confederate resistance.
However, in the long term it weakened the Confederacy who now
stood little chance of winning British support. By encouraging
slaves to flee to Union lines the Proclamation worsened the
South's manpower shortage. As Lincoln said: 'Freedom has given
us the control of 200,000 able-bodied men … It will give us more
yet. Just so much has it subtracted from the strength of our
enemies.'

The 13th Amendment

The Emancipation Proclamation was a war measure that
would have questionable force once the war ended. Consequently,
the Republicans determined to pass a constitutional
amendment prohibiting slavery. The Senate passed the
amendment in 1864 but it failed to get the necessary two-thirds
support in the House.

In June 1864 the Republican national convention, urged on
by Lincoln, agreed to endorse the constitutional amendment to
end slavery. Interpreting Republican election success in
November (see page 182) as public support for the amendment,
Lincoln redoubled his efforts to secure Congressional approval,

applying patronage pressure to several Democrats in the House – to good effect. On 31 January 1865 the House approved (with three votes to spare) the 13th Amendment for ratification by the states.

Thirteenth Amendment added to the Constitution: December 1865

Key date

Lincoln was delighted. It was, he said, 'a king's cure for all the evils. It winds the whole thing up.' It hardly did that, but it was a major step forward.

The Great Emancipator?

From January 1863 Union soldiers fought for the revolutionary goal of a new Union without slavery. Many – but by no means all – Northerners came to accept this. Most would not have accepted it in 1861. During the war opinion changed. Lincoln's policies reflected and influenced that change. He moved cautiously, his actions based more on pragmatism than on morality. From start to finish his main aim was to preserve the Union, not free the slaves. But by mid-1862 Lincoln believed that the two issues had become nearly one and the same. By freeing the slaves he could help to preserve the Union.

Key question
Was Lincoln the 'Great Emancipator'?

Some scholars have claimed that Lincoln did his best to evade the whole question of black freedom and that it was escaping slaves who forced him to embrace emancipation. However, the argument that the slaves freed themselves has been pushed too far. Only Union victory brought slavery to an end. Ultimately slaves were freed by the Union army. Lincoln was commander-in-chief of that army. The fact that he was also committed to freeing the slaves was crucial.

By 1865 many abolitionists were prepared to give credit where credit was due. In 1865 Garrison (who had castigated Lincoln for being a 'wet rag' in 1862) commended him for having done a 'mighty work for the freedom of millions ... I have the utmost faith in the benevolence of your heart, the purity of your motives and the integrity of your spirit.' Frederick Douglass commented: 'Viewed from the genuine abolition ground, Mr Lincoln seemed tardy, cold, dull and indifferent; but measuring him by the sentiment of his country, a sentiment he was bound as a statesman to consult, he was swift, zealous, radical and determined.'

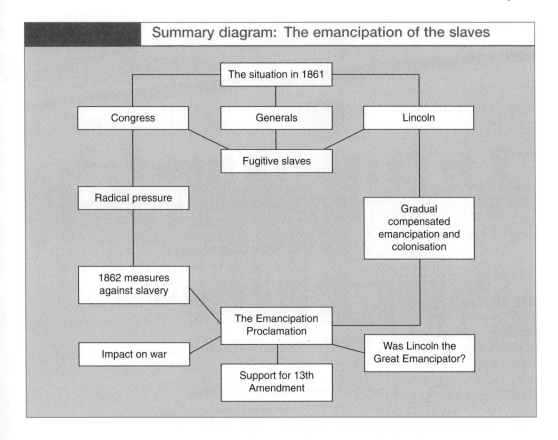

Summary diagram: The emancipation of the slaves

2 | The African American War Effort

The recruitment of black soldiers

Key question
Why were black
soldiers not recruited
until 1862–3?

From the start of the war Lincoln had faced strong and
conflicting pressure on the question of whether to enlist blacks in
the Union army. Initially, most Northerners, hating the notion of
blacks fighting against whites, opposed black recruitment. Black
leaders and abolitionists, however, were anxious that blacks
should fight in a war that was likely to destroy slavery. Pointing
out that blacks were serving in the Union navy, they pushed for
similar enlistment of black soldiers. 'This is no time to fight with
one hand, when both are needed', declared Douglass: 'this is no
time to fight with your white hand and allow your black hand to
remain tied'.

Lincoln, anxious to preserve Northern unity, initially stood firm
against black recruitment. This did not prevent some attempts to
recruit black soldiers. General Hunter, for example, raised a
regiment of black volunteers on the Sea Islands off the coast of
South Carolina in early 1862. Receiving no financial support from
the War Department, Hunter was forced to disband his regiment.
The July 1862 Confiscation Act gave Lincoln the power to use
ex-slaves as a military force but he interpreted this narrowly,
insisting that blacks should simply be employed as army
labourers, not front-line troops.

Company E of the Fourth Coloured Infantry photographed in 1865.

Others in Lincoln's cabinet felt differently. In August 1862 Secretary of War Stanton authorised the creation of a regiment of 5000 black troops to be recruited in Union-occupied areas of Louisiana. Lincoln did not object, and in September the first official regiment of blacks was mustered into Union service. After the Emancipation Proclamation, Lincoln's resistance abated and there was a large influx of blacks into the Union army. As in so many respects Lincoln was in tune with Northern opinion. Given the mounting casualty lists there was far more support for black soldiers than there had been in 1861.

Of the 46,000 free blacks of military age in the North, 33,000 joined the Union armies. Most black troops, however, were ex-slaves. Some 100,000 were recruited from the Confederacy. Another 42,000 slaves from Kentucky, Delaware, Maryland and Missouri also enlisted. (This was the swiftest way for border state slaves to get their freedom.) In June 1863 black troops acquitted themselves well at Milliken's Bend, Louisiana. In July the black 54th Massachusetts regiment suffered 40 per cent casualties in an assault on Fort Wagner. Many black regiments took part in the 1864–5 fighting around Petersburg. They fought as well as the white regiments.

Racial discrimination in the Union army
Within the Union army there was considerable racial discrimination. Regiments were strictly segregated. Black regiments were invariably commanded by white officers. By 1865

scarcely 100 black soldiers had become officers. Black regiments often received inferior supplies and equipment. What rankled most, however, was the fact that white privates received $13 a month while blacks were only paid $10. In November 1863 some black troops protested about their unequal pay. This protest was seen as 'mutiny' and the sergeant leading it was executed.

Although Stanton was sympathetic to black claims for equal treatment, Lincoln was not convinced. Blacks, he thought, had 'larger motives for being soldiers than white men … they ought to be willing to enter the service upon any condition'. In June 1864, however, Congress at last provided equal pay for black soldiers.

Black troops were in greater danger than whites if they were taken prisoner. Some rebels boasted that they took no black prisoners and there were occasions when black troops were killed as they tried to surrender (for example, at Fort Pillow in 1864). More often, black prisoners were returned to slavery. Given that the Confederacy was not prepared to exchange black soldiers Lincoln stopped all prisoner-of-war exchanges in 1863.

The significance of black participation

Key question
How significant was the black contribution to the war?

The fact that blacks had fought for freedom bolstered black confidence and pride. Military service also carried with it an assumption of US citizenship. Douglass commented: 'Once let the black man get upon his person the brass letters US, let him get an eagle on his buttons and musket on his shoulder ... and there is no power on earth which can deny that he has earned the right to citizenship in the USA.'

The impact of black soldiers on the outcome of the war should not be exaggerated. Of the 37,000 black soldiers who died, only 3000 were killed in combat; the vast majority died of disease. Nevertheless, black troops did help the Union war effort at a critical time when Northern whites were increasingly reluctant to fight. In September 1864 Lincoln wrote: 'Any different policy in regard to the coloured man [than black recruitment] deprives us of his help and this is more than we can bear ... This is not a question of sentiment or taste, but one of physical force which can be measured and estimated as [can] horse power and steam power ... Keep it up and you can save the Union. Throw it away and the Union goes with it.' By 1865 there were nearly as many black soldiers in arms against the Confederacy as there were white soldiers defending it.

Freed slaves in the South

As the war progressed, the Union army occupied large parts of the South. Some land was confiscated, but far more came into federal hands because Southerners had not paid their taxes or had simply abandoned their property. What to do with this land, coupled with the organisation of its black labour, became points of conflict as ex-slaves, former slaveholders, military commanders and Northern businessmen and reformers all sought in various ways to influence the transition to free labour. There was little agreement on the critical issue: would confiscated and abandoned land be sold or otherwise distributed to freedmen?

Given no firm presidential or Congressional guidance, the situation in the reoccupied areas of the Confederacy was chaotic, varying from place to place and from time to time. Federal agents in the South, especially army officers, instituted their own remedies. The most famous 'rehearsal for **Reconstruction**' occurred on the Sea Islands (off South Carolina), occupied by Union forces in November 1861. Blacks, who pooled their meagre resources, were able to buy plots of land. This well-publicised (albeit small-scale) development was not typical. In most occupied areas plantations were administered by 'superintendents of Negro affairs' or leased to Northern investors whose main purpose was monetary profit. Some plantations were still controlled by former slaveholders who were prepared to take an oath of allegiance to the Union.

Reconstruction
The process of restoring the seceded states to the Union.

Key term

In these circumstances life for most ex-slaves did not change very much. They continued to work on the same plantations, closely supervised by white managers. While they were now paid wages, most of the money earned was withheld to pay for food and clothing, and they were forbidden to leave the land on which they worked without permission. But at least they were no longer whipped and there were often incentives for those who worked hard.

Colonisation schemes

Fearing that blacks and whites could not live peacefully together and that blacks would never be afforded equal opportunities, Lincoln still supported the idea of colonising ex-slaves in the Caribbean or Latin America. Several attempts were made to put colonisation schemes into effect. All floundered, largely because few blacks agreed to participate. Most thought they had as much right to stay in the country of their birth as whites. (Only one per cent of black Americans in 1860 had been born abroad.) The failure of pilot colonisation schemes and the sterling service of blacks in the Union army convinced Lincoln that he must change policy.

The situation in 1865

- In January 1865 General Sherman declared that freed slaves should receive 40 acres of land and a surplus mule. Sherman was far from a humanitarian reformer: his main concern was to relieve the pressure caused by the large number of impoverished blacks following his army (see page 182–4). He stressed that Congress would have to agree to his plan. Nevertheless, his actions raised black hopes and expectations.

- By 1865 most Republican Congressmen favoured confiscating plantation land and redistributing it among freedmen and loyal whites. Such action would reward the deserving and punish the guilty. However, unable to agree on a precise measure, Congress failed to pass a redistribution bill.

Key question
How much had been done to help blacks by 1865?

- While some Northerners were anxious to help the ex-slaves, few believed that blacks were equal to whites. Indeed many Northerners still had a real antipathy to blacks and feared an exodus of ex-slaves to the North.
- Most border state whites had no wish to give blacks equal rights. Although Missouri and Maryland freed their slaves in 1864, Kentucky still had 65,000 blacks in bondage in April 1865. Its legislature opposed the 13th Amendment and slavery survived in the state until December 1865.
- During the war, a number of states eliminated some of their discriminatory 'black laws'. Nevertheless, in 1865 only five free states allowed blacks to vote on equal terms with whites.
- In March 1865 Congress set up the Freedmen Bureau. Its aim was to help relieve the suffering of Southern blacks (and poor whites) by providing food, clothes and medical care. Although envisaged as a temporary measure its creation symbolised the widespread Republican belief that the federal government should shoulder some responsibility for the freedmen's well-being.

The situation in the South

Most blacks remained slaves throughout the war. Given that they comprised more than a third of the Confederacy's population, they made a major contribution to its war effort:

- They worked in factories and mines, maintained the railways and helped to grow crops.
- They had an important military role, erecting fortifications and helping behind the lines.

Many Southern states passed laws enabling them to conscript slaves for military labour. In 1863 the Confederate Congress passed a general impressment law. The utilisation of slave labour enabled the South to fight on longer than would otherwise have been possible.

The war had a major impact on slave–master relations. As the conflict intensified, there were fewer white men left to supervise the slaves. Supervision, therefore, fell to women and young and old men. Most proved less effective taskmasters than their pre-war predecessors. Slaves took advantage of the situation, working less diligently. Slave owners on the coast or in the path of invading Union armies often sent their slaves to safer areas of the Confederacy. Such dislocations undermined traditional authority patterns.

For many slaves the war was a time of great privation. General shortages of goods resulted in planters cutting back on the food and clothing given to slaves. For impressed slaves labour was usually harder than on the plantation. Given the possibility of escape through Union lines, slaves at the front were more closely supervised than on their home farms. Service with the army also cut slaves off from their families.

Despite Southern whites' fears, there was no major slave rebellion. Aware that freedom was coming most slaves bided their time. Few showed much loyalty to their owners. Whenever an opportunity came to escape most took it. In the course of the war some 500,000 slaves fled. This had a damaging effect on the Southern economy.

Confederate recruitment of slaves

By 1864 some influential Southerners were arguing in favour of arming slaves to fight for the Confederacy. Most Southerners opposed the idea. 'Whenever we establish the fact that they are a military race, we destroy our whole theory that they are unfit to be free', said Governor Brown of Georgia. However, in February 1865 Robert E. Lee, desperately short of men, came out in support of arming slaves and the following month the Confederate Congress passed a law providing for the arming of 300,000 slaves.

The measure came too late. A few black companies were raised but not in time to see action. Some historians think that had the Confederacy recruited slaves sooner, it might have won the war. Whether slaves would have fought loyally for the rebel cause – even if they had been offered their freedom – must remain in doubt.

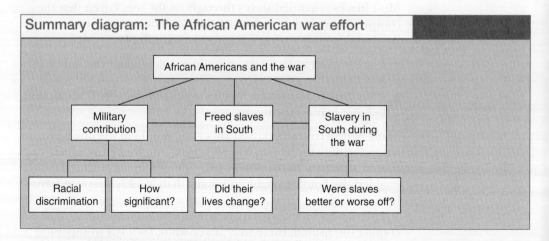

Summary diagram: The African American war effort

African Americans and the war

- Military contribution
  - Racial discrimination
  - How significant?
- Freed slaves in South
  - Did their lives change?
- Slavery in South during the war
  - Were slaves better or worse off?

3 | The Problem of Reconstruction

In 1865 the triumphant federal government faced the problem of restoring the 11 Confederate states to the Union. This process is known as Reconstruction. The period from 1865 to 1877 is often called the 'age of Reconstruction'. However, Reconstruction was not something that began in 1865: it was an issue from 1861 onwards; it was really what the war was all about. Nor did the process of Reconstruction necessarily end with the so-called Compromise of 1877. In most Southern states it ended much earlier. The debate over time-scale is by no means the only debate about Reconstruction. Virtually every aspect of the topic has been the subject of controversy.

If reconstructing Reconstruction is hard for historians, the reality was even harder for American politicians at the time.

Key question
What were Lincoln's aims with regard to Reconstruction?

There were no precedents and the Constitution provided little guidance. There were also fundamental disagreements about the basic issue of bringing the seceded states back into the Union. Ironically, the ex-Confederate states now claimed they had never legally been out of it. Equally ironically, many Republicans, who had insisted the Southern states could not secede, now claimed that they had in fact seceded, thereby reverting to territorial status.

There were other important matters to be resolved:

- Somehow a feeling of loyalty to the Union had to be restored among white Southerners.
- Somehow the war-torn economy of the South had to be rebuilt.
- Somehow the newly freed slaves had to be given the opportunity to enjoy their freedom.

Lincoln's view

From 1861, as Union troops pushed remorselessly into the South, Lincoln's administration faced the problem of how to restore loyal governments in the rebel states. In fact, there was a series of inter-related problems:

- On what terms should the states be re-united to the Union?
- How should Southerners be treated?
- Should Congress or the president decide Reconstruction policy?

Northern opinion was divided on all these matters. As well as differences between Republicans and Democrats, there were differences within the Republican Party, particularly between Lincoln and the radicals.

Lincoln was convinced that Reconstruction was a presidential concern. The Constitution gave him the power of pardon: he was also commander-in-chief. He realised, however, that once the war ended, his powers would be considerably reduced. If he was to control Reconstruction he needed to establish firm principles during the war.

Lincoln's strategic aim was consistent throughout the war: he wanted to restore the Union as quickly as possible. His usual policy was to install military governors in those areas that had been partially reconquered. The governors were expected to work with whatever popular support they could find. Lincoln hoped that military government would only last until enough loyal citizens could form a new state government.

The 10 per cent plan

Lincoln's 10 per cent plan: December 1863

Lincoln spelt out his Reconstruction ideas in more detail in a Proclamation in December 1863. He offered pardon to white Southerners who would take an oath of allegiance to the Union. When 10 per cent of the 1860 electorate had taken this oath, a new state government could be established. Provided the state then accepted the abolition of slavery, Lincoln agreed to recognise its government. In early 1864 Tennessee, Louisiana and Arkansas used this 10 per cent plan to set up new governments.

Republican opposition

Not all Republicans agreed with Lincoln's actions. During the war radical Republicans tended to be the president's most vocal opponents. Their leaders included:

Key question
What were the aims of the radical Republicans?

- Thaddeus Stevens, a Pennsylvanian industrialist
- Charles Sumner, the senator beaten in 1856 (see page 65)
- Benjamin Wade, a hot-tempered politician from Ohio.

Many had sat in Congress for many years. This enhanced their influence, ensuring that they were well represented on key committees. Most had good abolitionist credentials and some had long supported equal rights for blacks. Although the radicals did not work in close and constant harmony, most held similar views with regard to Reconstruction:

- They wanted to impose a harsh settlement on the South, punishing the main rebels (who they held responsible for the war) by confiscating their land.
- They believed that ex-slaves should have the same rights as white Americans.

It has been claimed that radical concern for black rights, particularly black suffrage, was triggered by shabby political motives rather than idealism. Certainly radicals feared that once the Southern states were back within the Union, the Democrat Party would again be a major threat. There seemed two ways to prevent this: first to ensure that ex-slaves could vote (they would surely vote Republican); and second, to disfranchise large numbers of rebels. Many radicals did not separate idealism and political pragmatism: they believed that blacks should be entitled to vote and were not ashamed to assert that such a policy would ensure Republican ascendancy.

Whatever their motives, most radicals were convinced that the Southern states, by seceding, had reverted to the condition of territories and should be subject to Congress's authority. Congress, not the president, should thus control the Reconstruction process.

The Wade–Davis bill

Radical dissatisfaction with Lincoln's 10 per cent plan was soon apparent. In April 1864 a Louisiana convention had drawn up a constitution banning slavery, but not giving blacks (47 per cent of the state's population) the vote. Over 10 per cent of Louisiana's electorate voted in favour of the constitution. Lincoln immediately recognised the new Louisiana government and treated the state as if it had been restored to the Union. However, Congress rejected Louisiana's constitution and refused admission to its two senators.

Wade–Davis bill: 1864

Henry Davis and Benjamin Wade now introduced a bill requiring not 10 but 50 per cent of the people of the Confederate states to take an 'ironclad oath' – an oath that they had never voluntarily supported the rebellion – before the states could return into the Union. Moreover, anyone who had held political office during the Confederacy or had voluntarily borne arms against the Union was to be excluded from the political process. It was likely to be many years before most rebel states could meet these conditions.

The Wade–Davis bill was not a fully fledged radical measure: it did not, for example, guarantee blacks equal political rights. Its main purpose was to postpone Reconstruction until the war was over when Congress would have more control. The bill easily passed both houses of Congress. Lincoln, aware of the political storm that would (and did) follow, vetoed the bill. His hopes of formulating a definitive method by which former Confederate states would be allowed back into the Union had failed.

Lincoln's views in 1865

Precisely where Lincoln stood on many Reconstruction issues by 1865 is a matter of debate. He seems to have been moving cautiously towards supporting the view that blacks should have equality before the law and talked in terms of giving some, especially those who had fought for the Union, the vote. On such matters as confiscation of property (slaves apart) and punishment of Confederate leaders, he was prepared to be generous. In his second inauguration speech in March 1865 he talked of 'malice towards none' and the need for a 'just and lasting peace'.

But it was clear that he faced problems. His executive power had not enabled him to bring a single rebel state back into the Union. The Unionist governments, created in Tennessee, Arkansas and Louisiana, had not been recognised by Congress. His party, even his own cabinet, was divided on a host of Reconstruction matters.

Just what Lincoln would have done will remain forever a mystery. On 14 April 1865 he was murdered by the actor John Wilkes Booth in the Ford Theatre in Washington. Booth escaped, but within days had been tracked down and killed by Union troops. Four others – three men and a woman – who were involved in the assassination were tried, found guilty and hanged. While most Northerners assumed that Confederate leaders had instigated the murder, it seems likely that the plot arose in the fevered mind of Booth alone. He had long wanted to strike a blow for the Southern cause. The murder of Lincoln did little to help that cause.

Key date
Lincoln assassinated. Andrew Johnson became president: April 1865

Andrew Johnson and Reconstruction

Key question
Did Johnson continue Lincoln's Reconstruction policies?

After Lincoln's assassination Vice-President Andrew Johnson, an ex-Democrat and ex-slave owner from Tennessee, became president. A self-made man who had risen from tailor's apprentice to prosperous landowner, he had been the only senator from any of the Confederate states to stay loyal to the Union. In 1864, in an effort to balance the Republican/Unionist ticket, Johnson was nominated vice-president. His behaviour at

Profile: Andrew Johnson 1808–75

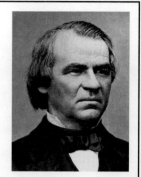

1808 – Born, in extreme poverty, in North Carolina
1826 – Moved to Tennessee
1827 – Married Eliza McCardle, who taught him to read and write
1853 – Elected Governor of Tennessee
1857 – Became a Senator
1861 – Remained loyal to the Union
1862 – Appointed military governor of Tennessee
1864 – Nominated as Lincoln's vice-president
1865 – Became president
1868 – Faced impeachment trial
1875 – Died

Throughout his political career Johnson stressed his working-class origins and claimed a special identification with ordinary Americans. In 1865 it seemed likely that he would take a tough stand against the Confederate leaders, especially the great plantation owners whom he had long attacked. This pleased radical Republicans. 'We have faith in you', Benjamin Wade told Johnson in April 1865. 'By the Gods there will be no trouble now in running the government.' However, Johnson and the radicals quickly fell out.

Historians have generally given Johnson a poor press. He has been criticised for sharing the racial views of most white Southerners and being unconcerned about the plight of ex-slaves. He has also been attacked for stubbornly ignoring the Northern political mood. However, some recent biographers have been more sympathetic, arguing that Johnson's Reconstruction policies were essentially right, his main failure being his inability to carry them out.

Lincoln's second inauguration did not inspire confidence. Recovering from an illness, he had fortified himself with several tots of whiskey. Unfortunately the alcohol had more effect on his weakened condition than he had anticipated, resulting in his being obviously drunk.

Nevertheless, a few radicals were (privately) pleased that Johnson had replaced Lincoln, even if they disliked the circumstances. They hoped he would take a tougher stance against the rebel leaders. 'Traitors', Johnson had declared in 1864, 'must be punished and impoverished'. This was the kind of talk that radicals liked to hear. However, the Johnson–radical honeymoon was short-lived. Differences over Reconstruction policies were soon to lead to bitter separation.

The situation in the South

The situation facing Johnson in the South might have been worse. By May 1865 the war was effectively over. Confederate soldiers returned home and there was no major guerrilla resistance. This meant that Johnson's administration could quickly demobilise Union armed forces. By December 1865 the Union army had shrunk to 150,000 men; by late 1866 it was only 38,000 strong.

However, there were serious problems in the South:

- A quarter of all white Southern men of military age had died in the war. Another quarter had been seriously wounded. (Mississippi spent a fifth of its revenue in 1865 on purchasing artificial limbs for Confederate veterans.)
- The Southern economy was in tatters. Union armies had caused widespread devastation.
- The Southern banking system was in chaos.
- Large numbers of black and white Southerners were dependent on federal aid for subsistence.
- The emancipation of the slaves meant that the South had lost over $2 billion of capital.

Black expectations

In 1865 most blacks relished the opportunity to flaunt their liberty and enjoy its material benefits. Many walked off the plantations to test their freedom, to search for loved ones who had been sold, or to seek their fortunes. In the summer of 1865 black leaders organised mass meetings and petitions demanding civil equality. Such demands were supported by thousands of blacks who had served in the Union army. Ex-soldiers, often now literate thanks to army schools, frequently became the leaders of black political movements post-1865.

The fact that many blacks had great expectations (which might be difficult to realise) was one problem. The attitude of Southern whites was another. The vast majority did not consider blacks to be their equals. Resentful and fearful of emancipated slaves, many were appalled at what they saw as black insolence and insubordination and a wave of violence raged almost unchecked in many parts of the South. Blacks were often assaulted and sometimes murdered for trying to leave plantations.

Johnson's aims

Johnson, who kept Lincoln's cabinet, claimed his intention was to continue Lincoln's policy. Viewing Reconstruction as an executive not a legislative function, he hoped to restore the Southern states to the Union before Congress met in December 1865. Keen that the USA should return to its normal functioning as soon as possible, Johnson saw no alternative but to work with ex-Confederates. He thus favoured leniency. Committed to state rights, he believed it was not the federal government's responsibility to decide suffrage issues or to involve itself in economic and social matters. Nor had he any wish to promote the position of ex-slaves. Shaped by a lifetime in Tennessee, he did not consider blacks to be equal to whites and was opposed to black suffrage.

Presidential Reconstruction

In May 1865 Johnson extended recognition to the Southern governments created under Lincoln's administration (none of which had enfranchised blacks). The same month he issued a general amnesty to Southerners who were willing to swear an oath of allegiance and support emancipation. While major Confederate office holders were exempted, they could apply for a presidential pardon. Over the summer Johnson granted thousands of pardons. Johnson also ordered that confiscated land be returned to pardoned Southerners. This necessitated the army evicting thousands of freedmen across the South.

Why Johnson so quickly abandoned the idea of punishing the Southern élite is something of a mystery. There were rumours at the time that some Southerners used bribery to win pardons. Others suspected that flattery by Southern planters, and the charms of their wives, played on the president's ego. More likely, Johnson came to view co-operation with Southerners as indispensable to two inter-related goals: the maintenance of white supremacy in the South; and his own re-election as president in 1868. To achieve the latter, he needed to retain the support of Northern Republicans, win over moderate Northern Democrats and build up a following in the South.

Johnson made the process by which Southern states would return to the Union easy. He appointed provisional state governors who did their best to co-operate with white Southerners. Their main task was to hold elections (in which only whites could vote) for state conventions. The conventions were to draw up new constitutions that accepted that slavery was illegal. Once this was done the states would be re-admitted to the Union.

Johnson's scheme was approved by his cabinet and seemed (in 1865) to have the support of most Northerners. While many Republicans favoured black suffrage, few – the radicals apart – saw it as a reason to repudiate the president. Moderate Republicans, anxious to keep their party united, realised that black rights was a potentially divisive issue in the North.

'Reconstruction Confederate style'

White Southerners set about implementing Johnson's terms. State conventions acknowledged the end of slavery. The South then proceeded to elect legislatures, governors and members of Congress. Thereafter, the new Southern governments searched for means of keeping the freedmen under control. No state enfranchised blacks. All introduced 'black codes', designed to ensure that blacks remained second-class citizens. Most states required blacks to possess contracts which provided evidence of employment. Those who were unemployed or who broke the contracts could be forcibly set to work. Black children could be taken as 'apprentices' and put to work on plantations. Some codes prevented blacks from renting or buying land, marrying whites, serving on juries, and from receiving poor relief or education. The codes were enforced by a white legal system that made little pretence of meting out justice fairly. Texas courts, for example, indicted some 500 white men for the murder of blacks in 1865–6: not one was convicted.

The aim of 'Reconstruction Confederate style' was to resurrect as near as possible the old order. White Southerners, given their basic attitudes, could hardly have been expected to act otherwise. Johnson did not approve of all the developments in the South and expressed some concern for the freedmen. But given his state rights' ideology, he believed he had no alternative but to accept what had occurred. In December 1865 he announced that the work of 'restoration' was complete.

Key question
Why did Congress take over the Reconstruction process?

Congress vs the South

By the time Congress met in December 1865 there were misgivings about Johnson's leniency. After four years of war Northerners still had a profound distrust of the South. The fact that the Southern Congressmen who turned up in Washington included Stephens (the Confederate vice-president), four Confederate generals and 58 Confederate Congress members did not reassure Northerners of the South's good intent. Nor did the black codes. Unless the federal government took action blacks would not have equal opportunity. Moreover, there seemed every likelihood that Southerners with their Northern Democrat allies would soon dominate the political scene. In 1865 Northern Democrats held only a quarter of the seats in Congress. The return of the Southern states would bring in 22 senators and 63 members of the House, the majority of whom would be Democrat.

Most Republican Congressmen were moderates – not radicals. They had no wish to bring about social revolution in the South. Many were not enthusiastic about black suffrage; nor did they wish to greatly expand federal authority. But most thought that Confederate leaders should be barred from holding office and that the basic rights of ex-slaves should be protected. Thus Congress refused to admit the Southern Congressmen or to recognise the new regimes in the South. In an effort to control developments, a Committee on Reconstruction was formed to recommend a new policy. This Committee had the support of most Republicans and was not dominated by radicals. The moderate Republican majority still hoped to work out a compromise that would guarantee basic rights to Southern blacks and be acceptable to Johnson.

Congress vs Johnson

Johnson now made a major blunder. Instead of working with the moderate Republicans he chose to side with the Democrats. When Congress tried to enlarge the powers of the Freedmen's Bureau he vetoed it, claiming that it was an unwarranted continuation of war power. Moderate Republicans were horrified. Despite huge problems the Bureau had operated quite effectively, providing basic welfare provision for ex-slaves. Johnson's veto helped to convince many Republicans that they could no longer work with the president. The Democrats, by contrast, were delighted by Johnson's veto and held a number of mass meetings in Washington to endorse his stand.

Moderate and radical Republicans now joined forces to introduce a Civil Rights Act which aimed to guarantee minimal rights to blacks. Defining all people born in the USA (except untaxed Indians) as national citizens, the measure asserted the right of the federal government to intervene in state affairs where and when necessary to protect the rights of US citizens. The bill received the virtual unanimous support of Congressional Republicans. Johnson stuck to his guns. Arguing that civil rights were a state matter, he vetoed the measure. Congress struck back. In April 1866 a two-thirds majority ensured that Johnson's veto was over-ridden and the Civil Rights Act became law. A few weeks later Congress passed a second Freedmen Bureau Act over Johnson's veto.

Civil Rights Act: 1866

The 14th Amendment

To ensure that civil rights could not be changed in future both Houses of Congress now adopted the 14th Amendment (which embodied the Civil Rights Act). This guaranteed all citizens equality before the law. If individual states tried to abridge the rights of American citizens, the federal government could intervene. It also banned from office Confederates who before the war had taken an oath of allegiance to the Union, required of officials ranging from the president down to postmasters. This made virtually the entire political leadership of the South ineligible for office. Rejected by all the ex-Confederate states (except Tennessee), it failed to get the approval of 75 per cent of the states that was necessary for it to become law.

Race riots

In the summer of 1866 there were serious race riots in the South, first in Memphis (May) and then in New Orleans (July). Gangs of whites attacked black 'agitators', resulting in 80–90 black deaths. Most Northerners were appalled. They were similarly appalled by the rise of secret paramilitary organisations such as the Knights of the White Camelia and the Ku Klux Klan which aimed to terrorise blacks, and those whites who sympathised with them.

The 1866 mid-term elections

The 1866 mid-term elections seemed to provide Johnson with an opportunity to strengthen his position. Hoping to unite Democrats and conservative Republicans he supported the National Union Convention which met in Philadelphia in July. The Convention called for the election of Congressmen who would support Johnson's policies. Johnson threw himself into the election campaign, speaking in many of America's largest cities. This unprecedented effort backfired. Confronted by hecklers, Johnson often lost his temper and in so doing surrendered his presidential dignity. Moreover, his hopes of establishing a new party did not materialise. The National Union movement soon became little more than the Democrats in a new guise. The Republicans had no difficulty campaigning against both Johnson (who they depicted as a drunkard) and the Democrats. Republican leaders harked back to the war, insisting that the fruits of victory would be lost if Northerners voted Democrat/National Union.

The election results were a disaster for Johnson and a triumph for the Republicans who won all but three states. In the new Congress the Republicans would have a comfortable two-thirds majority in both Houses, ensuring that they could over-ride any presidential veto.

Radical (or Congressional) Reconstruction

The Republican-dominated Congress, which met between December 1866 and March 1867, now took over the Reconstruction process. In the spring of 1867 Congress passed a Military Reconstruction Act. This stated that:

Military Reconstruction Act: 1867

14th Amendment added to the Constitution: July 1868

- no legal government existed in any ex-Confederate state (except Tennessee)
- the 10 Southern states were to be divided into five military districts, each placed under a federal commander
- to get back into the Union, Southern states had to elect constitutional conventions which would accept black suffrage and ratify the 14th Amendment.

The bill, which appalled Johnson, was passed despite his veto. Congress then moved to weaken Johnson's power:

- a Command of the Army Act, recognising the importance of the army in the Reconstruction process, reduced Johnson's military powers
- the Tenure of Office Act barred him from removing a host of office-holders, including members of his own cabinet.

The Tenure of Office Act was designed to protect Secretary of War Stanton, a fierce critic of Johnson, who had still not resigned from his cabinet. Johnson did not accept this muzzling without a fight and proceeded first to suspend and then to dismiss Stanton.

Johnson impeached

Republicans in the House of Representatives, convinced that Johnson had broken the law, determined in February 1868 (by 126 votes to 47) to impeach him for 'high crimes and misdemeanours'. The impeachment proceedings took place in the Senate in the spring of 1868. Johnson faced a mixed bag of charges but essentially they narrowed down to the removal of Stanton from office and not co-operating with Congress. Underpinning these 'crimes' was the fact that many Republicans were out for revenge and anxious to get rid of Johnson, whom they believed was impeding the implementation of Congress's Reconstruction policy. After a two-month trial, 35 senators voted against Johnson and 19 for him. This was one vote short of the two-thirds majority needed to impeach him. Although he had survived, for the rest of his term he was very much a 'lame duck' president. Nevertheless, he still did all he could to water down Congress's actions. By December 1868, for example, he had given pardons to almost every leading Southerner.

President Grant

In 1868 the Republicans chose General Grant as their presidential candidate. Grant, who had shown little interest in party politics and voted Democrat before the Civil War, was ambitious, felt honoured to be nominated and thought it was his duty to stand. Without ever being a fully fledged radical, he was prepared to support radical Reconstruction. His Democrat opponent, Horatio Seymour, campaigned against black equality. Although Grant easily won the electoral college vote (by 214 votes to 80), he won only 52 per cent of the popular vote. His popular majority was the result of Southern black support.

The 15th Amendment

Given the 1868 election result, Republicans had even better cause to support black suffrage. In 1869 the 15th Amendment was introduced. (It was ratified in 1870.) This stated that, 'The right to vote should not be denied … on account of race, colour or previous conditions of servitude.' To Democrats, this seemed a revolutionary measure: the crowning act of a Republican plot to promote black equality. Although some feminists were critical of the Amendment because it said nothing about giving women the vote, most Northern reformers hailed the Amendment as the triumphant conclusion to the decades of struggle on behalf of black Americans. A few years earlier such an Amendment would have been inconceivable. As late as 1868 only eight Northern states allowed blacks to vote. With civil and political equality seemingly assured, most Republicans believed that blacks no longer possessed a claim on the federal government. Their status in society would now depend upon themselves.

Ulysses S. Grant elected president: November 1868

15th Amendment added to the Constitution: 1870

Key dates

Summary diagram: The problem of Reconstruction

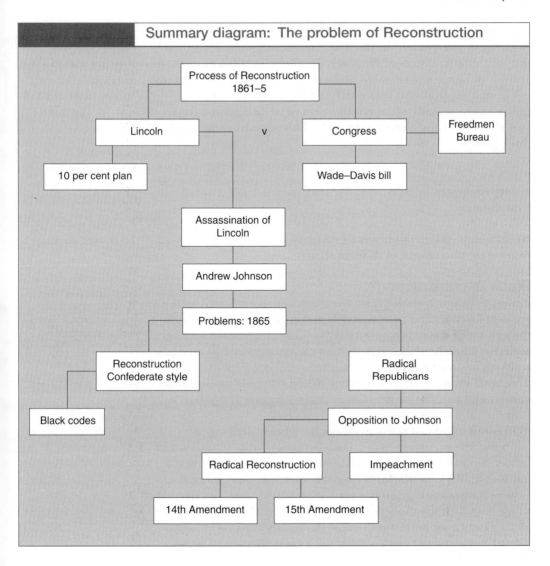

4 | Reconstruction in the South 1867–77

Key question
To what extent did the South suffer from military despotism?

Following the Military Reconstruction Act all the ex-Confederate states, except Tennessee, were under military rule before being eventually re-admitted to the Union. The extent to which the South was under the heel of a 'military despotism' should not be exaggerated. There were never more than 20,000 troops in the whole of the South. Moreover, military rule was also short lived. From the autumn of 1867 onwards Southern Republicans produced the necessary constitutions and in every state, except Virginia, took over the first restored state governments. By June 1868 Republican governments in Alabama, Arkansas, Florida, Georgia, Louisiana, North Carolina and South Carolina had ratified the 14th Amendment and been received back into the Union. Texas, Virginia, Georgia and Mississippi were re-admitted in 1870.

Republican rule in the South

Republican government in the South frequently depended on the support of federal troops. However, Southern Republicans in 1867–8 did have a reasonable, indeed often considerable, amount of popular support and thus a democratic mandate to rule (particularly as many white Southerners were disqualified from participating in the electoral process). This support came from three groups:

- blacks
- **carpetbaggers**
- **scalawags**.

Nevertheless, the Republicans faced fierce opposition from Democrats who sought to **redeem** their states.

Black Reconstruction?

Professor Dunning in the early twentieth century referred to the period of Republican rule as 'Black Reconstruction'. He thought the new governments represented the worst elements in Southern society – illiterate blacks, self-seeking carpetbaggers and renegade scalawags – given power by a vengeance-seeking Republican Congress. Dunning depicted 'Black Reconstruction' as essentially undemocratic, with the Republicans ruling against the will of a disfranchised white majority.

However, most of Dunning's views have been challenged, including the very term 'Black Reconstruction' which implies that blacks dominated the Reconstruction process. This was at best a half-truth. Black Southerners certainly wielded some political power. Having been given the vote, most blacks were determined to use it and large numbers flocked to join the Union League, which became an important arm of the Republican Party in the South. To encourage black voters, the League organised secret lodges with elaborate initiation ceremonies. In South Carolina and Mississippi, black voters constituted a real majority of the electorate. In three other states (by September 1867) black voters outnumbered whites because so many rebels were (temporarily) disenfranchised. The result was that in the two decades after 1867, Southern blacks were elected to national, state and local office. Two black Senators and 15 black Representatives were elected to Congress before 1877. Many blacks were elected to state legislatures and for a time blacks controlled the lower house of South Carolina's legislature.

But while this was a revolutionary break with the past, black political influence never reflected black numbers. Few of the top positions in state governments went to blacks. The majority of black officeholders were local officials, for example justices of the peace and superintendents of education. But even at this level blacks did not hold a proportionate share of offices. Black leaders increasingly balked at the fact that they were merely junior partners in white-dominated Republican coalitions.

Key terms

Carpetbaggers
Northern whites who settled in the South. (A carpetbag was the suitcase of the time.)

Scalawags
Southern whites who supported the Republican Party.

Redeem
To restore to white rule.

Key question
To what extent did blacks control 'Black Reconstruction'?

The lack of black experience, education and organisation, and divisions within the black community, particularly between free-born blacks and ex-slaves, help to explain why black office-holders did not equate with black voters. But perhaps the main reason was the fact that blacks were a minority in most states. If Republican governments were to be elected, the Republicans needed to win some white support. Assured of black votes, the Republican Party often put forward white candidates for office hoping to attract more white voters. Moreover, many white Republicans privately shared the Democrat view that blacks were not competent to govern.

The excesses of the Reconstruction governments were invariably blamed on black members, even though power in Southern states remained largely in white control. In reality, those blacks who came to office performed as well – and as badly – as whites. Most were moderates who displayed little vindictiveness towards whites. Few showed much enthusiasm for disfranchising ex-Confederates and banning them from state politics. Nor did most display any determination to confiscate plantation land and redistribute it to freedmen. They were aware that such a policy would alienate white Southerners who Republicans were desperately seeking to attract.

The first black senators and representatives. H.R. Revels (seated at far left), the first black senator in the USA, was elected to Jefferson Davis's seat in 1870. The first black representatives of the 41st and 42nd Congresses were: (seated) Benjamin S. Turner, Alabama; Josiah T. Walls, Florida; Joseph H. Rainey and Robert Brown Elliott, South Carolina; (standing) Robert C. Delarge, South Carolina; and Jefferson H. Long, Georgia.

Carpetbaggers and scalawags

If the notion that Reconstruction was imposed on the South by
blacks is wrong, so also is the notion that it was controlled by
Northern carpetbaggers who sought to profit at the South's
expense. Relatively few Northerners actually settled in the South:
in no state did they constitute two per cent of the total
population. Nor were they set on fleecing the South economically.
Many Northerners who went South were young, well-educated
and middle class. Some were teachers, clergy, offices of the
Freedmen Bureau or agents of the various benevolent societies
engaged in aiding ex-slaves. Some were army veterans who had
served in the South, liked what they saw and determined to
remain there. Others were talented lawyers, businessmen and
newspaper editors who headed South (often taking considerable
capital with them) hoping for personal advancement. Most
supported the Republican Party because they believed that
Republican policies were best for both the country and the South.

Without winning some support from Southern-born whites, few
Republican governments would have been elected. The scalawags
are difficult to categorise: they came from diverse backgrounds
and voted Republican for a variety of reasons. Some were rich
planters, merchants and industrialists who had once belonged to
the Whig Party. Others were self-sufficient farmers, usually from
upland areas, many of whom had opposed the Confederacy
during the war. Most scalawags, while prepared to guarantee
black political and civil rights, did not support full racial equality.
The alliance with blacks was a marriage of convenience. They
realised that if they were to have any chance of maintaining
political control, they must retain the black vote.

Corruption and inefficiency

Key question
How corrupt were the
Southern Republican
governments?

Southern Democrats bitterly attacked Republican rule in the
South for corruption and inefficiency on a grand scale. Historians
have found plenty of evidence to collaborate this charge. Many
Republican politicians were undoubtedly corrupt, using their
powers of patronage to benefit both themselves and their
supporters. Bribery, especially by railway companies, was
commonplace. Some administrations were also incompetent.
Southern state debts multiplied and taxes sharply increased. The
Freedmen Bureau, seen as a Republican-sponsored organisation,
was similarly indicted (then and since) for being corrupt and
inefficient and for encouraging a dependency culture.

However, historians now point out that the late 1860s and
1870s saw corruption and inefficiency everywhere in the USA.
Corruption in the South did not begin to compare with that in
New York. Moreover, there had been massive corruption in
Southern state governments pre-1861 and similar corruption
after the states had been 'redeemed'. Southern Republican
governments had little option but to raise and spend large sums
of money. Most inherited empty treasuries and large public debts.
Much of the Southern transportation system had been destroyed
during the war. Public buildings needed to be repaired. Schools,

hospitals, orphanages and asylums had to be built for blacks as well as whites. The fact that new schools, hospitals, prisons and railways were built indicates that the money spent was not always wasted. Historians have also come to the defence of the Freedmen Bureau, which seems to have had a good record in terms of providing blacks and poor whites with basic health care, education and jobs.

Economic Reconstruction

Key question
How successful was economic Reconstruction?

From 1867 to 1873 the South benefited from general prosperity and from high cotton prices. Railways were rebuilt and there was an increase in textile – and other – manufacturing. But promising as this was, it did not keep pace with industrial progress elsewhere. Short of cash and credit, the South remained an essentially agricultural region, heavily dependent on cotton. In many parts of the South the old plantations remained, sometimes with new owners, sometimes not. Blacks continued to do most of the hard labour.

During the 1870s most blacks became sharecroppers. White landowners provided the land, seed and tools: black tenants

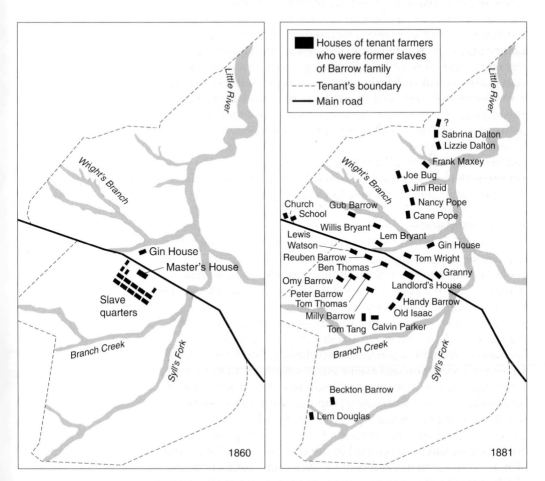

Figure 7.1: Changes on the Barrow Plantation from 1860 to 1881, demonstrating the way that plantation land was divided

supplied the labour. Whatever crop was produced was divided in a fixed ratio – often half to the landowner and half to the tenant. Sharecropping provided black farmers with freedom from day-to-day white supervision and some incentive to work hard. But neither the freedom nor the incentive should be exaggerated.

In the early 1870s, a world-wide glut of cotton led to a disastrous fall in prices which resulted in most sharecroppers being in a perpetual state of indebtedness to landowners and local storekeepers. In turn, landowners and storekeepers were often in debt to Southern merchants and bankers who themselves were in debt to Northern banks. These piled-up debts ensured that the South remained mainly a one-crop economy because everyone pressed the people below to produce crops – chiefly cotton – that had a ready market value. The South did remarkably well in terms of total cotton output. In 1860 it had produced about 4.5 million bales of cotton. By 1880 it produced over 6.3 million bales. But the increased production simply added to the cotton glut: consequently prices continued to tumble. And the only way for farmers to make ends meet was to try and produce more.

The result was that the South became the poorest section in the USA. In 1860 the Southern states produced 30 per cent of the nation's wealth. In 1870 they produced only 12 per cent. In 1860 the average white Southerner's income was similar to that of the average Northerner. By 1870 Southern income had fallen to less than two-fifths that of Northerners. The Republican governments in the South were victims rather than perpetrators of this situation – a situation which continued long after the states had been redeemed. Nevertheless they can be criticised. Too much reliance was placed on railway building. Instead of bringing prosperity to the South, state investment in railways led to ever-rising debts, higher taxes and often seedy corruption which tarnished the image of the Republican regimes.

White resistance

Most white Southerners harboured strong racist attitudes. The Republican reliance on black support meant that the party was unlikely to attract mass white support. Republican rule, in fact, sparked a vigorous backlash as Southern whites determined to recover political ascendancy.

Violence had been endemic in parts of the South since 1865. But radical Reconstruction stimulated its growth. In 1866 paramilitary groups formed in most Southern states to fight for white rights. The most notorious was the Ku Klux Klan. Established in Tennessee and led for a time by war hero Nathan Bedford Forrest, the Klan spread rapidly in the years 1868–71: by 1870 Forrest claimed there were over 500,000 Klansmen in the South as a whole. According to the Klan's 'Organisation and Principles' (1868): 'This is an institution of chivalry, humanity, mercy and patriotism; embodying in its genius and its principles all that is chivalric in conduct, noble in sentiment, generous in manhood, and patriotic in purpose; its peculiar objectives being

... to protect the weak, the innocent, and the defenceless from the indignities, wrongs, and outrages of the lawless, the violent, and the brutal.'

In reality, the Klan was a terrorist organisation, which sought to destroy Republican political organisations by intimidation and physical force. It drew support from all sections of the white community and was often encouraged in its violent actions by 'respectable' Southern Democrat leaders. In the early twentieth century, historians saw the Klan as a natural reaction to the rise of the Union Leagues and radical tyranny. Indeed it was lavished with praise in Thomas Dixon's novel *The Clansman* (subsequently adapted for the cinema in D.W. Griffith's 1915 epic, 'The Birth of a Nation'). Recent historians have been far more critical of its terrorist activities, which reached their peak in the years 1869–71. Blacks who held public office were particular targets. So were black schools and churches. Southern Republican governments tried to proscribe the Klan's activities by introducing laws which banned people from joining organisations that disturbed the peace. Some states even outlawed the wearing of masks in public. But most states found it hard to enforce the laws effectively. Nor could they easily deal with Klan violence. When Klan suspects were arrested, witnesses were usually reluctant to testify and

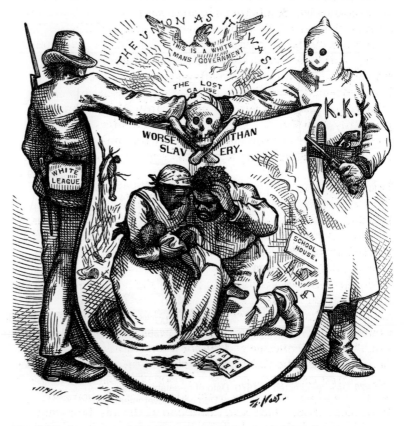

The White League and the Klan. The drawing from 1874 shows members of these organisations joining hands over a terrified black family.

Klansmen were ready to perjure themselves to provide one another with alibis. If there was a Klansman on a jury it was impossible to convict.

Some state governors appealed to Congress for help. Thus, in 1870–1 Congress passed three Force Acts, authorising President Grant to use the army to break up the Klan. Heavy penalties were imposed on those who used force, bribery or intimidation to hinder or prevent anyone from voting. Grant showed he meant business, imposing martial law in several parts of the South. Hundreds of suspected Klansmen were imprisoned. While this reduced Klan terrorism, violence and intimidation continued after 1872, especially in Louisiana, Mississippi and South Carolina – states still under Republican control. Detachments of ex-Confederate soldiers often accompanied Democrat speakers to political rallies and paraded through black areas. These shows of strength, coupled with sporadic attacks on opponents, made it difficult for Republicans to campaign and vote in some Southern states.

The South 'redeemed'

Radical Reconstruction was a limited process. In many Southern states it was over almost before it began. Tennessee was under Democrat control by 1869; Virginia and North Carolina were redeemed in 1870; Georgia in 1871; Texas in 1873; Arkansas and

Key question
Why were Southern whites able to re-establish control in the South?

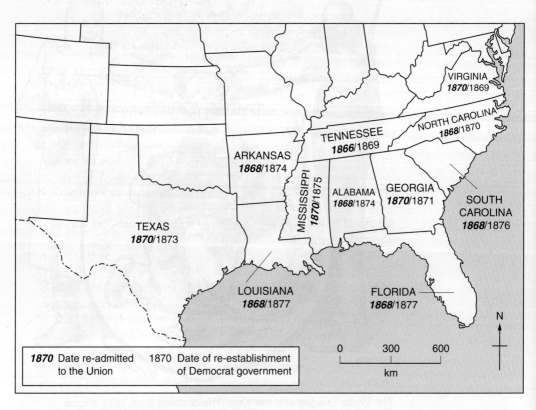

Figure 7.2: The Southern states redeemed. The map shows the date when the states rejoined the Union and when Democrat governments were elected

Alabama in 1874; and Mississippi in 1875. By 1876 only Louisiana, Florida and South Carolina were still – theoretically – under Republican control. The Democrat – or Bourbon – regimes, which replaced the Republican governments, shared a commitment to reducing:

* the political, social and economic power of blacks
* the scope and expense of government
* taxes.

Several factors played a part in Republican defeat. While most historians have emphasised the importance of white intimidation, others have stressed the destructive effect of factionalism within Republican parties at state and local level. Bitter internal feuds, which often centred on the spoils of office rather than actual policy, were a luxury the Republicans could scarcely afford. Racism was a major cause of the in-fighting. Scalawags were reluctant allies of the blacks. But there was also rivalry between different groups of scalawags and between different groups of blacks.

Historian John Hope Franklin suggested that a Republican coalition might have survived had the party been able to unite over economic and social policy. He argued that the Republican Party's best chance of success was to present itself as the poor man's party, championing policies that appealed to poverty-stricken whites and blacks. While some favoured this strategy, most Republican leaders had no wish to embark on radical policies which were likely to prevent outside capital being attracted to the South and which would end all hope of winning 'respectable' white support.

As it was, Republican fiscal policies at state level did not assist the party's cause. Heavy taxation helped to drive white farmers from the party. Nor were the Republicans helped by the economic depression which started in 1873. In the five years after 1872 cotton prices fell by nearly 50 per cent and many farmers were plunged into poverty. The depression dried up the region's already inadequate sources of credit, brought an abrupt halt to most railway building and forced into bankruptcy even such long-established bulwarks of Southern industry as the Tredegar Iron Works. Those Republican regimes still in power were usually blamed for people's misfortunes.

Arguably Southern Republicans were betrayed by the Northern wing of the party. Certainly after 1870 Northern Republicans offered little support for their Southern brethren. After 1867 radical influence within the Republican Party declined. Many radical leaders died or retired. Most Northern Republicans, who had never been radicals, had little sympathy for the plight of Southern blacks. They also felt that it was not the federal government's job to intervene too much in state affairs. By the early 1870s many Republicans felt the time had come to leave the South to sort out its own problems.

President Grant

Grant's administration has often been blamed for lacking commitment, vision and clear aims with regard to Reconstruction. This is not altogether fair. Grant took tough action against the Ku Klux Klan. However, he was anxious to end federal government involvement in the South and ready to build bridges to white Southerners. Two actions in 1872 symbolised this desire for accommodation:

- An Amnesty Act resulted in 150,000 ex-Confederates having their rights returned.
- The Freedmen's Bureau collapsed.

In 1872 Grant easily defeated Horace Greeley, winning over 55 per cent of the popular vote. Unfortunately, Grant's second term was dominated by two issues: the economic depression and a number of serious political scandals. The scandals, which involved some of Grant's close associates, damaged his standing.

In the 1874 mid-term elections the Democrats made tremendous gains, winning control of the House of Representatives and coming close to overturning Republican control in the Senate. Thereafter there was little that the Republican Party or Grant could do in terms of embarking on new initiatives to help Southern Republicans.

The last measure that aimed to help Southern blacks was the 1875 Civil Rights Act. Supposedly designed to prevent discrimination by hotels, theatres and railways, it was little more than a broad assertion of principle and had virtually no impact.

The situation by the mid-1870s

Although other factors played a part, the end of radical Reconstruction was almost inevitable given that whites were the majority in most Southern states. The two main political parties had distinct racial identities. The Democrat Party was the white party; the Republican Party the black party. Those who think that a strong Republican Party might have been founded on policies that appealed to poor whites and blacks were probably deluding themselves. The reality was that few poor whites identified with poor blacks.

Given that race was the dominant issue, many of the election campaigns in the South in the 1870s were ugly and few elections were conducted fairly. White Southerners organised new paramilitary groups – Rifle Clubs, Red Shirts, White Leagues – the ostensible aim of which was to maintain public order. Their real mission, however, was to overthrow the Southern Republican governments and banish blacks from public life. Unlike the Klan, these groups drilled and paraded openly. On election days, armed whites did their best to turn blacks away from the polls. Republican leaders, by contrast, tried to ensure that blacks did vote – often several times!

Events in Louisiana were typical of events throughout the Deep South. Every election in the state between 1868 and 1876 was marred by violence and fraud. After 1872 two governments claimed legitimacy in the state. A Republican regime, elected by blacks and protected by the federal army and black militia units, was the legitimate government. But a Democrat government, elected by whites and aided by the White League, controlled much of the countryside. Violence was common. Thirty people died in September 1874 in a battle between the White League and the state militia. In 1874 the Republicans stayed in power by throwing out the results from many Democrat areas. Grant reluctantly sent troops to prop up the corrupt Republican regime in Louisiana.

Strangely, Grant did nothing to help the Republican government in Mississippi, where there was similar violence. Mississippi Democrats tried to ensure that any white man not enrolled in a Democrat club was threatened and intimidated. The result was that Mississippi was redeemed in 1875. Historian Eric Foner thinks Grant's failure to intervene in Mississippi was a 'milestone in the retreat from Reconstruction'.

The 1876 presidential election

Disputed presidential election: 1876

Rutherford B. Hayes inaugurated president: 1877

Even though most states had been redeemed well before, the 1876 presidential election is often seen as the end of Reconstruction. The Republican candidate was Rutherford B. Hayes. The Democrats chose Samuel Tilden. In November 1876 it was clear that Tilden, helped by the effects of the depression, had won the popular vote, gaining 4,284,000 votes to Hayes' 4,037,000. But US presidential elections are determined by the electoral college, not by the popular vote. While Tilden had 184 electoral college votes to Hayes' 165, the voting returns from Oregon, South Carolina, Louisiana and Florida were contested. Between them, these four states had 20 electoral college votes. If all 20 went to Hayes he would win. If just one state went to Tilden, he would become president.

There was never much doubt that Oregon's votes would go to Hayes. The real problem lay in the South. Democrats justifiably claimed that Republicans had manipulated the vote and that many blacks had voted umpteen times. Republicans claimed, with equal justification, that blacks had been intimidated from voting. It was – and is – impossible to know how far Democrat intimidation offset Republican fraud. The dispute lingered on over the winter. Some Southern politicians talked of fighting a new civil war to ensure that Tilden became president. But behind the scenes powerful forces worked for a peaceful settlement. Eventually Congress established a Commission to review the election returns. Eight commissioners were Republicans: seven were Democrats. By votes of 8 to 7 the Commission awarded every one of the disputed elections to Hayes.

The Compromise?

Key question
What was the importance of the 1877 Compromise?

The 1877 Compromise ended the crisis. While some see the Compromise as important as the Compromises of 1820 and 1850, others wonder whether anything was actually agreed. Certainly nothing was agreed in writing. The Compromise, in so far as

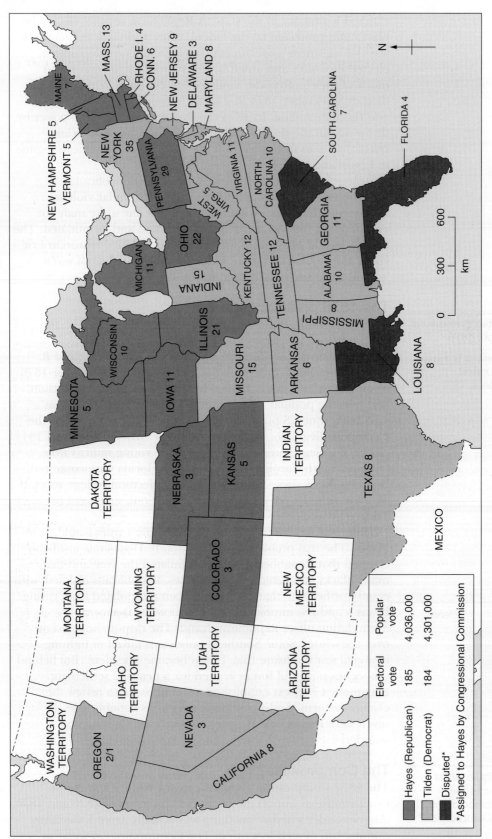

Figure 7.3: US election results of 1876

	Electoral vote	Popular vote
Hayes (Republican)	185	4,036,000
Tilden (Democrat)	184	4,301,000

Disputed*

*Assigned to Hayes by Congressional Commission

there was one, seems to have been as follows: the Democrats would accept Hayes as president. Hayes, in return, agreed to withdraw all troops from the South, recognise Democrat governments in the three disputed states, appoint a Southerner to his cabinet and (possibly) look kindly on Southern railway interests. Whether Hayes agreed to this is debatable. He claimed that he had made no concessions to the South. Whatever had – or had not – been agreed, Hayes did withdraw troops from the South with the result that South Carolina, Louisiana and Florida immediately fell under Democrat control. Thus, by 1877 all the ex-Confederate states had returned to white rule. Hayes continued his policy of conciliation, appointing a white Southerner to his cabinet and visiting the South on a goodwill tour. While Hayes's presidency is usually seen as marking the end of Reconstruction, his actions did not mark an abrupt change in policy. They only confirmed what had been done earlier by Congress or by Grant.

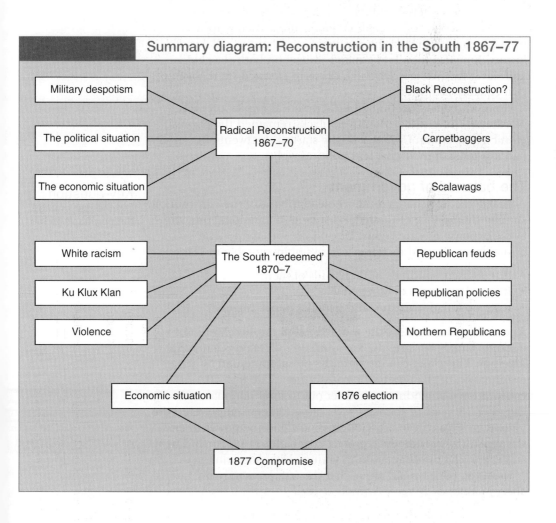

Summary diagram: Reconstruction in the South 1867–77

- Military despotism
- The political situation
- The economic situation

Radical Reconstruction 1867–70

- Black Reconstruction?
- Carpetbaggers
- Scalawags

- White racism
- Ku Klux Klan
- Violence

The South 'redeemed' 1870–7

- Republican feuds
- Republican policies
- Northern Republicans

- Economic situation
- 1876 election

1877 Compromise

5 | The Impact of the Civil War

Key question
Was the Civil War the USA's second revolution?

In his first message to Congress in December 1861 Lincoln had deplored the prospect of waging a revolutionary struggle. However, in March 1865 Lincoln talked of the 'fundamental and astounding' changes which had occurred as a result of the war. Many contemporaries agreed. In 1869, the American historian George Ticknor declared that the Civil War had riven 'a great gulf between what happened before in our century and what has happened since or what is likely to happen hereafter. It does not seem to me as if I were living in the country in which I was born.' Historians continue to debate whether the Civil War was America's second revolution. (The War of Independence is seen as the first.)

The emancipation of the slaves

The Civil War resulted in the emancipation of four million slaves. Given the Southern commitment to slavery, it seems unlikely that it would have withered and died in the final decades of the nineteenth century. The confiscation of the principal form of property in one-third of the country was without parallel in US history. Emancipation had a major impact on both slaveholder and slave. By the early 1870s blacks were elevated (in theory) to civil equality with whites.

However, emancipation had little practical impact on most – Northern – Americans. Moreover, blacks remained the poorest ethnic group in the USA and by the start of the twentieth century had lost most of their civil and political rights.

The balance of government

Key question
Did the war change the emphasis of the US constitution?

Arguably the war changed the whole emphasis of the constitution, shifting the balance of the federal system in a national direction at the expense of state rights. During the war, the federal government asserted its power in ways unimaginable in 1861:

- It mobilised hundreds of thousands of men.
- It levied new sources of revenue.
- It set up a national bank and issued a paper currency.

The changes wrought by the war, it is often implied, were not undone, largely because the war resulted in a major change in ideology. This claim can (apparently) be substantiated by examination of changes to the constitution. The first 10 constitutional amendments had set out to limit national authority. But after 1865 six of the next seven amendments empowered the federal government to act. Congress now had the power to end slavery (13th Amendment), protect civil rights (14th Amendment) and end racial discrimination in voting (15th Amendment).

However, many would argue that the war years were an aberration:

- It was inevitable that during the conflict federal power would increase. (Some think it is surprising how limited that increase was.)

- After the war there was a return to normalcy. The rapid demobilisation of the army in 1865 is a good example of the hasty abandonment of the government's wartime powers.
- For the rest of the nineteenth century the federal government had a minimal impact on the lives of Americans.
- Belief in state rights and the notion of a weak federal government remained articles of faith of most Americans – not just Southerners.
- Given that successive federal governments lacked the will to enforce the principles contained in the 14th and 15th Amendments, state power was not effectively reduced.

The economic effects

Historian Charles Beard saw the war as the triumph of the forces of industrialism over plantation agriculture. The war, in Beard's view, was 'a social **cataclysm** … making vast changes in the arrangements of classes, in the distribution of wealth, in the course of industrial development.' While most historians today regard such views as far too sweeping, some think the war did nourish the growth of Northern business enterprise, ensuring that the USA became the world's greatest economic force after 1865. During the war the Republicans passed a broad spectrum of laws which underpinned the country's future economic growth: higher tariffs, a national banking system and government loans to build the first transcontinental railway. Republican policies, as well as the demands of the war itself, may also have encouraged the growth of big business. Many of the great industrialists of the late nineteenth century were set on the path to wealth by the war. Nor did they forget the lessons it taught, especially the advantage of large-scale enterprise.

However, there are many counter-arguments to the notion that the war resulted in major economic change:

- The USA had already been a great economic power, second only to Britain, before 1861.
- The crucial innovations in transport, agriculture and manufacturing had begun well before 1861. The war produced no fundamental change of direction.
- It is possible that the war retarded the country's economic expansion. The 1860s show up poorly in statistical terms when measured against earlier and later decades.
- To argue that the war transferred economic and political power into the hands of industrial capitalists is simplistic. If the big manufacturers proved to be the chief economic beneficiaries of the war (and this is debatable), their victory was an incidental rather than a planned result of the conflict.

The social effects

The emancipation of slaves apart, the war produced no major upheaval in the social order. If it had opened up doors of opportunity for women, those doors were quickly closed. Nor did the loss of 620,000 men have much effect. Natural increase and high immigration ensured that by 1870 the American population far exceeded that of 1860.

The political effects

The main political result of the war was the effect it had on the sectional balance of power. Between 1789 and 1861 a Southern slaveholder had been president of the USA for 49 years; 23 of the 36 **speakers** of the House of Representatives had been Southerners; and the Supreme Court had always had a Southern majority. After the war 100 years passed before a resident of an ex-Confederate state was elected president; for 50 years none of the House speakers came from the South; and only five of the 26 Supreme Court justices appointed during the next 50 years were Southerners. However, whether this change merits the label of revolution is debatable. Arguably Northern dominance would have happened anyway.

Speaker
The leader of the House of Representatives.

key term

Conclusion

Had the Confederacy won, the Civil War would have been one of the great turning points in modern history. Indeed the long-term implications of a Confederate victory for both the USA and the world are so far-reaching as to be incalculable. Union victory meant in effect that the *status quo* was preserved – hardly revolutionary! Indeed, in many respects the war scarcely affected the deeper currents of US economic, social and political development.

Yet many of those who lived through the war shared a sense of having lived through events that had radically changed their world. American writer Mark Twain, for example, wrote that the war had 'uprooted institutions that were centuries old … and transformed the social life of half the country'. Twain was surely correct to stress that the war had a massive impact on 'half' the country. While it is easier to see continuity than revolution in the North, the war had a dramatic impact on the South. By 1865 slavery was gone and the South had lost much of its economic and political power.

Southern whites salvaged what they could from the wreck of defeat and their counter-revolution had some success. By 1877 all the Southern states had white-controlled governments. Notwithstanding the 14th and 15th Amendments, Southern blacks did not have equal civil rights until the second half of the twentieth century. Nevertheless, the ending of slavery and the passing of the 14th and 15th Amendments were extraordinary developments in terms of what might have been anticipated in 1861. In that sense, the changes wrought by the war were revolutionary.

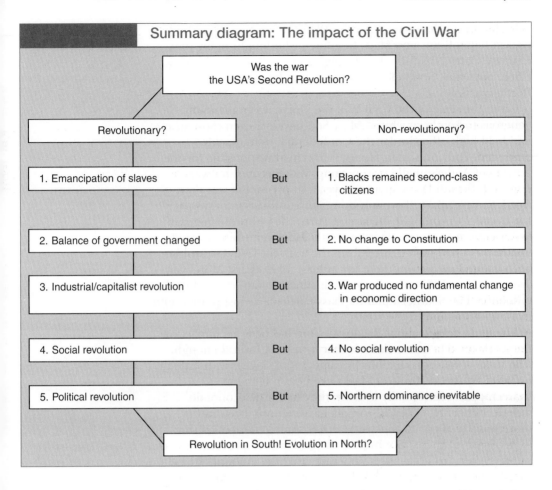

Summary diagram: The impact of the Civil War

Was the war the USA's Second Revolution?

Revolutionary?		Non-revolutionary?
1. Emancipation of slaves	But	1. Blacks remained second-class citizens
2. Balance of government changed	But	2. No change to Constitution
3. Industrial/capitalist revolution	But	3. War produced no fundamental change in economic direction
4. Social revolution	But	4. No social revolution
5. Political revolution	But	5. Northern dominance inevitable

Revolution in South! Evolution in North?

6 | Key Debate

Was Reconstruction a tragic failure?

In the early twentieth century, white Southern historians, such as Dunning, saw Reconstruction as 'The Tragic Era' – a dreadful time when Southerners suffered the indignity of military occupation, when the South was ruled by incompetent, corrupt governments, and when blacks, unprepared for freedom, proved incapable of exercising the political rights which the North thrust upon them. In Dunning's view the Reconstruction heroes were President Johnson who tried to continue Lincoln's policies, and white Southern Democrats and their Ku Klux Klan allies who waged a forceful campaign to redeem the South. The villains were the vindictive radical Republicans, scalawags and carpetbaggers.

In the 1950s and 1960s, historians such as Kenneth Stampp and John Hope Franklin depicted Reconstruction very differently. 'Rarely in history', said Stampp, 'have participants in an unsuccessful rebellion endured so mild penalties as those Congress imposed upon the people of the South and particularly upon their leaders.' In Stampp's opinion the villains were

Johnson, white Democrats and the Klan. The heroes were the radical Republicans and black freedmen who fought nobly (but ultimately unsuccessfully) for the rights of ex-slaves. In this view, black, not white, Southerners were the real losers of Reconstruction.

Given the scale of the Civil War, the North was remarkably generous to Southern whites. Most Southerners, even those who had held high office under the Confederacy, were quickly pardoned. Only one man, Henry Wirtz, held responsible for the horrors of Andersonville prison camp, was executed for war crimes. Jefferson Davis spent two years in prison but was then freed. Slavery apart, there was no major confiscation of property. For decades to come the Democrat Party, the political agency of white supremacy, controlled the South. However, white Southerners had not escaped from the war scot-free. Control had been wrested away from them for at least a few years. Moreover, the years after 1865 saw a major reduction of Southern political influence. The Southern planter class particularly lost power, both in Washington and in the South.

The main debate about Reconstruction has been its impact on the ex-slaves. The usual claim is that it was not radical enough. The main criticism is that blacks came out of slavery with little or no land. By the 1870s most blacks eked out a living as sharecroppers. Perpetually in debt, they had little economic independence. However, historians have recently been rather more positive about Reconstruction's economic impact on the lives of blacks. Sharecropping was a significant improvement over slavery. After 1865 blacks steadily increased the amount of land they farmed – at the expense of white farmers. With the end of slavery, blacks also had mobility. Many moved to Southern cities: in the five years after 1865 the black population of the South's 10 largest cities doubled. While most blacks remained in the South, some moved to Northern cities or out west. Black living standards improved and did so despite the adverse economic conditions of the 1870s.

A second major criticism of Reconstruction is that it failed to guarantee blacks civil rights. By the first decade of the twentieth century, despite the 14th and 15th Amendments, blacks were regarded and treated by most whites as second-class citizens in the South. Segregation was the norm in most aspects of Southern life: schools, churches, transport, cemeteries, entertainment, sport, restaurants, housing and public facilities. While a rigid legalised segregation system did not exist in most states until the 1890s, the so-called **Jim Crow laws** did not represent a shift in the actual degree of segregation. These laws simply confirmed segregation – a fact of Southern life since 1865. Moreover, by 1900 black Americans had effectively been disfranchised. State governments introduced a variety of measures – poll tax tests, literacy tests and residence requirements – to ensure that blacks were unable to vote. Blacks were also taught to know their place. There was massive intimidation: physical, psychological and economic. 'Uppity' blacks were likely to receive brutal treatment.

Jim Crow laws
Segregation laws, passed in most Southern states in the 1890s. (It remains something of a mystery why they were called Jim Crow laws.)

Key term

Black sharecroppers harvesting cotton in the fields of Georgia in the 1880s.

Lynchings of suspected (and sometimes convicted) murderers and rapists were a common aspect of Southern life in the late nineteenth and early twentieth centuries.

However, the situation was rather more complex than historians have sometimes inferred. Southern blacks were not just victims or objects to be manipulated: they were also important participants in the Reconstruction process. Segregation was not something which was simply imposed on blacks by Southern whites. Quite naturally, given their experiences under slavery, many blacks had no wish to mix socially with whites. Like most American ethnic groups they preferred to keep themselves to themselves. As a result segregation was often simply a statement of black community identity. After 1865, for example, there was an almost total black withdrawal from white churches as blacks tried to achieve self-determination. Churches – the first and most important social institutions to be fully controlled by blacks – became a focal point of black life. Blacks also established their own welfare institutions, trade associations, political organisations and benevolent societies. The fact that there were black institutions, paralleling those of whites, meant there were opportunities for blacks to lead and manage.

The Supreme Court, in the 1896 *Plessy* v. *Ferguson* case, accepted segregation provided that blacks and whites had equal facilities. The Supreme Court did not approve of segregation: it simply thought there was little it could do to end it. It hoped to improve – not worsen – the lot of black Americans. Many blacks viewed the situation in a similar way to the Supreme Court. Most took racial segregation for granted. The real issue was not segregation as such, but equal treatment within a segregated society.

It is also worth remembering that effective disfranchisement of blacks did not occur on a major scale until the 1890s. For most of the 1870s and 1880s blacks voted in large numbers and continued to be appointed to public office. Eric Foner has argued that black participation in Southern political life after 1867 was a radical development: 'a massive experiment in interracial democracy without precedent in the history of this or any other country that abolished slavery in the nineteenth century'.

Some black leaders, most notably Booker T. Washington, accepted that blacks were second-class citizens. Washington believed that blacks must seek to better themselves through education and hard work. Only by so doing could they prove their worth to white Americans. His faith in education was shared by many blacks. After 1865 many black communities made great financial sacrifices, raising money to build their own schools and to pay teachers' salaries. Individuals, young and old, made similar sacrifices to educate themselves. At first, most teachers were white: many were Northern women – young, middle class and idealistic. But blacks wanted to control their own education and after 1870 most teachers in black schools and colleges were themselves black. Black education was one of the successes of Reconstruction.

Reconstruction was thus far from a total failure. The essential fact was that blacks were no longer slaves. Most left slavery with a rather more realistic opinion of what was achievable than many later historians. If Reconstruction did not create an integrated society, it did establish the concept of equal citizenship. If blacks did not emerge from Reconstruction as equal citizens, at least the 14th and 15th Amendments were enshrined in the Constitution and could be invoked by later generations of civil rights' activists.

Some key books in the debate

Eric Foner, Reconstruction: *America's Unfinished Revolution 1863–1877* (Harper and Row, 1988).
James M. McPherson, *Ordeal by Fire: The Civil War and Reconstruction* (McGraw-Hill, 1982).
Kenneth M. Stampp, *The Era of Reconstruction* (Knopf, 1965).
C. Vann Woodward, *The Strange Career of Jim Crow* (OUP, 1974).

Study Guide: AS Question

In the style of OCR

To what extent does Lincoln deserve the title 'The Great Emancipator'? (30 marks)

Exam tips

The cross-references are intended to take you straight to the material that will help you to answer the question.

The question asks you to focus on Lincoln's role. You will need to consider the pressures upon Lincoln in 1861. Should he be praised or blamed for moving hesitantly? Note that it is unfair to judge Lincoln purely by 'politically correct' twenty-first century standards. Remember that Lincoln, by mid-nineteenth century American standards, was a liberal on the slavery issue. But he did not let his heart rule his head. In my view his policies were determined more by pragmatism than by his conscience, but I think he was right to act as he did. Do not let me persuade you. It is for you to decide. The main content areas to consider are on pages 197–202.

Study Guide: A2 Question

In the style of Edexcel

How far do you agree that the Civil Rights Acts of 1866 and 1875 were effective in extending civil rights to freed slaves? (30 marks)

Source: Edexcel 2007

Exam tips

The cross-references are intended to take you straight to the material that will help you to answer the question.

This question requires you to consider what was enacted by this legislation and, more importantly, the extent to which it made a difference in practice. The intent of the legislation to extend civil rights to freed slaves is clear from the granting of the right to vote and equality before the law for all freed slaves and the end of segregation in 1875 act for African Americans.

To assess effectiveness in practice (pages 200–1) you should consider the extent to which the vote could be freely exercised and the extent to which black Americans were able to achieve positions of power and influence. How far were opportunities curtailed through the actions of white racists (pages 224–9) and how far did the low proportion of black office-holders reflect not a failing of the legislation, but the problems in the short term of lack of black experience, education and organisation? The legislation provided for wider ranging freedoms than the granting of the right to vote. In assessing 'effective' you should consider the extent to which educational opportunities and employment opportunities for African Americans improved and how far sharecropping represented an advance. This is a question giving you the opportunity to make clear the criteria by which you are judging the effectiveness of the legislation. It will depend on what in your view counts as 'effective'. Make that explicit when you come to your conclusion.

Glossary

Abolitionism   The desire to end slavery.

Abolitionist   Someone who wanted to end slavery in the USA.

Agrarian   Relating to land and farming.

Agrarian civilisation   An advanced and sophisticated society based on farming.

American Dream   The idea that the American way of life offers the prospect of economic and social success to every individual.

Anti-establishment   Opposed to the opinions of those in power.

Arsenal   A place where military supplies are stored or made.

Article of faith   A main belief.

Battleground state   A state whose voters might well determine the outcome of the presidential election.

Belligerent status   Recognised legally as waging war.

Billy Yank   Union soldiers' nickname.

Black Republicans   A term used by Southerners to describe Republicans who were seen as being sympathetic to slaves.

Border states   States between the North and the Deep South (for example, Kentucky, Maryland, Tennessee, Delaware and Missouri). These states supported slavery but were not committed to secession.

Call to Arms   A presidential order calling up troops and putting the USA on a war-footing.

Capital offence   A crime punishable by death.

Carpetbaggers   Northern whites who settled in the South. (A carpetbag was the suitcase of the time.)

Cataclysm   A great change.

Civil liberties   The rights of individuals.

Colonisation   The movement of people to a different country or area, which they then take over.

Commerce raiders   Confederate warships that attacked Union merchant ships.

Confederate   Supporter of the Southern states that seceded from the Union in 1861.

Confederate commissioners   Men representing the Confederate government.

Confederate socialism   The Richmond government's attempts to control the Confederate economy.

Contraband of war   Goods that can be confiscated from the enemy.

Cracker line   The term given to Grant's success in establishing a supply route to Chattanooga. Army rations very much depended on hard bread – or crackers.

Crimean War   In 1854 Britain and France went to war against Russia to protect Turkey. Most of the war was fought in the area of Russia known as the Crimea.

Cult of domesticity   The notion that women's place was in the home.

Declaration of Independence Thirteen American colonies declared independence from Britain on 4 July 1776.

Democratic A form of government in which ultimate power is vested in the people and their elected representatives.

Draft evaders Those who avoided conscription.

Draft exemptions Workers in key industries, such as the railways, did not have to serve in the armed forces.

Egalitarian A society in which people are equal.

Emancipation The act of setting free from bondage.

Esprit de corps A French term meaning loyalty to, and confidence in, something.

Evangelical A passionate belief in Christianity and a desire to share that belief with others.

Federal A government in which several states, while largely independent in home affairs, combine for national purposes.

Federal government The national government.

Filibuster A military adventure, aimed at overthrowing a government.

Fire-eaters Southerners who wanted to leave the Union.

Founding Fathers The men who drew up the American Constitution.

Free homesteads The Republicans hoped to provide 160 acres of land to farmers who settled in the West.

Freeport Doctrine A view that voters in a territory could exclude slavery by refusing to enact laws that gave legal protection to owning slaves, thus effectively invalidating the Dred Scott ruling.

Gold reserves Most currencies are based on a country's gold holding.

Gone With the Wind This novel, written by Margaret Mitchell (a Southerner), was published in 1936. It sold over 10 million copies and was soon made into a successful film. Both book and film suggested that the pre-war South was a civilised society.

Great experiment Americans saw themselves as doing things differently to, and more successfully than, the rest of the world. The USA was thus an example for other countries to follow.

Impressing Forcing into government service.

Impressment of supplies Confiscation of goods.

Inaugural address A new president's first speech, made after he has been sworn in as president.

Industrialising capitalism A society in which industry and big business are developing.

Inflationary pressure An undue increase in the quantity of money in circulation. The result is that the value of money goes down.

Ironclad warship Ship made of iron or protected by iron plates.

Jim Crow laws Segregation laws, passed in most Southern states in the 1890s. (It remains something of a mystery why they were called Jim Crow laws.)

Johnny Reb Confederate soldiers' nickname.

King Cotton Cotton was so important to the US economy that many Americans claimed that 'cotton was king'.

Laird rams The distinguishing feature of these vessels was an iron ram that projected forwards from the bow, enabling them to sink an enemy by smashing its hull.

Louisiana Purchase Territory The huge area bought from France in 1803.

Lower South The Deep Southern states: Alabama, Louisiana, Georgia, Texas, Florida, South Carolina and Mississippi.

Manifest destiny The USA's god-given right to take over North America.

Martial law The suspension of ordinary administration and policing and, in its place, the exercise of military power.

Mass production Making large quantities of goods by a standardised process.

Merchant marine Ships involved in trade, not war.

Mid-term elections The whole of the House of Representatives and a third of the Senate are re-elected every two years. This means that there are major elections halfway through a president's term of office.

Militia draft Conscription of men in the state militias.

Minié ball An inch-long lead ball that expanded into the groove of the rifle-musket's barrel.

Miscegenation The blending of the white and black races.

Mission A religious settlement, set up by the Spanish to try to convert Native Americans to Christianity.

Mobilisation Preparing for war, especially by raising troops.

Mormons Members of a religious sect, founded in the 1820s by Joseph Smith. In 1846–7, Brigham Young established a Mormon 'state' in Utah, centred on Salt Lake City. Mormon men could have multiple wives; this made the sect unpopular with most Americans.

Muzzle-loading Loaded down the barrel.

Nationalism Loyalty and commitment to a country.

Native Americans American Indians; the people who first inhabited North America.

Nativism Suspicion of immigrants.

Nullification Crisis In the late 1820s Calhoun had proclaimed the right of any state to over-rule or nullify any federal law deemed unconstitutional. When South Carolina disallowed two tariff acts, President Jackson threatened to use force. Unable to muster support from other Southern states, South Carolina pulled back from declaring secession.

Ordnance Bureau The government agency responsible for acquiring war materials.

Patronage The giving of jobs or privileges to supporters.

Patronage pressure Using the offer of government jobs and offices effectively to bribe Congressmen.

Peculiar institution Southerners referred to slavery as their 'peculiar institution'.

Plantation agriculture Sugar, rice, tobacco and cotton were grown on Southern plantations.

Planters Men who owned plantations with 20 or more slaves.

Platforms The publicly declared principles and intentions of a political party.

Polygamy The practice of having more than one wife.

Popular sovereignty The notion that settlers, not Congress, should decide whether a territory should or should not allow slaves.

Posse A group of men called out by a sheriff or marshal to aid in enforcing the law.

Postmaster The person in charge of a local post office.

Potato famine In 1845–6 the Irish potato crop was hit by blight – a fungus which destroyed the crop. The result was a serious famine. Millions of Irish people died or emigrated to Britain or the USA.

Proviso A provision or condition. (The Wilmot Proviso was an amendment to a finance bill.)

Rebel armies Confederates were called rebels or 'rebs' by Union forces.

Reconstruction The process of restoring the seceded states to the Union.

Redeem To restore to white rule.

Referendum A vote on a specific issue.

Republican A form of government without a monarch (or someone who supports such a government).

Saltpetre Potassium nitrate – a vital ingredient of gunpowder.

Scalawags Southern whites who supported the Republican Party.

Secede To leave or quit.

Second party system The period from the mid-1830s to the mid-1850s when the Democrats and Whigs were the two main parties.

Segregation The system whereby blacks and whites are separated from each other (for example, in schools and housing) on grounds of race.

Self-determination The right of a population to decide its own government.

Slave patrol Armed men who rode round slave areas, especially at night, to ensure that there was no disorder.

Slave Power conspiracy A Northern notion that Southerners were plotting to expand slavery. Those who believed in the conspiracy were never very specific about who exactly was conspiring.

Sovereignty Supreme power.

Speaker The leader of the House of Representatives.

State militia All able-bodied men of military age (in most states) could be called up to fight in an emergency. Traditionally every able-bodied male, aged 18–45, had been required to muster in state militia units once or twice a year. By the 1850s, most militias were shambolic; many men did not bother turning up for drill practice.

State rights Many, particularly Southern, politicians believed that most issues should be decided at state, not federal, level.

Strike breakers Workers employed during a strike to do the work of those on strike.

Supply lines Links with sources of food, equipment, ammunition, etc.

Tariff Customs duty on imported goods.

Temperance Opposition to the drinking of alcohol.

Territories Areas in the USA that had not yet become states and which were still under federal government control.

Underground railroad   A network of anti-slavery houses that helped runaway slaves to escape to the North and to Canada.

Vetoed   When a president refuses to sign a bill from Congress.

Vigilantes   Self-appointed and unofficial police.

War Democrats   Those Democrats who were determined to see the war fought to a successful conclusion.

War of attrition   A conflict in which each side tries to wear down the other.

West Point   The main US military academy.

Wigwam   A huge wooden building that could hold over 10,000 people.

Writ of habeas corpus   The right to know why one has been arrested.

Index